TALES THE WESTERN
TOMBSTONES TELL

Tales the WESTERN TOMBSTONES TELL.

BY

LAMBERT FLORIN

THE FRONTISPIECE

IN OLD TELLURIDE CEMETERY stand two similar marble slabs just back of a flat plaque marked "Pioneers of San Miguel", another mining camp near Telluride, now vanished. Headstones are those of two brothers, William and Lindley Remine. Once very close, they fought against each other in Civil War, William for Union, Lindley for Confederacy. Returning home, veterans retained animosity, never speaking to each other. At William's death in 1916, Lindley's heart softened and he made arrangements to be buried beside estranged brother. Wishes were carried out at his death in 1928.

BONANZA BOOKS - NEW YORK

This edition published by Bonanza Books
a division of Crown Publishers, Inc.
by arrangement with Superior Publishing Co.
a b c d e f g h
LIBRARY OF CONGRESS CARD NO.
67-20242

PRINTED IN THE UNITED STATES OF AMERICA

DEDICATION

This book is dedicated to Dr. David C. Mason who has done the endsheet drawing and in many other ways assisted in the preparation of this work.

FOREWORD

From our vantage point in the old graveyard on the hill we look down on scattered ruins of the town below. Almost formless, our once roistering mining camp shows indications of a main street now filled with yellow flowering rabbit brush and spiny cacti. Hardly visible are the ruts ground deep by rumbling Conestoga wagons. Wooden sidewalks fringe the margins, boards splintered and warped, grass grown.

Facing each other are two rows of sagging frame buildings still masquerading behind false fronts. Doors sag on loosening hinges, windows without glass allow vagrant breezes to blow fragments of torn curtains.

If we could press some sort of rapid-reverse button, rolling back the tape of some four score and ten long years, our old town so long deserted might suddenly spring to life, life as it was then. Now the street is filled with sounds of the era when women wore bustles, when miners were bearded. Passing pack trains stir up clouds of acrid dust. Burros bray, beef cattle bellow, wagon wheels screech, honkytonk pianos tinkle; these are the sounds of everyday life in a boom town.

Every other building along the street is a saloon where miners can moisten parched throats or stake a month's wages on the turn of a roulette wheel. From one of these suddenly comes a burst of gunfire, a man staggers out, falls beside the hitching rail.

Death by violence was a frequent thing in a day when law was only on its way West. So, too, was death by disease at a time when medical men were few and these lacking in present day skills. Tuberculosis took tremendous toll of young people, mothers frequently died in childbirth, the infants themselves all too often departing at an early age.

Whatever the cause of death there remained the grim need for disposal. Lacking provisions for embalming, obsequies must be expedited, especially in summer. If our mining camp was large enough to support a furniture store the proprietor was likely the undertaker as well. He knocked together a crude coffin of rough boards, perhaps lined it with white cloth, then placed the body within. No attempt was made to soften pallor and distortion with cosmetics, death was harshly barefaced. There might be a wake of sorts, this celebrated before the coffin placed astraddle of two sawhorses. Tears often gave way to ribald humor if the victim was a man or a woman of the back street cribs, especially after liberal libations of red-eye.

Larger towns usually offered a hearse for rent. The vehicle had glass sides and was decorated with elaborate carvings and brass ornaments. On top were tall, shako-like plumes, one on each corner. In towns of large Chinese populations the hearse was denied to Orientals after owners found the vehicle littered with bits of roast pork and other comestibles carried to the grave for use in the departed one's long journey to celestial realms. Whatever the vehicle employed, the distance to the graveyard was generally short, mourners following on foot.

If a minister was available he preached a simple burial service at the graveside. The coffin was lowered into the grave with ropes, the soil at least partly filled in, mourners then dispersing. Someone, a carpenter, or again the furniture man would carve a wooden headboard later and place it at the head of the grave. Perhaps there were funds available for a marble headstone. This was almost never obtainable in the mining camps or cattle towns. It had to be ordered from the nearest city, possibly San Francisco, Portland or Salt Lake City. Handwritten "copy" of the inscription desired was sent along with the order. After months of waiting the finished slab arrived. As often as not, the stoneworker had been unable to make out the name or date of death of the deceased, the resulting chiseled inscription then being far from that requested. Seldom was such faulty merchandise returned, the stone was erected anyway and the best made of it.

Such "typographical errors" were so frequent that most state laws forbid use of tombstone data as proof of death, birth or other vital statistics, and they are not allowed in courts of law. Examples of errors are frequently encountered in old cemeteries. A marble headstone at Alma, New Mexico reads "Charles Moore — Murdered at Lovney," No amount of research revealed the existence of a "Lovney", the only conclusion possible is that the nearby mining camp of Cooney was meant. Two letters chiseled in error make Cooney into Lovney. A stone in an old graveyard in the San Juans of Colorado states that Oscar Johnson was a native of "Sweeden". Lt. H. H. Garber, who died of a broken heart over loss of his Indian sweetheart, was memorialized by a marble headstone. On it his name appears as Gasber.

Long unused graveyards show the wearing effects of time, but they are peaceful places to walk in. Tombstones often are works of art, a craft no longer practiced except for Jewish interments and vanishing as the markers are destroyed by unthinking vandals. Carvings on them offer infinite variety, yet follow a general theme. Such classic symbols as clasped hands, floral wreaths, heaven-pointing finger, crown, dove of peace and especially the cross are frequently seen. Tombstones on the graves of Puritans who died in the East during the early 1700's are often ornamented by carvings showing a skeleton representing Death who snuffs out the flame of life while Father Time vainly attempts to restrain him. This style was definitely a product of an earlier period and not used on the western frontier, fortunately for the queasy.

In most old cemeteries, especially those in areas of plentiful rainfall, there will be open spaces without markers. These are generally filled with graves unmarked since the old wooden headboards once placed there have rotted away. Sometimes old church records might reveal locations and identities of those buried there, but for the most part they are known only to God.

In this book, as in the previous *Boot Hill, Historic Graves of the Old West,* we tell the tales and show the aspect of many of the old tombstones. Again, as in our other books, the photographs are mostly our own. In this volume we have much widened the field covered by making use of material kindly offered by several western State Archives. Especially useful have been the many beautiful photos and historically accurate information from the book *Here Rolled the Covered Wagons,* by Albert and Jane Salisbury, a treasury of Western Americana.

Lambert Florin.

Acknowledgments and Bibliography

Stampede to Timberline by Muriel Sibell Wolle
Ghosts of the Glory Trail by Nell Murbarger
Nevada's Turbulent Yesterday by Don Ashbaugh
Pacific Northwest Indian Wars by Ray Howard Glassley
East of the Cascades by Phil Brogan
History of Oregon by Charles Carey
Willamette Landings by Howard McKinley Corning
Fort Klamath by Buena Cobb Stone
Indian History of the Modoc War by Jeff Riddle
Jack London, Sailor on Horseback by Irving Stone
Men of Champoeg by Caroline Dobbs
Jason Lee, Prophet of the New Oregon
    by Cornelius Brosman
Land of the Yankee Fork by Esther Yarber
Historic Spots in California by Howard and Rensch
John D. Lee by Juanita Brooks
History of Utah by Bancroft
American Guide Series, Works Projects Administration
Richfield Reaper, Utah
American West Magazine
Calamity Jane by J. Leonard Jennewein
Pictorial History of the Old West by James D. Horan
    and Paul Sann
Montana Paydirt by Muriel Sibell Wolle
Here Rolled the Covered Wagons
    by Albert and Jane Salisbury
Longview by John McClelland, Jr.
Desert Magazine
Frontier Times Magazine
True West Magazine
Thanks to western states historical societies, particularly those of Wyoming, the Dakotas and Oregon, to many descendants of pioneer families and to special proofreaders Mr. Jack Pollard and Mrs. Gertrude Pollard.

TOMBSTONE STANDS in old Boot Hill in Alma, New Mexico. Others were killed by Apaches, Charley met death in private war. No amount of research has uncovered existence of "Lovney", but now-vanished mining camp of Cooney was nearby. Inscription is almost certain to be "typographical" error, likely due to poor handwriting in "copy" sent along with order for stone.

TABLE OF CONTENTS

JIM SKIN, Pvt. Co. I, is one of many veterans of Indian Wars buried at Fort McDowell.

WASHINGTON WAS ONLY A STATE OF MIND

Some historians give James Birnie credit for the "founding" of Cathlamet, Washington, but in truth it was a big Indian village long before the white man came. The area was a favorite camping ground of Chinook, Wahkiakum and Cowlitz tribes when Birnie came, the village for a time the largest on the Columbia River.

Before dying at the age of 70, Queen Sally of Cathlamet, was able to tell Birnie and other settlers stories of the time Lewis and Clark called there. She recollected that at various periods in her lifetime the Indian population of "Cathlamah" numbered a thousand. Sally said the places along the river bluffs had once been solidly lined with canoes filled with the remains of the dead. Some of these tombs remained in the latter days, white children playing with the bones.

Cathlamet was the classic example of the complete Chinook village. Many houses were built of split cedar planks, some averaging 35 feet long and 20 wide (see *Boot Hill*). No doubt odor emanating from the site was pungent and potent in proportion to the big population, an aroma described as so thickly putrid it would fell any white man coming close. It was the natural result of a complete lack of sewage disposal and the most basic sanitation, accumulation of years of human and animal excrement, garbage and piles of decaying fish entrails. When it became so bad the Indians could not stand it, they decamped for a while to roam the beaches and woods while the village aired out.

This was Cathlamet when the white man came. Lt. William Robert Broughton, commanding the armed tender *Chatham* of the Vancouver expedition, explored the Columbia from the mouth in the fall of 1792. Thirteen years later Lewis and Clark came down the river but the first white man to stay at Cathlamet any length of time was James Birnie.

He joined the Hudson's Bay Co. at Montreal and three years later in 1820, established an outpost for the Company at The Dalles. After that he moved on up to Fort Simpson in British Columbia, an island outside the harbor there bearing his name. He was then put in charge of Fort George, now Astoria, and in 1846, wishing to establish a permanent home, he quit the Company and settled at Cathlamet. When a Hudson's Bay store was started there, Birnie was persuaded to operate it for a time.

It was natural, an accepted practice in that time and place, for a white man to have an Indian woman, no opprobrium attached to the custom in a country so lacking in white women. A native Chinook woman who married or merely moved in with a white man was never considered his equal, particularly by herself. A natural shyness and reserve prevented her from moving on the same level with her husband, no matter what his status might be. She cleaned his house and set his table, then retired to her own quarters in back, often no more than a shack or tent.

Birnie was no exception to the white man's custom. He had an Indian wife and it was she who broke the rule. She was a Chinook but was said to be of the "Red River" tribe from somewhere in the East where Birnie married her. Although her skin was red, Mrs. Birnie assumed her rightful place beside her husband.

James Birnie built his home on the brow of the hill above Cathlamet which commanded a sweeping view of the Columbia. There the Birnies entertained the few white men visiting the lower Columbia River town, guests which several times included the giant "Father of Oregon", white-thatched Dr. John McLoughlin. Others were young Capt. U. S. Grant and Fort George factors Duncan McDougal and Donald McTavish. On these festive occasions Mrs. Birnie took her proper place as hostess, assuming the duties of any white wife. When the eldest Birnie daughter was married at Cathlamet the ceremony was solemnized by Thomas Fielding Scott, first Episcopal missionary bishop to the Oregon Country.

TOWN OF CATHLAMET is carrying on continuous, sometimes losing battle against time, weather and vandals, in restoring historic burial ground—note patched shaft. Birnie monument is first prominent stone at left. Burial ground adjoins area where Indians buried bones collected from original canoe interments, these graves unmarked. White settlers burying their dead frequently dug into masses of bones, transferring them to known Indian section.

BIRNIE FAMILY PLOT is centered by tall marble monument. Urn-shaped ornament, once crowning shaft, was broken off, is seen here in grass lower left. Right face of marker is dedication to first white settlers—James Birnie, born in Aberdeen, Scotland, and Red River Indian wife, Charlot, born in Manitoba, Canada.

As an Indian, by character a child of nature, Mrs. James Birnie no doubt found her social position a mixed blessing. At least once a year she broke away and returned to the ways of her people. Yet as became the wife of a chief she maintained a mammoth canoe in grand style. It had a capacity of 100 and was elaborately ornamented, requiring a crew of 30 paddlers. When the leaves began to fall, Mrs. Birnie had the vessel loaded with camping gear and her retinue swept it down river to Shoalwater Bay which abounded with fish and game. After a few weeks of life in the raw the wife who would a native be returned to obligations of husband and home.

MODERN MARKER on grave of Chief Wahkiakum was placed by Wahkiakum County Historical Society. Mrs. Harold Bradley of Cathlamet recalls funeral of old Indian chief. She states that a picket fence was erected around the grave, this hung with his clothing. Possibly this was persisting remnant of older custom of placing belongings in canoe with body.

OLD INDIAN SECTION of cemetery with carpet of snowdrops, blooming violets, green ivy in first week of February. Only grave now identifiable is that of benign Chief Wahkiakum, said to be last of his tribe, for whom county is named.

Disastrous epidemics in 1825 killed many natives, scattered survivors in terror. They wandered for many years, some eventually returning to Cathlamet. One was old John Wallaka who outlived almost all others. At his death white friends remembered final request, "Bury me in a black suit, a blue shirt with pearl buttons, a red necktie and blue socks with white toes and heels."

PUGET ISLAND lies directly below Cathlamet and old cemetery on hill. 5 by 2 miles in size it almost chokes Columbia River, was named for Lt. Peter Puget of one of Capt. Vancouver's ships. (Puget Sound also bears his name). Island, populated largely by Scandinavian fishermen, is laced with waterways, many scenes resembling those in old country.

PIONEERS OF FISHER'S LANDING

Solomon Fisher, born in 1821, went out to the Oregon Country in 1850 and the next year took out a land claim on the banks of the Columbia. He wanted to farm the rich soil but it was covered by a heavy stand of virgin timber, except for a narrow strip along the river bank. So he planted that part only to lose his crop in May when the river flooded the lowlands, as it did every year, he learned.

He began cutting the trees and while resting from his labors one day, saw the river teeming with boats, all using wood to fire their boilers. In clearing his land why couldn't he sell the by-product? Acting on the idea he built a dock and advertised he would always have a plentiful supply of the best fuel on the river. In no time he was selling all the wood cut from the gently sloping hill above the river. All right, he thought again, why not a ferry service from his dock across the Columbia?

Action again. Solomon and his two newly arrived brothers bought a small steamboat and, converting it to ferry use, built a dock on the Oregon side — and the Fishers were in business. A man on the Oregon bank wanting to cross to the north shore would simply hoist the white flag provided and the ferry would start out into the river.

About 1889 competition began a mile and a half up river where a quarry had been started. The people digging and shaping rock hired cheap labor—Chinese, Italians, Greeks and Slovaks—to cut wood to undersell the Fishers. Local settlers protested. The Chinese in particular annoyed them and a delegation was sent to order them off. The Orientals failed to respond and a local paper announced, "There is only one solution. We should keep up a vigorous crusade against the supporters of this Mongolian outfit and ostracize them from society. If they want to support the Chinese they should be forced to live with them. No good will come from actual violence to the Chinamen." The mild protest had the desired effect. The Celestials and other aliens faded away, peace again reigned on the Columbia and the Fishers continued to sell wood and run their ferry.

Solomon acquired a son-in-law — Henry M. Knapp. Born in Wyoming County of New York in 1849, he moved to Ohio and then joined a wagon train to the Oregon Country. He settled on the north bank of the Columbia at a spot called Grass Valley near Camas and with so few neighbors about, became acquainted with the Fisher family, and especially with Solomon's lovely daughter Rachel. In 1853 the two were married. Of their six children all but one were overtaken by tragedy, a son, Oliver, living out a long life in Vancouver. Rachel passed away in 1865 and Henry married Anna Huffman, daughter of the pioneer Proebstels of Fourth Plain.

FISHER FAMILY PLOT in Fisher's Landing Cemetery. Original settler was Solomon Fisher, his grave second from right.

Henry M. Knapp was elected to the Territorial Legislature in 1859, 1866 and 1886, and in 1860 he became county assessor. A prominent member of the Order of Patrons of Husbandry, he was also one of the founders of a store in Camas. His printed obituary, July 10, 1892, adds, "He made a fine home in Grass Valley, three miles from La Camas, which town property makes a valuable estate."

TWINS JAMES AND SARAH were among 6 Knapp children. Born on same day, was it coincidence they died on same day? Riddle remains unsolved in spite of every effort to solve it. Although Knapps left many descendants, mostly from second marriage, no person interviewed knew what happened to twins.

HENRY M. KNAPP is buried close to first wife and their children, grave of second Mrs. Knapp, Anna, not located. Henry's monument is seen at right, surmounted by urn symbolical of death, and as nearly always, resting on bible and drape. Next left is slab marking grave of wife Rachel.

BEAUTIFUL SCULPTURED CHERUB surmounts columned gravestone in cemetery at North Bonneville, Wash.

EMORY STRONG, author of **Stone Age on the Columbia River** writes this author, "If you photograph any of the stones in the cemetery at North Bonneville, the large cross has an interesting story. After the Cascade Massacre in 1856, Lt. Phil Sheridan hanged nine Indians, all innocent. One had a little girl who was of course left destitute. The soldiers and residents felt so sorry for her they took up a collection amounting to $250 in gold. She grew up and married Miller, a white man. All her life she saved the gold and when he died, she bought the headstone. This story from an old clipping in a scrapbook owned by the Wasco County Museum."

INSCRIPTION at base of obelisk reads, "Erected by the Corps of Engineers, U. S. Army, over the remains of ancient Indians whose graves were uncovered during construction of the Bonneville Dam, 1933-35."

GOLD RUSH SOLDIER

The gold rush to the Yukon in the waning years of the 19th century was literally that, waves of adventurers of every description piling up in wild confusion at Skagway, U.S. port of entry at the foot of White Pass to the gold fields of the Klondike, and the flimsy tent camp of Dyea at the foot of Chilkoot Pass.

Both towns filled up fast with a lawless element so swayed by mob rule that contingents of the military were sent from Vancouver post. Semi-permanent buildings were run up at Skagway, tents set up at Dyea. In one of the latter in early March, during the height of the '98 gold rush, was Sergeant Major Kelley, 38.

Extremely popular with his comrades, Kelley took plenty of rough ribbing about being forced to leave his bride of one week when he sailed for Dyea. A site for flag raising was selected directly in front of his tent and while digging a hole for the staff,

the men heard a sudden cry of pain. They found Kelley stricken with spinal meningitis which was becoming epidemic in Dyea and Skagway.

The soldier lived only three days. To a news item in the *Register*, predecessor of the Vancouver *Columbian* of March 31, 1898, was added this note, "He was strong and healthy up to within an hour after being taken with the disease. His unexpected and untimely death has plunged the regiment into grief and alarm. All the more sorrowful is the fact that he was married just a short time before leaving Vancouver Barracks. First raising of the flag on the new mast was only to half mast, a most gloomy and foreboding omen for the entire regiment. . . Sgt. Major Kelley's body will be embalmed and sent to Vancouver on the last day of the week for burial."

On April 7 the remains arrived on the steamer *Elder* and the funeral was held on the following Monday with full military honors and solemn requiem Mass at St. James Cathedral.

VANCOUVER POST Military Cemetery adjoins Saint James Catholic cemetery on the south, burial ground containing long rows of stones marked "Unknown" (see **Boot Hill**). These are for those buried at John McLoughlin's old Fort Vancouver, and then presumed transferred, and also for military personnel moved when highway was cut through old graveyard. Original wooden headboards have long since rotted and identity lost but later burials in newer section are identified, at least with regulation army slab, sometimes with more imposing monuments as this provided by Kelley's regiment.

FRONTIER SISTER OF MERCY

In the wilds of the Colorado Rockies the stage jolted to a squeaking halt, clouds of dust billowing up from the horses' hooves. Four masked bandits ordered the passengers out, one of them holding a rifle on the driver, demanding him to throw down his shotgun and all the luggage. But Mother Joseph, who in her life as a nun, had not been intimidated by plague or person, stepped forward, asking calmly, "My son — will you please hand me that black leather one?" The robber recognized authority in the voice. He gave her the bag and she climbed back inside the stage with all the money the sisters had collected for the new House of Providence in Vancouver.

Esther Pariseau was the third in a brood of children that reached 13, born to Joseph and Francoise Pariseau April 16, 1823, in the comfortable stone farmhouse at St. Elzear, Ile Jesus, near Montreal. With the mother busy taking care of the last child and carrying the next, Esther's childhood was filled with farm tasks — tending the animals, pruning the orchard, gardening and cleaning the house.

At a very early age she showed an aptitude for carpentry and her father, who was getting ready to set up a carriage-making business, often asked for her help in finishing some intricate piece of wood.

She made a sewing box for her mother out of red maple, finished and polished it beautifully. In 1840 she entered Mlle. Elizabeth Bruyere's school to acquire skill with the pen and spoken word and showed a genius for organization, a born leader — decisive in manner and carriage, erect and above the average height.

In 1843 Esther enrolled with the newly organized Sisters of Providence, taking final vows two years later, and was called Sister Joseph. When the "Irish Plague" broke out, spawned in the filthy quarters of the poor Irish at home and on shipboard where emigrants were crowded into holds full of disease-carrying rats, she put her sense of humanities to work and grew experienced in caring for the sick. On one day in Montreal there were 1,291 cases with 25 deaths. A huge pit was dug where later would be the northern terminal of Victoria Bridge and into it were dumped a total of 3,862 victims. Toward the end of the plague, Sister Joseph was made infirmarian, pharmacist and bursar.

In 1853 Abbe Augustine Magloire Alexander Blanchet came to Montreal to seek volunteers among the sisters to go to Fort Vancouver. Sister Joseph volunteered but was refused as being too valuable where she was. Abbe Blanchet (brother of Norbert)

SAINT JAMES ACRES where remains of sisters buried on convent grounds at De Smet, Walla Walla and Steilacoom, were transferred to special plot. Stone slabs are uniform. Even marker for distinguished leader of original expedition of Sisters of Sacred Heart in 1856, Mother Joseph, is undistinguished except for floral decoration placed regularly on her grave by unidentified parishioner.

Pepper plant in photo made at Christmas time has bright red berries. First thing noticed by Sister Joseph on arrival in lower Columbia country in dead of winter was "springlike green of grass and trees", contrasting with frozen landscape at home in Montreal.

SEVERAL MARBLE CARVINGS, statues, adorn graves in Saint James Cemetery. This one catches gleam of sunshine, seldom seen in rainy Washington winter.

selected his five nuns and sent them off by themselves while he went about other business in Montreal. The girls eventually arrived at Oregon City instead of Vancouver and, because of confusion and lack of communication, they were sent to San Francisco and ultimately wound up in Chili.

In 1856 Abbe Blanchet tried again and this new group of five nuns did include Sister Joseph. This time the party was escorted by the Abbe himself, the ship *Illinois* arriving at Jamaica Nov. 13, where the sisters were presented with a branch bearing oranges from the Jesuit garden. One of the girls wrote in her journal, "The presentation of this branch made us think of the fall of Mother Eve." At Colon they took a narrow gauge railroad across the Isthmus. Passage had been arranged at Panama City to board the *Golden Age* for San Francisco and as they were rowed out to the ship they were surrounded by naked boys diving for coins. The girl's journal reports, "We were horrified and did not know what to do with our eyes. But we couldn't help being amused when we saw the Abbe Blanchet whacking them with his furled umbrella and shouting 'Allez-vous-en, petits salops!' "

The *Brother Jonathan* took the party out of San Francisco and for the first time the girls enjoyed a mirror-like ocean. This was short-lived for the next day a storm tossed the vessel and all were sick. "I exhausted all my prayers," wrote the journal-keeper, "and then started all over again." When the mast fell on deck in a welter of rigging, a young priest in the party, Father Rossi, banged on the bishop's door, crying, "My Lord, don't you know we are perishing!" A loud noise and sudden stoppage of the engines interrupted him and then he shouted again, "The captain has told us we are about to cross the terrible Columbia River bar, that grave of so many ships." But the few remaining sails took the ship to a safe entry, the sisters gathering on deck to sing the ancient hymn "Stabat Mater".

At Fort Vancouver they were greeted almost sullenly by Abbe Jean Baptiste Abraham Brouillet who ten years earlier arrived at his Walla Walla post to be drawn into the terrible aftermath of the Whitman Massacre. It developed Brouillet had tried every way he could to have the sisters sent to Nisqually where he felt they would be more useful and he had made no provision to house them at the Fort. They were finally put up in a crowded attic and then in a bare cabin, 10 x 16. With her

furniture-making skill learned at home Sister Joseph fashioned five cots, covering them with ticking filled with straw from the barns. Five boxes provided seats. Another nailed on the wall became a cupboard for silverware and the curtains were of simple calico.

School was opened in 1857 with one pupil, Emily Lake, three year old half-breed abandoned by her mother. The waif was quickly joined by six other girls, some older, and the first boy, James Wilkes, brought in his mother's arms.

With a hospital only being planned, youthful John Lloyd, suffering from tuberculosis, came to the convent pleading for help. Sister Joseph was equal to the emergency, giving up her newly built bakery and laundry, a 16 by 20 foot shack, covering the ceiling and walls with muslin, then wallpaper, furnishing it with four beds she herself built. This first hospital was blessed in 1858 by Bishop Blanchet. Ceremonies were hardly over before the suffering John Lloyd was put to bed.

A hospital association was set up, members drawn from all sects in the community—Episcopal, Jewish, Methodist and Catholic — and the institution named Vancouver Ladies of Charity Hospital. Protestant Mrs. William Rodgers was its first president. The first patient to die was John Lloyd, followed by a small Indian child already near death, then Mrs. Rodgers herself.

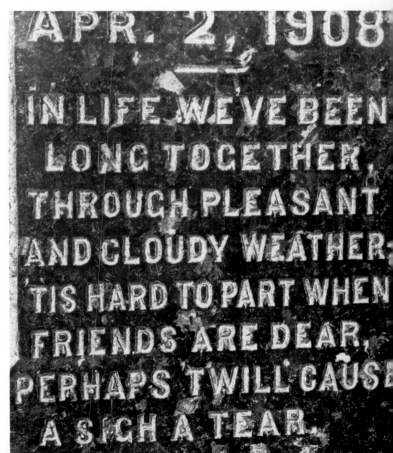

APR. 2, 1908

IN LIFE WE'VE BEEN
LONG TOGETHER,
THROUGH PLEASANT
AND CLOUDY WEATHER.
'TIS HARD TO PART WHEN
FRIENDS ARE DEAR,
PERHAPS 'TWILL CAUSE
A SIGH A TEAR.

"TOMBSTONE POETRY" found on stone in Saint James Cemetery.

THREE IMPRESSIVE CROSSES mark graves of early priests. Left to right — monuments to Very Reverend Em. Kauten of Belgium, Chancellor of the Diocese; Very Reverend Louis de G. Schram V. G., Rector of the Cathedral; Very Reverend Felix Erwilgher J. C. L., Rector of St. James Church.

In a few years the little building became hopelessly inadequate and with no funds for a new hospital available, Mother Joseph, as she was now titled, set off on a trip to the gold mines of Idaho to raise money. With Sister Catherine, she took the *Owyhee* to the lower Cascades, coach to the upper falls, the *Oneonta* to Wallula, stage to Walla Walla and Idaho City. The arduous journey took them as far as St. Ignatius Mission in Montana, to Idaho's Orofino and mines in the Coeur d'Alenes and to the Colorado Rockies where they had the experience with the bandits. On another trip a raging forest fire came within a few feet of an overnight camp and although Mother Joseph's tent caught fire, all escaped the blaze.

The cornerstone for the Providence Academy was laid in 1873 but when completed, the building was without heat, the Association $20,000 in debt. So it was off to the mines again for Mother Joseph,

this time up the Fraser River to the Cariboo diggings. A heating plant was installed with the gold from sympathetic miners there.

At home again Mother Joseph organized many bazaars. Generous ranchers up and down the Columbia donated livestock to be sold for funds. One farmer near The Dalles, the story goes, brought a cow to the steamer *Undine*, saying to the freight handler, "I don't know just how to get this to Mother Joseph". The cargo man had the answer. "We'll just hang a tag around her neck saying 'For Mother Joseph'. That'll do it. Everybody knows the old girl."

Over a period of several years Mother Joseph helped establish hospitals and schools in Colfax, Spokane, Yakima, Olympia, Port Townsend, Sprague — these in Washington — and in New Westminster and Kootenay in British Columbia. In all she made six trips back to Montreal for funds

TWO GRAVES marked by huge petrified logs attracted author's attention while photographing historic graves in Saint James Cemetery. Grandson Frank Lackaff of Ridgefield, Wash. later explained, "I was born in 1910 and as long as I can remember I saw these two logs standing on end in the yard of my grandparents in Vancouver. When grandmother Therese died, grandfather Frank took one of them for her tombstone and gave instructions that the other one was to be used as a marker for his own grave when he died. I believe the logs came from the Stevenson area along the Columbia, now covered by water from Bonneville Dam."

and to visit her home, the last journey in 1898.

During all her years at Vancouver, and in spite of her pressing duties as administrator, Mother Joseph managed to keep up her work at "making things", a hobby her busy hands and mind required. She fashioned religious figures for churches and hospitals throughout the diocese, all admirable works of art, surpassing many of the "boughten" ones. Among her figures, and her special love, were realistic representations of the infant Jesus. The wax was moulded in her basement workshop, cloth bodies and clothing carefully stitched. As for hair, Mother Joseph thought of blonde, curly headed Johnny Steffan, three year old orphan under her care and made judicious snips of his golden locks. There were at least seven of the figures, all with hair provided by little Johnny over two years. At six he was given a real boy's haircut and the tresses were used to replace moth-eaten one of St. Lucien in St. James Cathedral.

During the summer of 1900, Mother Joseph began to suffer excruciating pains in her facial muscles. She spent the following months in the infirmary with advancing paralysis. Beside her bed was a box of hard candies which she gave to the little orphan children almost constantly gathered about her bed, asking when she would come out again in the garden and play with them. She never did, dying "in extreme suffering" on January 19, 1902 at 79 years of age.

DOLL FIGURE of infant Jesus is held by Sister Maria, present administrator of St. James Hospital, Vancouver. Mother Joseph maintained workshop in earlier hospital, fashioned variety of statues, figures, wood carvings. Few are known to exist now, this possibly only one of baby Jesus. Fabricated about 100 years ago, figure is made of molded wax, delicately tinted, dress carefully hand-stitched, real hair clipped from blonde orphan child, Johnny Steffan. Box is original in which image was stored. Photo Vancouver Columbian.

TOWN IN THE TIMBER

During the late 1840s a veritable parade of emigrants came floating down the Columbia, all looking for homesites on free land. Many stopped at what would be Monticello on the lower river, some kept on in search of greener pastures or like Alexander Abernethy seeking a good growth of timber for boards to use and sell. They did not have far to look, shores of this section being solid masses of prime fir and cedar.

Abernethy picked a location 13 miles below Monticello on Mill Creek at Oak Point, the name given it by Broughton in 1792. On the level bank he dammed the stream for power and erected his crude little up-and-down mill, the first in Cowlitz County, the boundary between that and Wahkiakum County at the western edge of his claim.

The sawmill cut lumber for local needs and Abernethy turned his attention to Monticello and other markets, shipping boards to Panama and more distant ports. Later he and partner James Clark built a grist mill close by to handle grain now being grown on the higher, almost level areas.

The Abernethy home often had a distinguished visitor in George, Alexander's brother, then governor of Oregon. He conducted some official business from there which may have influenced Alexander toward the political scene. In 1854 he was elected delegate to the first and second territorial legislatures and later was active in organizing the Republican party in Washington. He strongly opposed Gov. Stevens in the controversies over management of the Yakima Indian Wars and ran against him as territorial delegate to Congress. Defeated in the effort he retired from state politics to county offices and management of Abernethy and Clark and Co. which operated a line of sailing vessels between Oak Point and the Sandwich Islands until 1872.

The Alexander Abernethy family died or moved away, mills decayed and disappeared and Oak Point also vanished except for a small store near the water. The only tangible link with the past was the tiny cemetery on the hill, spectacularly located several hundred feet above the Columbia with sweeping views of the mighty stream. In time trees and brush encroached upon the small plot, a tall obelisk fell to the ground and was nearly covered with moss and ferns. The historic site was almost lost when in 1964 local citizens, particularly G. E. Hendrick of the Oak Point store, took steps to save it.

He organized a committee that went promptly to work to clear it, with various firms donating their services. Marble headstones and the tall obelisk were reerected and based in solid concrete. A neat picket fence was built around the burial ground and painted white.

During the restoration a legend sprang up around the Abernethys who were extremely indulgent of their employees. A sailor on an Abernethy ship picked up a parrot and a monkey in Panama bringing them home to Oak Point. When the pets died their owner went to Abernethy with a request to bury them in the family cemetery. The kindly patriarch agreed and the jungle creatures were interred with proper ceremonials.

MANY TINY ISLANDS, some little more than rocks bead shoreline of lower Columbia River. This one annually serves as nesting place for pair of Mallard ducks. No one has so far witnessed method used by ducklings in reaching water.

TINY CLEARING is only open spot in dense forest on steep slope above Columbia River at Oak Point. Here are buried Alexander Abernethy and family, tall shaft marking grave of patriarch. In days when Abernethy home was almost only residence in wilderness area, family extended welcome to all sojourners. As other homes were established nearby famed hospitality was extended to little burial ground to include neighbors, mill employees and friends.

OAK POINT lies at right just beyond mouth of Mill Creek where saw and grist mills were located. In distance is misty outline of one of many islands in Columbia River. George Abernethy and partner operated extensive shipping line, vessels sailing to Panama and far flung ports. Location of old dock is indicated by stumps of rotting pilings.

THE RIVER GAVE THE FINAL WORD

The month of December 1849, along the Columbia River must have been a dry one, lacking in normal rainfall, because Harry Darby Huntington and his party floated down it to find a verdant but not too wet level area at the mouth of a tributary that would be called the Cowlitz. As the boats were pulled ashore he looked over the lush pasture land and expressed his own version of Brigham Young's famous cry, "This is the place!" What the stocky young man from Indiana did not know was in spring the Columbia would carry a tremendous burden of rain and melting snow that usually swelled the volume over its banks to flood all the low lying lands. He finally did discover it could rain here.

With dispatch Huntington erected a crude cabin and traveled to the provisional capital, Oregon City, to take out a donation claim for his farm. The following May brought rising waters in the Columbia but that year the floods were moderate, rising only to the doorsill of the Huntington home. The warning however was sufficient to cause him to erect a better house farther back and somewhat higher. He named the place Monticello after his home town back East.

Harry Huntington was a hospitable man and when the occasional traveler came through the vast wilderness of what would be southern Washington he was made warmly welcome — with reservations. He got no heart-warming drink to restore his spirits. Huntington's credo was, "Liquor is bad for the health and the soul. It will never be served here."

With Huntington in 1849 had come Nathaniel and Amanda Stone, and Orlando George, with their wives, each claiming 640 acres of free land. When the next year or two brought an "influx" including Victor Wallace, Seth Catlin, William McCorkle, Thomas Roe, Thomas Carrol and Jesse Fowler, it was apparent available farm sites on the rich bottom land would soon be used up. Land claims were then reduced by half and even then many of the new settlers could not find suitable space in the immediate vicinity. The Ostranders had land a short distance north and east and started a town by that name. Alexander Crawford was crowded to the very edge of the surrounding hills, one of them called Mount Crawford. The elevation would become the site of the cemetery.

To transact official business in the Territory of Oregon, all the settlers on the north side of the Columbia must make the long and arduous water voyage to the capital, Oregon City, on the Willamette River. They felt officials there patronized them. They wanted their section declared a separate territory and even had a name picked for it — Columbia. A general meeting was called at Cowlitz Landing near Toledo and somewhat north of Monticello on August 29, 1851.

Seth Catlin was elected president. Harry Huntington, Robert Frederick Huntress and Jonathan Burpee of Monticello were delegates as were such pioneers as Arthur Denny of Seattle and several from Olympia. They drew up a petition addressed to Congress which read in part, "The

BASE OF HUNTINGTON MONUMENT marks family plot in old Catlin Cemetery at edge of long vanished Monticello. Near side commemorates Harry Darby Huntington and wife Rebecca. At right are names of infant children, Lucia dying first winter in wilderness home, November of 1849, baby too young to be christened.

Some years ago surmounting shaft was toppled by vandals. Descendants re-erected several hundred pound piece of marble with block and tackle, drilled hole and inserted steel reinforcement. Several days later obelisk was again on ground, family then giving up efforts to preserve historic monument. Old burial ground, only tangible evidence of site of Monticello Convention which started proceedings to separate Washington from Oregon, is now enclosed in stout steel fence with padlocked gate. Visitors may obtain key from nearby market.

committee respectfully requests that Congress will pass an act organizing a separate territorial government north of the Columbia River . . . to be known as Columbia Territory." The message was sent on a journey of several weeks with much doubt that it would reach the national capital.

More than a year passed with no word from the East. In November of 1852 settlers decided to try again, this time gathering a much larger group of 50, with delegates from nearly every hamlet of the area. This was the celebrated Monticello Convention held in the home of Harry Darby Huntington.

The tiny village of Monticello was hard pressed to house so many visitors and after private homes and the small hotel were full, 15 delegates were packed into an attic over a business establishment. All had blanket beds on the floor and some had flasks of "tangle leg" and who needed sleep? A new territory was about to be born and that called for a celebration. It lasted into the cold gray dawn and many who got to the convention were *non compos mentis.* The record shows the petition bore only 44 signatures.

Word came back to Monticello that Territorial Delegate Joseph Lane presented it to the Committee of Territories and the only objection was to the proposed name — Columbia. The Committee reported that this would be confused with the District of Columbia.

During the years of settlement the Columbia River had behaved moderately well in its annual

STONE marks actual grave of pioneer founder of Monticello, Harry Darby Huntington. He and Rebecca had family of 15, most surviving to adulthood. Youngest was Wallace who fathered Frances Rebecca, she marrying Harry Siverson, couple still living in nearby Kelso. Mrs. Siverson filled in much family history.

spring freshets, the Snake and other major tributaries spacing out their heavy flows. But there came a spring when all tributaries roared in noisy jubilance and the grand gathering of waters poured into the main stream at once. The Columbia spread over all the bottom lands in its valley, rolling from one bank of hills to the other. Monticello was erased from the map as if the fates decided the town had served its purpose and was no longer needed. Remaining intact on Mount Crawford was the Catlin Cemetery.

SETH CATLIN, among first settlers of Monticello and for whom cemetery was named, and wife Agnes Ridpath, are interred here. Catlin's signature appears on document drafted at Monticello Convention. City of Longview was built on historic site, architects and planners having little time or concern for history. In 1922 granddaughter Mrs. Minnie Catlin Wolford wrote, "The Catlin farm on which your city is to be built has been in the Catlin family since the year 1849 . . . would deem it a gratifying compliment if you would give a prominent avenue, street or park the name". Committee on names demurred, but promised to call lake in park Catlin Lake. Later it was named Sacajawea. However granite monument honoring pioneer Catlin was placed in park. Somewhere on city property are graves of three small children, site lost to history.

JAMES HUNTINGTON, one of Harry's 6 cousins, was among second wave of settlers coming to fertile land at mouth of Cowlitz River.

GRAVE OF ABEL OSTRANDER lies in middle of road. With son Nathaniel he came to Monticello area in 1852, settling at present town of Ostrander, now nearly vanished. He died 6 years later. When Pleasant Hill road was laid out it intersected grave, was divided to pass on both sides.

For many years poorly marked site deteriorated, finally became mere patch of weeds. In early 1966 Cowlitz County historians renovated spot, erected fitting monument, placed protecting barricade of timbers fittingly rough-hewed. Formal dedication of site was held Sunday, June 12, 1966 with many descendents of Ostrander present, including two great-great-great-great grand children.

OSTRANDER was originally settled as homestead on donation land claim and became center of logging camps such as this in dense stands of virgin timber—old Portland Camp, few miles out of Ostrander. Photo was made about 1910. Woman with baby is Mrs. Elin Berglund, aunt of author, child Kenneth (see story on Wauna in **Ghost Town Treasures**). Other woman is unidentified.

Aunt Elin recalls, "The single men lived in bunkhouses, but Joe and I had this house. We paid $50 for it. It was built so that when the trees close by were all cut it could be placed on a flat car and hauled on the logging train to a new camp. There were three small rooms, end to end. When this picture was taken it was near to Thanksgiving. The turkeys were gathered from farmers at Ostrander. The loggers held a turkey shoot every year. They took turns, paying so much for a shot until all the birds were killed. Joe, a skilled marksman, claimed six and was eliminated as a contender."

MASSACRE ON THE WHITE RIVER

Johnny King, 7, was accustomed to the usual Klickitat Indians who came begging at the door of the family's new frame house in the White River Valley, 20 miles south of Seattle. But one day Chief Nelson came and talked to his mother who told his stepfather Harvey Jones, the Indian had acted strangely. The parents prepared for trouble, setting about to protect themselves, daughter Edith, 4, Edward, 2, and Johnny who was Mrs. Jones' son by a previous marriage.

On the fatal morning in October, 1855, the family sat down to breakfast without the father who was in bed with a pleurisy attack. Handyman Enos Cooper had eaten early and was working outside. A disturbing noise came from outdoors and Mrs. Jones went to the door, the curious children hanging to her skirts. She was greeted by the face of a strange Indian, others pointing guns at her. Holding the children back, she slammed and barred the door. There was a burst of musket fire and window glass shattered across the floor. The mother snatched up her husband's five shooter and emptied it through the window. Without waiting to see if she had hit any Indians she herded the children into a back room and covered them with a feather bed on the floor.

The curious Johnny crawled from under it to see his stepfather stagger to his feet and lean weakly against the wall. Just then Jones was hit full in the chest by a musket ball and called out, "Oh, my God — I'm shot!" The mother helped him back to bed and Johnny crawled under it. He heard his stepfather stop moaning and his mother start to sob loudly.

Then the door burst open to admit a mob of Indians. One grabbed the featherbed off the children and tossed them outside. Johnny saw them stuffing blankets and papers under the house and setting the material afire. He lay frozen in terror while the blaze reached powder kegs in a corner, the explosion scattering Indians in all directions. The boy rallied, taking the smaller children to the temporary safety of a small cave where they often played, hiding until all was quiet. Then he ran to the house of William Brannon, half a mile away.

Johnny found the house a shambles, the inside wrecked with feathers scattered everywhere and under them the mutilated body of John Brannon. Later the wife and her baby were found in the well. Johnny hurried back to Edith and Edward, still hiding in the cave and crying with hunger. He found some potatoes roasted in the fiery ruins of the house and went searching for his mother.

She lay in the grass some distance away, chest covered with blood and more seeping from her mouth. She was barely able to ask about the other children, then told him he must somehow get them to the Thomas home. She persuaded him to leave her but did not say she was dying. The Thomas place was some distance away but Johnny got the children there only to find it empty, the family gone. The boy found a loaf of bread which the three children wolfed down and he settled the younger ones under some brush. The three shivered through a cold October night.

LITTLE JOHNNY KING was hero of White River Massacre, in which 8 settlers lost their lives. Monument honoring them stands about 2 miles north of Auburn, Wash.

An Indian came near them at daylight but Johnny saw it was Tom, houseboy of the Thomas family. Out of sheer relief the 7 year old let his feelings go for the first time and started to cry. Tom comforted him, saying he knew all about the massacre, had himself escaped from his murdering brothers who would have killed him as a friend of the whites.

Johnny told his story and tried to get Tom to go back and help his mother but the Indian knew there was no help for her, that she would be dead by now. He kept the children under cover until night brought a full moon. Then he put them in his dugout canoe and at great risk took them down river to Seattle and safety.

Johnny grew up to become a physician in Burghill, Ohio. In later years when someone in Seattle wrote him Tom was in trouble, he sent funds and kept him on a regular pension as long as the old Indian lived.

CAMP FIRE OF DEATH

In December following the slaying of white settlers on White River by Klickitat Indians, young Lt. William Slaughter and several men were sent to join a company of volunteers organized to subdue the hostiles. Slaughter's guide through country strange to him was friendly Puyallup Tom.

Darkness fell before the party reached the volunteers' camp. The guide took them to a cabin where plans were made to camp for the night. The men were tired, wet and cold so they stacked their weapons and built a rousing bonfire to dry their clothes. Puyallup Tom protested vigorously with the warning there were Indians near and the fire would attract them. Slaughter ridiculed any hint of danger and refused to extinguish the cheering blaze, confidently asserting there was no need to post guards.

Later in the evening as the men began to dry out they distinctly heard the hoot of an owl. Now the Indian guide was really alarmed, saying the sound was a signal used by the Klickitats. Again Slaughter paid no attention to the warning, instead sending a messenger to the volunteers' camp to request the presence of three officers for a conference on the next day's tactics. The three arrived and all gathered around the fire for a convivial conference.

Suddenly a volley of gunfire came through the trees, killing three soldiers and wounding others. One of the fatalities was Lt. Slaughter, a bullet striking him in the heart. He gasped sharply and fell over dead. Puyallup Tom kicked out the fire— but it had already served the Indians' purpose.

MONUMENT to overconfident Lt. Slaughter stands near marker for settlers killed earlier in Klickitat War. Location is close to Auburn, Wash. which grew up after hostilities ceased. Town was first named for young lieutenant but proved embarrassing to townspeople when Northern Pacific Railroad came through, hotel runners boarding incoming trains crying, "This way to the Slaughter House". Town and hotel were renamed Auburn after town immortalized in Oliver Goldsmith's poem, "The Deserted Village": "Sweet Auburn, loveliest village of the plain."

HE SOLD HEADS TO THE ARMY

Patkanim, chief of the Snoqualmie and Snohomish tribes was a contradictory character about whom many disputes have arisen. Some of this confusion originated from his having several brothers who were often mistaken for him, and were almost as puzzling as he was.

He first appears in Washington history as a menace. He and his braves theatened Thomas M. Glasgow and A. B. Rabbeson when they landed on Whidbey Island, forcing them to return to Tumwater. Emboldened by this success he led a party of Indians to Fort Nisqually, gaining entrance on the pretext that he wished to settle a difference with the Nisquallies. Sensing trouble, soldiers called in the settlers and held Patkanim in the stockade. The prompt action averted a massacre, although one white man was killed and one wounded. The chief escaped in the ensuing disorder.

Apparently Patkanim planned to kill the whites, secure guns and ammunition from the fort and drive the settlers from Puget Sound. One of his brothers, Quallawort, was hanged for his part in this affair, Patkanim shipped to San Francisco. He saw so many white men there he decided to get on their side and returning to Washington Territory, he proclaimed his everlasting friendship for the settlers. He became a trusted friend of Arthur Denny. At Mukilteo he signed the Stevens Treaty in behalf of his tribes, yet Governor Stevens distrusted him as did the captain of the *Decatur*.

Patkanim warned Denny of the impending Indian trouble in 1856. When the chief was seen lurking at the heels of a military party in the White River Valley, near the scene of Indian depradations, he was ordered arrested. Arthur Denny interceded for him, claiming the Indian seen was Joe Kanim, that Patkanim was on a hunting trip. Fortunately for him he did appear with game he had killed in the Cascades, but just when no one could prove. He was not arrested.

The military authorities offered $20, during the Indian uprising, for each head of a hostile Indian. Patkanim promptly led his warriors in a ten-hour battle with Chiefs Leschi and Owhi of the Klickitats

and obtained several heads, which he sold. But fighting for heads he concluded, was too hard and dangerous. It was much easier to kill his slaves for their heads.

After he made sufficient profit from this enterprise he collected his money in Olympia and came back in style. An early settler recounts, "A fleet of twenty canoes was seen rounding Alki Point and approaching the *Decatur* in Seattle harbor, and as the occupants were decked in gala costume, with clean faces, we were at a loss to account for the unusual display until Patkanim came up over the gangway arrayed in citizen's garb, including congress gaiters, white kid gloves, white shirt with standing collar reaching halfway to his ears, and the whole finished off with a flaming red necktie."

Patkanim died in 1858 and was first buried at the mouth of the Snohomish River. When floods threatened to destroy the grave, the body was moved to its present location on the Tulalip Indian Reservation.

HEAD-HUNTER'S HEADSTONE at grave of Chief Patkanim who sold heads of his enemies to army authorities.

THE WATCH ON THE SOUND

Frank Peabody was fascinated by the novels of Alexander Dumas, popular in the 1890's. He had just finished reading *The Count of Monte Cristo* and when he made his lucky strike, he exclaimed to his prospecting partner. "There's more gold here than in all of Monte Cristo!" He had little time for reading then.

Born in Massachusetts in 1854, Frank Peabody grew up "Down East" and when he attained his majority he headed for the fabled gold fields of Arizona and Nevada. Frank had the strength for hard work away from town but a weakness for gambling in the flesh pots. With a little gold dust gained by hard labor he went to the poker and faro games in town and lost it all. With a valuable watch as his only asset he decided to go to the Washington Cascades where, it was rumored the gold would put Arizona and Nevada to shame. He scraped up funds and reached Seattle sometime in 1888.

At the first opportunity young Peabody sold his treasured watch and headed straight for the first gambling joint sporting a faro game, around First and Yesler. In the cooler, damper atmosphere of Puget Sound Lady Luck was kinder and where he had consistently lost his shirt he wound up the first night with $1,000 in his pants.

Determined to have something to show for his winnings he went just north of Seattle to Edmonds and bought a small house. From the westward windows he could see the waters of Puget Sound and in the east rose the jagged line of the snowy Cascade Mountains where he intended to prospect. In 1890 when Edmonds citizens drew up the petition for incorporation and found the list two names

short, they enterprisingly added the names of two of the town's oxen, Bill and Bolivar. This bit of history would not have occurred had Peabody and a new friend Joseph Pearsall been at home. For over a year the two had been scouting the ledges and snow-banked slopes of the high Cascades.

The partners decided to penetrate the almost impassable wilderness from camps at Index, push almost due north, then over Poodle Dog Pass toward the Stillaguamish River. Once over the pass they began picking at the rock again. On the slopes of what would be called Willman's Peak, Peabody saw a streak of glittering rock which proved to be a brilliant ledge of gold. He burst forth excitedly with the cry about Monte Cristo that made him famous. Later when mining there became established the boom town was named Monte Cristo, the main street Dumas. However since the discovery was made on July 4, the creek tumbling through town was named '76.

Peabody was active in all town affairs during the stirring mining years. When things quieted down, due mainly to refractory nature of the ore, the discoverer and wife Kittie spent only summers at Monte Cristo, escaping the deep snows in the little home at Edmonds. In their failing years, the late 1920's, the couple employed a faithful nurse, Kate Knolton.

HUGE ROCK, almost oblong, marks grave of Frank and Kittie Peabody. Short distance off trail roughly following what was once Monte Cristo's main street, Dumas, is sign indicating side trail to "Peabody Rock", a steep but easy walk past several decaying and almost vanished ruins of old town.

Couple lived last days in little house in Edmonds purchased with Peabody's faro winnings in 1888. Both were cremated, ashes placed under rock. Plaque was purchased by Kate Knolton, dedicated in ceremonies held in August, 1953. Charles Nordlund, who with wife still lives in Monte Cristo in summer, helped with arrangements, built benches, traces of which remain. Dense forest of mountain hemlock surrounds site of grave.

MEMORIAL PLAQUE shows detail of inscription.

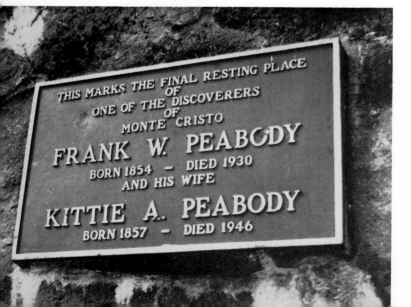

THIS MARKS THE FINAL RESTING PLACE
OF
ONE OF THE DISCOVERERS
OF
MONTE CRISTO
FRANK W. PEABODY
BORN 1854 – DIED 1930
AND HIS WIFE
KITTIE A. PEABODY
BORN 1857 – DIED 1946

HE WENT DOWN WITH HIS SHIP

Young Jimmy Kyes seemed to feel a great compassion for the small seedling. He loved to spend his summers roaming the snowy-peaked Cascade Range in northern Washington and this day in the 1920s he stood at the edge of a tarn, a tiny high country lake, snow still mantling its fringes. Growing there was a little alpine fir, its foliage displaying the blue coloring sometimes found in this species.

Jimmy wanted to nurture the struggling little tree and he lifted it from the earth very carefully so as not to disturb the roots, carrying it down to the old mining town of Monte Cristo where he was staying. He planted it in the garden of the hotel there and it was his to care for. In 1923, while in the U.S. Forest Service as lookout on the summit of Mt. Pilchuck, he met Mr. and Mrs. H. A. Annen of Everett, Washington who would later carry on Jimmy's protective efforts by building a fence around the tree.

James E. Kyes was born in Everett and educated in grade and high schools there. He studied at the University of Washington, specializing in mining engineering, and a year later was appointed to the U.S. Naval Academy at Annapolis, graduating in 1930.

After serving on the carriers *Saratoga* and *Ranger* he returned to Annapolis to complete a two-year postgraduate course in engineering and then assumed command of the U.S.S. Destroyer *Leary,* taking it on convoy and patrol duty. On Christmas eve 1943, the vessel was returning to port where Kyes would be given a new command. A message was received that an aircraft carrier in the North Atlantic was under attack by German submarines. The *Leary* was ordered to go to her assistance.

As the destroyer drew near the carrier she was struck by two torpedoes fired from the enemy wolf pack, the vessel breaking into three sections and sinking rapidly. Commander Kyes was donning his preserver when he saw his negro messboy was without one. Kyes put his around the boy and went down with his ship as it foundered.

James Kyes, who held the rank of full commander for two years at the time of his death, received posthumous honors including the Navy Cross for heroism displayed during the sinking of his ship. Already held were the Purple Heart, Bronze American Defense Service Medal, European-African Campaign and Middle East Area Campaign honors. Another mark of recognition for his courage was the naming of the destroyer *Commander James Kyes* in 1946, which was christened by Kyes wife Frances, their son David beside her. An even more enduring memorial is the 7,239 foot mountain seven miles west of Monte Cristo named Kyes Peak, Jimmy and a companion making the first recorded ascent of the rocky spire in 1920.

And the alpine fir still grows in the old hotel grounds.

NEAR FLATTENED RUINS of hotel on Dumas Street in one time mining camp of Monte Cristo, stands fir tree planted by James Kyes in boyhood. About time of his death picket fence was placed around tree and later this monument erected memorializing heroic death of Commander Kyes at sea.

OLD TIME PHOTO of Monte Cristo. Extensive mines, mills were served directly by railroad. Present day Monte Cristo, while no longer important as gold mining center is mecca for campers, fishermen, mountain climbers.

ALPINE PHLOX, botanically Phlox Douglasii, forms dense mats of deep pink to white flowers, spreading color over large areas of Cascade Mountains at altitudes of from 4,000 to 7,000 feet.

LETTER IS FRAMED and secured to picket fence around tree.

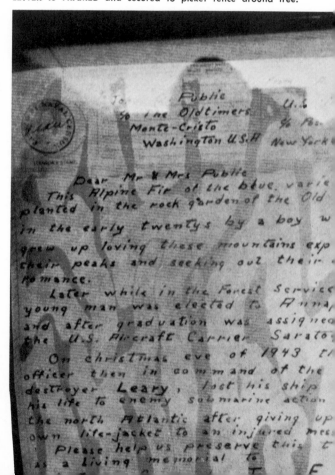

AN IMPORTANT FACTOR IN OREGON HISTORY

In Portsmouth, England, he ordered ale and found both it and the barmaid heady stuff. He took her aboard the *Isaac Todd* and sailed for the outpost on the Columbia River where he spent half his time keeping his Jane out of the amorous clutches of other men. But finally he had to share her, lose her and then his life in the stormy Columbia.

When the North West Fur Company appointed Donald McTavish to the post of Chief Factor at Fort George all he knew about the place was it was situated at the mouth of the Columbia River in the Oregon Country and that it lacked all the comforts of home. The fort was started as Astoria by John Jacob Astor but the British had taken over at the outbreak of the War of 1812 and renamed it.

On a late evening in February of 1813, McTavish was stopping at an inn in Portsmouth where the *Isaac Todd,* the vessel that would carry him to the far outpost, was anchored. He expected to sail in a few days and had tried to think of everything he could take along to keep him comfortable and happy in the raw new world. He had quantities of fancy cheeses, liquors and other delicacies in the hold but what about women? He was going to miss his lady friends, he mused, as he went into the barroom of the inn. What he saw relieved his mind and sparked an idea — blonde, buxom Jane Barnes, one of the barmaids. Damn all ridicule — she was a lovely bit. As she served him he caught her wrist. Would she go with him to Fort George?

That she would, gracious sir, and she flew into a tizzy of excitement, spending hours in the town's best stores buying new dresses and other finery, all to the account of Donald McTavish. And when the *Isaac Todd* sailed into the Atlantic, Jane Barnes sailed into McTavish's cabin as fancy lady.

The crew, from captain to cabin boy, harbored ideas about luring the pretty barmaid into their raw-knuckled hands. McTavish, however, kept her in his own iron fist and stayed close to the cabin during the long months at sea, and when the *Isaac Todd* crossed the Columbia bar on April 17 and anchored off the primitive Fort George, the barmaid was still his Jane exclusively.

But McTavish had qualms when he went ashore in the long boat about leaving Jane Barnes on board. And then, after a few days getting familiar with things, he invited young Alexander Henry Jr., head clerk, and other officials on board the ship to dinner and to meet Miss Barnes. The meeting was electric. Any white girl would have made an impression on men so long removed from any females other than the vermin-infested Chinook squaws, but these men were fairly bedazzled by the blonde

OCEAN FOGS were drifting over Astoria when this photo was made, diffused but brilliant light giving effect of studio set-up. McTavish stone is set in solid concrete base, secure against theft. Painted background shows ship **Isaac Todd**.

beauty of the English girl. After a few drinks had loosened restraints the conversation began to get out of hand, according to an item in Henry's journal: "A vile discourse took place in the hearing of Jane, on the subject of venereal disease among the Chinook women." Alexander Henry stopped the talk, no doubt aware the barmaid had heard worse.

When she made her first visit ashore she flaunted her new finery before all the men at the fort and ignored the venomous looks of the Indian women, always eager to entangle a white man. Then McTavish began to worry about his charge. He was increasingly busy with fort affairs, feeling Jane was unsafe ashore or on board without him. His original plan had been to arrange matters at the fort quickly and return overland to Montreal with his lady love. It was now pointed out this was too dangerous and difficult.

McTavish came to a decision. Jane had been his for several months and now he would share her with Alexander Henry so the clerk could keep an eye on her when he couldn't. The arrangement was most agreeable to Henry and apparently to Jane Barnes but not, it soon appeared, to the Chief Factor. Henry began to "watch out for her" full time, McTavish usually sleeping alone. In spite of this both men continued to get along well in their business relations, and McTavish took to one of the Chinook women left behind by a departing American who had worked for Astor. The squaw was deloused, somewhat cleansed of fish oil and was fairly easy to live with once the factor realized he had lost Jane.

On May 22 McTavish, Henry and five crewmen boarded a longboat for what should have been a routine crossing of the Columbia to the *Isaac Todd*. They may have intended to visit the Indian camp at Point Ellice to look over some squaws but they failed to make the crossing. A strong wind was kicking up huge swells, an almost normal condition at the mouth of the river, over five miles wide at this point. The boat was swamped and all were drowned.

The body of Donald McTavish drifted ashore and was buried in the tiny cemetery at the northeast bastion of the fort, a suitable tombstone erected some time later. This is of sandstone, not native to the area, presumed to be finished from a "blank" among many shipped as ballast in North West ships, the company expecting many deaths among personnel at Fort George.

Jane was now left without a benefactor but also without restraint, free to make the rounds of the men at the fort. One day, Casaka, a son of Concomly, one-eyed Chinook chief from Point Ellice across the river (see *Boot Hill*) was at the fort, offering Jane 100 of the finest otter skins for her hand. But the one time barmaid took a look at his painted face and decided all that fur wouldn't keep out the smell of his body coating of whale oil. She said, "Indian go home" or a similar phrase of the day.

Some time later Capt. Robison of the ship *Columbia* offered her passage to Canton, China, and she went with him. At least he did "escort a young woman ashore" in Canton, one record states. Stories about Jane from here on are less well documented but she is supposed to have taken up with a wealthy Englishman for a time, eventual-

IN MEMORY of D. M. McTAVISH AGED 42 YEARS DROWND CROSSING THIS RIVER MAY 22, 1814

HISTORIC TOMBSTONE is easily oldest in Pacific Northwest, material of sandstone, foreign to country. Astoria historian, Burnby Bell, surmises that British-based North West Co., anticipating many deaths among employees and officers at fort, ballasted outgoing ships with "blank" slabs of sandstone, material serving double purpose.

After 100 years of exposure to damp coastal weather of lower Columbia, inscription has become very shallow, hard to read. Curator Bell has "limned" letters for readability. Author has mixed emotions about treatment, admitting old buildings, relics and gravestones, if left to ravages of nature and not "restored" or "renovated", or repaired in any way, soon fall prey to effacement.

LOG STRUCTURE is near duplicate of original Fort Astoria, standing at right of McTavish grave marker. Grounds are maintained by Astoria garden clubs.

ly returning to England where her trail vanishes.

On the Columbia River history was in the making. The Americans regained the country, Fort George was once again Astoria and the town grew. Sometime in the 1870s workmen excavating for a building uncovered half a dozen skeletons and presumably the McTavish headstone. A Catholic priest blessed the bones which were then moved to a new small burial ground near the top of the hill where the Astor Column now stands. In time the sandstone marker fell over and was covered with weeds and brush.

About 1904, Sam Gill, an uncle of Harold Gill of the present J. K. Gill Co. in Portland, was in Astoria as a crew member of the government survey ship *Lincoln*. Familiar with the McTavish story, young Gill searched for the long lost grave, located the cemetery on the hill and cutting through the

weeds, finally reclaimed the fallen stone. Determined that the relic be properly preserved, he enlisted the aid of an expressman and got the marker in a large gunny sack and on board the stern wheeler *Lurline*, putting it in the hands of the Oregon Historical Society at Portland.

There the stone rested until an Astoria business man visited the Society's museum and George Hines, the curator, showed him the exhibit. The Astoria man and fellow townsmen wanted it returned and promised to take proper care of it. So the slab went back to Astoria and was mounted near the front door of the newly erected City Hall at 16th and Exchange Street with a cage to protect it. Much later, when Astoria garden clubs finished landscaping the grounds of the Fort Astoria memorial site, the stone was again moved to a spot a block and a half above the original location.

BLOOD ON THE UMPQUA

Someone was groaning near him. Hedden crawled out from the bush to see a man trying to pull an arrow from his back and sinking to the ground with pain. It was Williams. He staggered to his feet and Hedden, cut and bruised, crawled to hold him upright. The two stood there in aching bewilderment.

* * * * *

Early in June, 1851, navigator Capt. William Tichenor anchored the *Sea Gull* off a prominent rock on the Southern Oregon coast. The land there looked good so he sailed north to Portland, then to Oregon City, where he took out a section of land around the spectacular rock, naming the place Port Orford.

The *Sea Gull* then set sail for her home port of San Francisco, leaving a party of men at Port Orford under the command of Capt. J. M. Kirkpatrick. They were supplied with some firearms and food, their mission to construct a trail over the Cascade Mountains to the thriving gold camps in the interior but to await the return of the *Sea Gull* with more supplies before beginning construction. As the ship bore away the landing party saw a number of Indians lurking among the trees on the mainland and frantically signaled it to return. The vessel came close enough to unload a cannon with copper magazine and the shore party placed it at the summit of their rocky "fort".

On the 10th of July a war party of more than a hundred Indians was sighted on the beach, the savages splitting the air with yells and letting loose a swarm of arrows. Whites and Indians closed in the hand-to-hand combat, fighting with knives and clubs, Capt. Kirkpatrick scrambling up to the cannon and lifting a flaming torch to the priming fuse. The explosion swept a shower of lead into the advancing band of Indians with devastating effect, killing thirteen with four more dispatched by revolver and rifle. The attackers fled to the woods, leaving the bodies on the beach, one of them in a bright red shirt. The whites remembered this man had acted differently, fighting with more skill than the others.

Two of the Indians returned carrying a white flag, advancing far enough to indicate they wanted to remove their dead. All were carried away except for the red-shirted one and that body received a violent kick from each passing Indian. Later it was learned the man was a shipwrecked Russian sailor, cared for by the Indians but guilty of seducing their women. Strongly fearing another attack the white men managed to slip by the Indian guard on the beach and escaped into the woods. After four days of rugged travel they got to the settlements on the Umpqua.

When the *Sea Gull* ran afoul of bad weather off San Francisco a steam vessel was sent with supplies for the road builders left at the promontory that would be known as Battle Rock. There the crew found only desolation and a note written by Capt. Kirkpatrick, relating the details of the attack but none about the men's flight. The steamer went on to Portland, its captain reporting that Kirkpatrick's party had been victims of a massacre.

CYRUS HEDDEN settled in Scottsburg, Ore. Founded at head of navigation on the Umpqua in 1850, town was center of activity in section for many years as outfitting point for many gold camps along rivers in Siskiyous. Hedden became prominent merchant in community, his store now almost only building standing in faded town. Business still operated by granddaughter, Emma Hedden, is partly filled with fascinating relics of Scottsburg heyday, including wooden cradle which once held Cyrus Hedden's baby son, Emma's father. At left Cyrus Hedden monument in Scottsburg cemetery is marker for wife Margaret, life span Jan. 28, 1833 - Dec. 20, 1890.

BATTLE ROCK, on southern Oregon coast at Port Orford is prominent scenic and historical point. A peninsula at low water, rock becomes island on flooding tides. On this beach swarms of yelling Indians attacked party of white men, July 10, 1851.

A new party was assembled, this time under command of Col. W. G. T'Vault, who started the first newspaper in the Oregon Country at Oregon City and had earlier guided regular army troops under Major Kearney to California in 1846. He landed the new contingent, which included U. S. troops from Astoria, at Battle Rock on Aug. 3. When additional troops arrived from San Francisco, Port Orford took on the aspects of a military camp.

About August 15 T'Vault and twenty-three men set out to survey a route to the gold camps, planning to head south to the mouth of the Rogue River, then along its north bank, having selected some of the roughest terrain in the country to scout on foot. Huge rocks, thick brush and downed timber presented a barricade so nearly impenetrable that the men were soon near starvation. Adding to their misery was the shortage of wild game and adequate hunting experience. After thirty miles had been gained up the river inch by inch the expedition was abandoned. The party split, thirteen men retracing the tortuous trail along the Rogue, T'Vault and nine men striking out in a northerly direction for the settlements along the Umpqua. After days of struggle against more difficult country they finally arrived at the Coquille River about where the little town of Norway now is.

The men were nearly at the end of their endurance, weak, starved and desperate. When they encountered a band of Indians displaying signs of friendliness, they forgot all caution, engaging the Indians to ferry them to the coast, payment to be all their remaining belongings except firearms. Unobserved, the Indians sent runners ahead to alert their downstream tribesmen of their impending arrival.

In mid-September, a month after leaving Port Orford, the sorry whites were heartened to see a large Indian encampment on the river bank a short distance upstream from the ocean. A welcoming committee waited on the bank around a pile of food which dispelled any hesitation the men might have about going ashore.

Now came the moment of truth. At the instant of beaching, the new found "friends" loosed a barrage of yells and arrows, then closed in with knives. During the melee T'Vault and another white slipped into a canoe and got away while six others were slain on the spot. L. L. Williams got free by swinging his gun by the barrel and when the stock was smashed, by cracking heads with the barrel. He ran as far as he could, stumbled and fell, to see an Indian trying to fire a gun taken from one of the slain whites and causing it to misfire, Williams

37

regained his feet, struck down his attacker and with the gun ran into a dense growth of brush. His pursuers returned to celebrate and mutilate their victims.

Williams found one arrow penetrating his back, passing through the stomach. He managed to pull out the shaft, leaving the head in his body. Another arrow had broken a rib, his scalp was opened to the bone, a wound in his side bled profusely and there was an arrow in his shoulder, with numerous knife wounds in between. Standing there, nearly fainting from loss of blood, he heard a voice whispering, "Is that you, Williams?" It was Cyrus Hedden calling from under a bush. Hedden was bruised and cut all over his body but had no such major injuries as Williams.

The two survivors began a struggle to make their way to the gold camps on the Umpqua, Williams able to walk only a short distance before fainting. Coming to, he would struggle on, leaning heavily on Hedden's shoulder, halting to let Hedden massage his arms and legs to stimulate circulation. They were without food except for the sour oxalis carpeting the ground and shelled snails common to the Oregon woods. Williams constantly urged Hedden to push on and leave him but his friend valiantly urged him along.

After several days of this grinding effort Williams could no longer stand. Hedden ripped off his own shirt, twisted it into a rope which he looped under Williams' arm pits, hoisting the half-conscious man to his feet. He pulled the end of the shirt rope over his shoulder, half-dragging, half-carrying his friend with agonizing slowness. The two reached the south shore of Coos Bay where Hedden found an Indian canoe to take them across. They were still thirty miles short of the Umpqua and Williams could no longer bear the pain of being dragged along. Hedden got him on his back and staggered on, foot by foot, resting every few hundred yards.

He was nearing the absolute limit of endurance when he came to a wrecked schooner on the beach. In it he made Williams as comfortable as he could and struck out for help from any Indians in the area, his only weapon a bead-handled knife which he hoped to trade for food. A boat came across the bay near where Reedsport is now, the man rowing it sighting the stumbling man, bare to the waist. He was S. Schofield and he immediately beached the boat and ran to Hedden, pulling off his shirt as he ran. The two went back to find Williams near death but were able to get him to the village of Gardiner across the bay.

For most of the next seven years Williams was an invalid, until the arrowhead worked itself out of his body. He eventually became treasurer of Umpqua County and later chief clerk for the U.S. Land Office. When he died in 1880 he left a will reading in part, "To my friend Cyrus Hedden . . . for kind care and attention while suffering from wounds received from Indians, I give and bequeath the sum of five thousand dollars."

SECOND SLAB FROM RIGHT marks grave of Daniel Lyons. "Danny" was outstanding character of Scottsburg's early, busy days. He left County Cork, Ireland, to make his fortune in America. Living in Kentucky for a time at the home of Henry Clay he met his lovely Virginia who would be his wife. Lyons, who was blind, took his bride to the Siskiyou gold camps in So. Oregon and No. Calif.

His sole resources a good voice and guitar, he wandered from camp to camp singing to miners in saloons and dance halls. Accumulating substantial nest egg, he and wife settled in Scottsburg where he bought town's leading hotel—the Lyons becoming most popular in area. He died while town was still prosperous, wife surviving him to see it subside with gold camps, then be almost entirely washed away by raging Umpqua floods. Her stone is at right, daughter Virginia buried at left of father's grave.

GRAVE OF THE UNKNOWN PIONEER WOMAN

Across the road from a lonely grave on the Mt. Hood Loop Highway curving around the mountain is a large wooden sign carved by Larry Espinosa of the Zig Zag Ranger Station, Mt. Hood National Forest.

The sign points out a pile of rocks, stating that this is the grave of a pioneer woman who died on her way to Oregon, her identity unknown. The sign and grave have long intrigued this author. Would it be possible to unravel the story of this woman and her death for *Tales The Western Tombstones Tell?*

During ensuing research we met John Standish, direct descendant of the famous Puritan, Miles Standish. Now deceased, John was intensely interested in geneology and spent years of research tracking down his ancestry. He was convinced that the "Unknown Pioneer Woman" was a sister of his great grandfather. Of several stories unearthed his is the best authenticated. It goes like this.

For several weeks before April 12, 1853, in Knoxville, Iowa, preparations were made to organize several families to form a wagon train for the arduous trip across the plains and mountains to the Oregon Country. The Bonds, Hayes, Jewetts, Windoms and Davis — almost all the families were connected by blood ties or marriage. Young William Bond and wife Hannah Hayes Bond had a difficult time making the decision to go. Hannah was pregnant but at the last minute declared she would be all right and the young couple joined the party.

The journey was beset by most of the troubles encountered by other trains, the worst coming when the Blue Mountains in northeastern Oregon were reached. Here, on August 24, Hannah gave birth to her baby, a girl later named Emma, and suffered complications. Rest for her was short, the party forced to move on for if they did not get to the Cascade Mountain barrier early enough snow would block their way. The train reached the Cascades early in September and on the 14th, at the approximate summit of the pass, a stop had to be made. Hannah could go no farther. She died here on September 15.

The men dug a grave in the soft forest soil. William Bond refashioned one of the wagon boxes, which they would not need on the down grade, into a coffin. Hannah's body was wrapped in blankets, placed in the box and lowered into the grave. The neck yoke worn by the team that pulled the wagon was used as a marker. Some details and most dates were recorded in a daily diary kept by one of the Bonds, still in possession of a descendant now living in Pullman, Washington.

William Bond was now a widower with three small sons, Seth, James and Ebenezer, in addition to the new-born turned over to the care of Hannah's mother, Mrs. Lydia Louis Hayes, John Standish's great-great-grandmother. There was no time for mourning and the party moved on down into the Willamette Valley. Most of the members settled around Brownsville, Halsey and Crawfordsville.

Seth Bond, 4 years old when his mother was buried in the mountains, taught school in California for many years. In middle age, while on a train trip, he sat beside an older woman and a friendly conversation developed. She told him she had been present at a burial in the Cascades in 1853, described the wagon box coffin, neck yoke

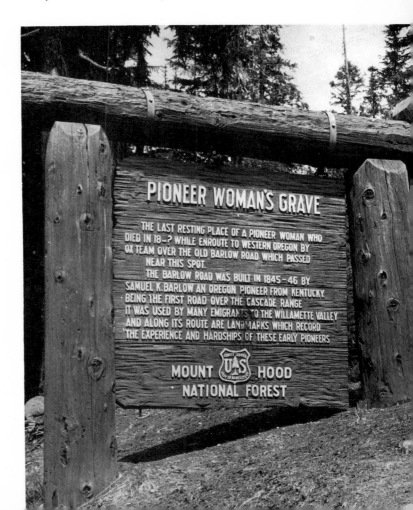

SNOW STILL LINGERS in June in high mountain setting where pioneer woman was buried. Timber of various altitudes blends here with graceful arching young cedar at left of monument, medium-zone mountain hemlocks in middle ground, alpine firs in background.

marker, adding, "I felt so sorry for her little 4-year-old son. I wonder where he is now." In a dramatic moment she learned the man beside her was that little boy. As soon as he could he went to Portland and burial place in the mountains, following directions given him by his train companion. At that time the Barlow Road was still well marked, even in the dense timber.

He found the grave, cleared away overgrowing brush and exposed the partially decayed neck yoke but made no attempt to mark the spot more clearly. In 1912 he visited his relative, John Standish, in Portland, relating all details of the incident.

In the early 1920s a road to connect the Columbia River Highway at Hood River with the road from Portland to Central Oregon points to form a loop around Mt. Hood, was being surveyed. Where the new grade brushed the old, long unused Barlow Road, a surveyor noticed a slight rise in the ground level. Scraping away dirt he found the corner of an old wagon box, and then pieces of the neck yoke. Careful excavation revealed the whitened bones of a woman. After due consideration the remains were reburied a safe distance away from the projected road line and identified by a pile of rocks.

Later, when the road was nearly finished, a cross was erected which carried the words, "In

Memory of a Pioneer Woman, 1848"—the year being one of large migration.

Had probing been stopped at this point it would seem certain that Hannah Bond was the woman buried near where the Barlow Road and the Mt. Hood Loop Highway come together, but actual scrutiny of the diary mentioned reveals a serious flaw. The document certainly proves the death of Hannah Bond, but indicates the location of that calamity and of the burial is somewhere on Summit Prairie, the same camping place where Perry Vickers lies buried (see *Boot Hill*). The following are three critical entries from the diary. "September Wed. 14 traveled to the somet Prarie met Hardon Davis layed by half day.—Th 15 Hana died layed by—F16 Beried Hanah traveled to and camped Loral Hill."

The reference to Summit Prairie seems very definite, and the party could hardly have traveled from the "Unknown Pioneer Woman's Grave" site to Laurel Hill in the time specified.

Mt. Hood National Forest files contain the following story, possibly relating to the incident. "Stephan Coleman, supervisor of the old Barlow toll road from 1863 until his death in 1905 relates that in 1864 near the Salmon River he met a man who had just buried his wife. The man stated that he buried her in a wagon box made from the bed of the wagon and had made a crude fence around the grave. She had been very sick and they camped there several days before she died. He inquired the name of the stream and said he would return at some time in the future and remove the remains. The man had two small children, a boy and girl both under 5 years of age." Here the main discrepancies with the Hannah Bond story are the date and description of the small children.

Another story on the subject appeared in the Portland, Oregon *Sunday Journal Magazine* April 10. It told of an interview with a Mr. J. F. Boothe who said that the grave in the mountains is that of his paternal grandmother, Mrs. Lucy Harris Boothe. There seems little to show that she is the "Unknown Pioneer Woman."

The Mt. Hood National Forest Recreation Director Mr. H. Cranson Fosburg agrees with the author that the "Unknown Pioneer Woman" remains in anonymity. He says that the road passing the grave is being widened and improved. A forest campground will be established at the site. The grave will become a monument to all the many pioneer women who died on the Old Oregon Trail.

DESOLATE GRAVES of two members of unfortunate "Lost Wagon Train" party led by Stephen Meek in 1845. First of party to die in Oregon was Mrs. Chambers (see **Boot Hill**), then two days farther west children of party were said to have found gold nuggets, later touching off stories of fabled "Blue Bucket Mine". When immigrants reached this point many were dying of thirst and general exhaustion, and about here turned north toward The Dalles which some eventually reached.

HE LEFT HIS MARKER ON OREGON

A prominent and influential pioneer, Jesse Applegate was politician, trail scout, road builder and farmer. He and brother Lindsay are remembered in a host of Oregon place names. Jesse came west in one of the earliest important migrations, in 1843, and in two years he was a member of the provisional legislature for Clackamas District. In later years his activities centered in southern Oregon and he developed a farm near Yoncalla about 1850. Originally the name "Yoncalla" applied only to the nearby hill, described as "ten miles in circumference and half a mile high" in a letter written in 1852 by Jesse's daughter Roselle Applegate Putnam. She said:

'The hill is called after a chief (Yoncalla) who came to beg for a crust of bread or an old garment . . . there are some old ones who remember the chief, say that he was a great physician and caught salmon in the streams and the women dug roots in the valley and gathered nuts and berries on the hill. They were a numerous and happy people. . . At this time there are four men living around the foot of Yoncalla who have between four and five hundred of cattle. . . My father's claim lies at the foot of it—he keeps the post office and calls it after this hill — he is very fond of hunting and this is his hunting ground. He has killed two bears and upwards of forty deer on it since he has been living here."

JESSE APPLEGATE died on his home property near Yoncalla and is buried in the tiny private cemetery there — not the Yoncalla Cemetery. No original buildings remain, more recent farmhouse stands on property.

MONUMENT to Susan and Elijah Estes stands near Jesse Applegate grove. Family is likely one of those mentioned in daughter Roselle's letter. Numerous graves of Applegate descendants and some unidentified fill small graveyard.

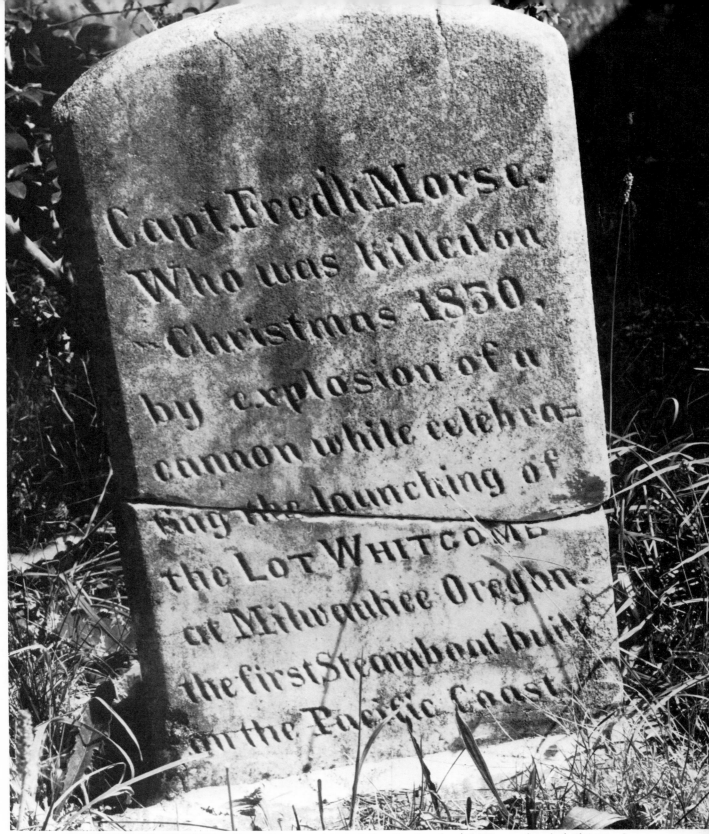

Capt. Fredk Morse.
Who was killed on
Christmas 1850,
by explosion of a
cannon while celebra-
ting the launching of
the LOT WHITCOMB
at Milwaukee Oregon.
the first Steamboat built
on the Pacific Coast

SIDE-WHEELER LOT WHITCOMB, with machinery purchased at San Francisco for $15,000, was launched Christmas Day would enable Milwaukie to get headstart over close neighbor Portland and outgrow it. Officiating at launching was Oregon's territorial governor John P. Gaines who made speech and christened steamer, Fort Vancouver sending brass band to ceremonies.

As vessel floated on river swollen by winter rains, "She made a proud sight", said local press. Schooner **Merchantman** was loading lumber at Milwaukie sawmill, captain loaning launching committee small, seldom used cannon. Young Capt. Morse was delegated to fire rusty weapon. It exploded, sending piece of cast iron into his neck, almost decapitating him. He died immediately and was buried in nearby Pioneer Cemetery then only containing body of Mary Meek who had died in childbirth two weeks before.

FIRST MINISTER ORDAINED IN OREGON

Born in New York State, Jan. 14, 1806, Josiah Parrish was one of the dedicated pioneers who came west to reinforce the original group founding Oregon's Methodist missions. His wife and three children came with him on the *Lausanne*.

Parrish was licensed to preach before leaving the East and was the first Methodist minister ordained in Oregon, the ceremony one of many "firsts" credited to the mission colony. With Joseph Holman, Parrish started breeding pure-blooded sheep in Oregon from a nucleus of several Marino ewes and a buck in 1860. And he was said to have obtained and planted the first white clover seed.

The minister held many offices, one being acting Indian agent for the vast territory extending from California to the Canadian border. He was treasurer of the early Willamette University and in the 1860s donated a valuable parcel of land close to the center of Salem on which to build an asylum for orphans. A few years later he was elected president of the University and then became honorary vice-president.

Rev. Parrish lived to be 90 years old but long before his death he took particular interest in prisoner welfare at the state penitentiary at Salem. Often preaching at the prison, he was known affectionately by many inmates as "Father Parrish."

GRAVE OF REV. JOSIAH L. PARRISH who died May 31, 1895, is marked by this comparatively modern tombstone in contrast to rococo one on grave of first wife.

ELABORATE MONUMENT on grave of Elizabeth, first Mrs. Parrish who married minister in 1833. Date of death is shown as 1869. Exact date of donation and establishment of present Lee Mission Cemetery is unknown but articles of incorporation show dates prior to 1860, pointing up this tombstone as placed here directly, rather than being transferred from earlier locations as were others in enclosure.

Photo of monument was shown in Sunday **Oregonian** May 24, 1931, illustrating article about historical value of old cemeteries which stated monument was carved by Frank N. Wood. Picture shows large elaborate cross as continuance of truncated stump shown here. Present custodian of cemetery, Dr. Robert Gatke, says rather ruefully that various attempts to repair stone were "somewhat amateurish".

HE BOUGHT HIS OWN TOMBSTONE

Born at Stanstead, Canada, June 28, 1803, Jason Lee was left fatherless at three and sent to live with the children of his brother Elias, twenty-one years his senior. One nephew was Daniel, only three years younger than himself, the two growing up together and remaining very close, Daniel later joining Jason in the trip to Oregon. The British-American War upset the Lees' lives and Jason found himself on his own at 13. An item in his diary reads, "I was thrown upon the world without money to provide for all my wants except by my own industry."

Fortunately he went to school for a short time, later referring to the little Stanstead school as the place where "our gentle youth was cherished." After working at manual labor for a time he was converted by fiery-speaking Rev. Richard Pope. He worked three more years and in 1829 registered at Wilbraham Academy in Massachusetts.

Of imposing height, about 6 feet 3 inches, he was "slightly stooping" according to one description, and somewhat awkward in movement. His complexion was light, features sharply chiseled with nose prominent, jaws massive and lips kept tightly closed. One account refers to his eyes as "spiritualistic blue", forehead high and receding, long hair pushed back. The impression is of an austere, cold and loveless man, yet he was to write the guardian of his small daughter, from whom he was separated at the time, "Please tell little Lucy Ann how much her pappa loves her, and how he longs to kiss her."

After ordination in 1833 Jason and Daniel felt inspired to establish a mission in far off Oregon to convert the "Flatheads". The two arranged to accompany Nathaniel Wyeth who was about to start on his second expedition to Oregon. Big-hearted Wyeth even made provision for the missionaries' personal belongings and mission supplies in the hold of his brig *May Dacre*. The vessel set sail for Oregon by way of Cape Horn from Boston in January of 1834, cargo including farm implements, garden seed and live chickens.

The land party assembled at Independence and left for Oregon. In his diary Lee noted some vivid descriptions of the journey, writing of the boundless prairies, of how trails were crossed and recrossed by tracks of countless buffalo. In the Rockies the men met Capt. Thomas McKay's Hudson Bay Brigade (see *Boot Hill*), the Indians with it staging a horse race, two of the mounts colliding and killing one rider named Kamseau. Young Lee preached the funeral service, first to be held in the Rocky Mountains.

At Walla Walla the party stayed with Factor Pierre Pambrun who helped get Lee's ten horses, four mules and three cows down the Columbia River to Fort Vancouver. There began a long and unbroken friendship between Lee and Dr. John McLoughlin. The warm welcome and spectacularly coincidental arrival of the supply ship seemed almost to guarantee the success of the projected Willamette Mission.

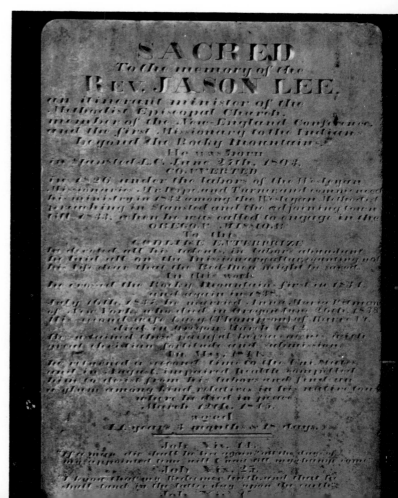

IMPRESSIVE SIX FOOT STONE marks resting place of man who in 11 brief years changed history of Oregon. Before his death in Stanstead, Canada, Lee stipulated in will, "Ninethly, I order and direct that a marble stone be placed at my grave with such inscription thereon as my friends may see fit." In 1904 negotiations were started with object of removing Lee's remains to scene of labors in Oregon, this accomplished in 1906 when bones were reinterred and slab re-erected here. Director of cemetery association, Dr. Robert Gatke, fears vandalism for historic relic, hopes to eventually set slab in more solid concrete backing and incise inscription more deeply, now much weathered. Lack of funds is holding project back. So far efforts at preventing vandalism of Lee graves has been posting of two college lads as guards until midnight last two Halloweens.

McLoughlin provided the mission party with canoes for the trip to the Willamette, and upstream as far as the farm of Thomas McKay who was McLoughlin's step-son. After a short rest there, the party moved on to French Prairie, then only dotted with a few rough log cabins of French-Canadian fur trappers. Farther on up the valley Lee found a site for his mission, about ten miles northwest of the present site of Salem on the east side of the Willamette River. Construction of log cabins began immediately.

Food was a real problem that first winter, most of it consisting of unleavened cakes made of flour provided by McLoughlin, peas grown by French Prairie settlers, salt pork from the *May Dacre* stores and the luxury of a little milk from the cows driven across plains and mountains. Later more milk would be supplied by Ewing Young's cattle from California, which included a bull or two, the missionaries' bull being on loan from McLoughlin. After shelters were completed the mission itself was erected, 32 by 18 feet, story and a half high, from the big and plentiful "Oregon oaks", *Quercus garryana*, growing on the river bottoms. The logs were squared on one side to give the interior a fin-

ished appearance. There were two rooms on the ground floor with four windows, chimney of clay, floor of "split planks", likely of cedar as were the roof shakes. The structure was snug but built on the rich black-soiled bottom land, created by successive floodings of the river. And another of its rampages carried away every log and shake so painfully put together. The only consolation was, the building had served its purpose in being the center of mission life for six years.

A new structure went up on higher ground and added to it was a school for local Indian children. Many presented themselves almost naked, perhaps wearing a fringed apron around the waist or a piece of deerskin slung over the shoulder. All were infested with vermin, Lee personally scrubbing and de-lousing most of them.

In July of 1836 the *Hamilton* sailed from Boston carrying the first reinforcements to the mission, including Dr. Elijah P. White, first physician to join the forces, and Anna Maria Pittman. The ship stopped at the Sandwich Islands, the party continuing to the Columbia on another. It was met at Champoeg by a messenger requesting the doctor to hurry to the several sick at the mission.

ALL BURIALS in early days of Methodist Mission were on mission grounds, a few miles from Salem. Presumably bodies were moved several times, one location thought to be on banks of Mill Creek. It is known that members of Rev. Josiah L. Parrish family donated sufficient land for permanent burial ground for him and other mission personnel. Later, all remains were moved there except those of Jason Lee who died at place of birth. Sixty-one years later his remains were transferred to this cemetery, stone shown at left.

One of small "pillow" stones in front marks grave of second wife, Lucy Thompson Lee, exact location uncertain. Next tall marble slab right is marker for first wife, Anna Maria Pittman Lee. Next tombstone, broken by vandals, marks grave of first mission worker, Rev. Cyrus Shepard, who never recovered from infection in amputated leg, dying in January, 1840. Horizontal stone between this and rail support is for Alanson Beers. At right of support is Parrish monument, then marker for Mrs. Elizabeth Parrish. Little plot has long been surrounded by much larger cemetery.

On a bright Sunday morning in July Anna Maria Pittman and Jason Lee were married in a grove of oaks near the river bank. Attending the wedding party were 30 or 40 Indian children and groups of French-Canadians, half-breeds and Indians. The wedding service was read by Jason's nephew Daniel and it marked the first Christian marriage in the Oregon Country, those at Fort Vancouver having been under "civil marriage contract", witnessed by two persons and approved by Dr. John McLoughlin.

Bride Anna Maria wrote her brother, "George, I hope you are as happy with your wife as I am with my husband." But in June of the next year she was to write no more as she died in childbirth, the first white woman casualty in the Northwest. Lee was in the East at the time on one of his many journeys to raise money for the mission.

On one such journey later he met Lucy Thompson and the Aug. 14, 1839 issue of *Zion's Herald* carried a notice: "Married — at Barre, Vt. July 28, by Rev. E. J. Scott, Presiding Elder of Montpelier District, Rev. Jason Lee of the Oregon Mission and Miss Lucy Thompson." A student at Newbury Seminary for two years and valedictorian of her class, Lee's new wife wrote a letter to her half-brother, dated Oct. 8, informing him, "The long looked for day has arrived, our vessel is in the stream; we go aboard at half past nine tomorrow morning. We sail on the ship *Lausanne*, Capt. Spaulding . . . . . My further acquaintance with Mr. Lee proves him to be worthy of the confidence I reposed in him. He is one of the kindest, best of men . . . he is all an earthly friend can be."

On Oct. 9, 1839 the New York *Journal of Commerce* reported: "The ship *Lausanne* has gone to sea, having on board a large Methodist Expedition to the Oregon Territory." Cape Horn was rounded safely in spite of a delaying storm but the Straits of Magellan were not reached until early in February and Valparaiso, Chili, was found to be in the throes of a smallpox epidemic. Since it was necessary to replenish food and water supplies, crew of the *Lausanne* went ashore which frightened some of the missionaries-to-be. Lee remarked in his diary shrewdly, "I have been watching the reinforcements in order to discover their traits of character . . . I am persuaded it is one thing to be a missionary on board the *Lausanne*, another to be a good one in Oregon." The ship finally reached the Columbia on May 20, 1840.

Lucy Thompson Lee began to fail in health shortly after reaching the mission. Her husband

UNIQUE TOMBSTONE tells pathetic history of Jason Lee's first wife. Author made numerous trips to Salem, finding cemetery and stones severe problem in photography because of spotty illumination, trees partially obstructing sunshine. Conditions were right for this photo, lettering standing out plainly in glancing sunlight, which vanished few minutes after photo was made.

was gone much of the time, establishing branches at Wascopam, Oregon City and other outposts. About March 20, 1842 she gave birth to a daughter and about a month later, while standing next to her husband at a Sunday service she collapsed. "One gasp, and it was all over," recorded historian Rev. Harvey K. Hines. "When a few hours later they laid away her remains by the side of his former companion, they laid away the casket that had borne one of the purest gems that ever blazed in the dark night of Oregon." Jason Lee, his tiny daughter cradled in his arms, turned away from the grave, perhaps vowing never to marry again, for he never did.

Death overtook him when he was only 41 years old, on March 12, 1845, in his old home and birthplace at Stanstead, Canada, a postmortem showing "diseased state of the lungs . . . the right lobe attached to the walls of the chest." He was buried in the little Stanstead cemetery far from the wives he had buried in Oregon.

PIONEER WITH A MISSION

Fate had other plans reserved for Solomon Smith than drowning him in a Newfoundland fog. He was needed in the new country of Oregon and by devious means was led there in the early 1830s to help establish, with his Indian wife, a semblance of order and Christian living.

Born at Lebanon, New Hampshire, Dec. 26, 1809, Solomon Smith studied medicine as a youth but earned no degree, spent a short time at a Norwich, Connecticut, military school but never served as a soldier. He went cod fishing off the Newfoundland banks but in a dense fog the schooner was rammed by a larger vessel and sank. All the men were saved but Smith wanted no more cod fishing and decided to go West to that talked about Oregon Country.

In 1831 he fell in with Nathaniel Wyeth who was recruiting for the first trip to the new land. The party left Boston in March of 1832, traveled by water to Baltimore, took trails across the mountains to the Ohio River, boats up the Mississippi and the Missouri to Independence. Then began the long march across the plains of Nebraska, men dropping out one by one until there were only twelve left, these near starvation, subsisting on rose hips. As they gained elevation even this meager supply of food ran out and the party was saved only by stumbling into an Indian camp, the air filled with the ambrosial fragrance of buffalo steaks broiling over the fire. The Indians proved friendly life savers, sharing the meat with the whites.

When Wyeth's men at last reached Vancouver, the weather cold and dreary, the welcome was warm but Dr. McLoughlin was cold to Wyeth's proposed project of salmon packing. It was the Hudson's Bay Co. policy to discourage all commercial enterprise that threatened its hold on the country.

At this time McLoughlin was without a teacher for the little school started for the Indian wives and children of his men, his first teacher, John Ball, having vanished. The "Great White Eagle" was a man to recognize talent when he saw it and in Solomon Smith he found an educated man with teaching abilities. The ex-codfisherman was hired at a salary of $80 a month for nine months a year on a two-year agreement.

Being a bachelor he prepared his own meals and on his first visit to the bakery of Frenchman Porier he was waited on by Porier's wife Celiast. Daughter of Clatsop Indian Chief Coboway, the girl was exceptionally beautiful and Smith was unusually handsome. She looked at him and he looked at her for the several days he bought bread and they decided to keep it up, the lovers running away to the French Prairie area on the Willamette River to start an Indian school. Solomon Smith was now the first school teacher in Oregon proper, classes held in the home of Joseph Gervais whose Indian wife was Celiast's sister.

Two years later the couple moved to a cabin at the mouth of Chehalem Creek where Smith went into partnership with Ewing Young in the latter's sawmill and grist mill venture, Solomon and Celiast being formally married by missionary Jason Lee on Feb. 11, 1837.

Attending a revival meeting of the fiery preacher David Leslie, the Smiths became inflamed with the idea of becoming missionaries. Celiast yearned to start with her own people, the Clatsop tribes on Clatsop Plains south of the Columbia's mouth. They persuaded Jason Lee to establish a mission there under Rev. J. H. Frost where they could actively convert the Indians. The Clatsops were anything but cooperative and the next few years saw the Methodist personnel involved in several brushes with ambush, always managing to come out alive.

Before building a home on the Plains, Solomon returned to the Chehalem to harvest his crops and bring back his fine team of horses. The animals were transported down the Willamette and the Columbia on a platform laid across two canoes. At the historic meeting at Champoeg, missionary Smith voted to go along with the Americans and was elected captain.

With the discovery of gold in California he went into business, selling produce to those heading for the Sierra at $2 a pound for butter and $5 a bushel for potatoes, soon having more money than ever before in his life. If he allowed his beautiful wife to wait on the customers, history does not record what happened.

The Smiths lived out their lives on Clatsop Plains, Solomon holding public office, such as clerk or director of the district, the rest of his life. When it ended in 1874 he was a member of the state senate.

PLAQUE READS: "Beneath this native stone lie Oregon's first school teachers, Solomon Howard Smith of New Hampshire, pioneer missionary, millwright, farmer, merchant, state senator and his wife Ellen, born Celiast, Princess daughter of Coboway, Chief of the Clatsops."

In background is Gray Memorial Chapel, erected on site of early Presbyterian Church dedicated in 1851 by Rev. Lewis Thompson. One of the principal founders was W. H. Gray, writer of Oregon's first history, 1869. Chapel was erected by Gray's daughter, front entrance portico pedimented with with walled sides and recessed between tall columns.

49

FIVE BEERS FOR OREGON

Alanson Beers, with wife and family of three children arrived in Oregon by ship, probably in May, 1837. The ship may have been the *Diana* as given in Caroline Dobbs' book *Men of Champoeg,* or the *Hamilton* as Cornelius J. Brosnan writes in *Jason Lee, Prophet of the New Oregon,* where he was fellow passenger of Anna Maria Pittman. The blacksmith son of a Revolutionary War soldier, born in Connecticut in 1800, was an anvil-solid help in the early days of the Jason Lee Mission.

Beers and some lay workers at the mission spent most of the summer transporting goods from ship to shore, a slow process done by canoe, while others were building a log cabin for him. As mission blacksmith he was kept busy hammering out nails, the square-sided, square-headed pieces of metal sometimes still found in the ruins of old buildings. Beers also repaired and built farm machinery and later was placed in full charge of the farms, erecting mills which required machinery. At the same time he served in organizations such as the famed Oregon Temperance Society of which the often bibulous Joe Meek was a member.

Alanson Beers was an honest, capable, trustworthy worker and Jason Lee named him as one of the executors of his estate. But his first claim to fame comes from his being one of those voting for the United States at the Champoeg meeting in 1843. He was then elected to the legislative committee of nine which framed for the country the new code of laws proving so useful and practical for many years. He also helped form the first military organization in the Northwest and later went into partnership with Oregon's first territorial governor, George Abernathy, in the operation of a flour mill at the falls of the Willamette in Oregon City.

GRAVE OF BLACKSMITH, house builder, organizer Alanson Beers is in Jason Lee Cemetery close by those of the people with whom he worked. Stone seems more modern than others, likely replaced wooden headboard. Shown clearly is plaque placed on all graves of Champoeg signers by D.A.R., this one having double meaning as Alanson Beers was son of soldier in that war.

THEIR LABORS WERE FRUITFUL

In 1824 a group of young men were hired in England by the Hudson's Bay Company. As guests at a gala farewell party, each man was seated between two lovely young ladies at the dinner table. One turned to his partner and said, "I hear it's a very rough country where we're going, without any of the refinements we have here, not even such apples and grapes as these." The lady beside him picked several apple seeds from the core on her plate and placed them, with some grape seeds, in the young man's pocket, telling him, "When you get to Fort Vancouver be sure to plant these. When they grow into trees and vines and you eat the fruit, think of me, won't you?" When the youth arrived at the fort he discovered the seeds in his dress jacket pocket and did plant them.

There are numerous versions of this story, all romantic and all might have been regarded as legends except for one point. Mrs. Narcissa Whitman, later martyred with her husband at Waiilatpu, kept a meticulously accurate diary. Under the date Sept. 12, 1836, she wrote of a visit to Fort Vancouver where she saw young apple trees and grape vines grown from seeds brought from England by a young employee, the seeds having been given him at a farewell banquet. At the spot where the apple trees were said to have been planted, an ancient apple tree stands to this day. It still blossoms every spring and bears the tiny, scrubby fruit characteristic of ungrafted orchard trees.

In 1845 a young emigrant named William Barlow (presumably the same 23 year old son of

SETH LEWELLING, brother of Henderson, remained in Iowa several years before joining nursery venture at Milwaukie. Spellings of family name have muddled local history. Originally from Wales, name was Lewellyn. In this country and joining Quaker sect, simplified spelling "Luelling" considered more "seemly". After severing Quaker ties in Oregon, brothers reverted to fancier spellings but disagreed on choice — Lewelling for Seth, Luelling for Henderson.

CONFUSION, DISAGREEMENT OVER SPELLING of family name extends even to inscriptions on tombstones. Years later when a Portland public school was to be named in honor of family, controversy rose again, factions finally settled for Llewellyn.

informant at Independence Rock. However he did have a bag of seeds which eventually became saleable trees, a large quantity at fifteen cents each. Even so the Oregon Country still had only scrawny apples. Nathaniel Wyeth claimed to have "grafted and planted apples and other fruits" at his ill-fated Fort William on Sauvie Island but the grafts and stocks would have had to come from the Hawaiian Islands and these temperate zone fruits would not thrive there. In any event neither fort or trees survived the Columbia River floods.

It remained for Henderson Luelling to introduce the fruit for which the Pacific Northwest became famous — apples, pears, cherries, grapes, gooseberries, currants etc. Luelling, one of three nursery-

TALL, SQUARE-CUT MONUMENT in center is that of Mary, daughter of Henderson Luelling buried on part of family claim, her commitment the first in what grew to be a well populated cemetery. Not long after father started his nursery in Oregon he was joined by William Meek, 30, also from Iowa where he married, bride dying within a year. He fell in love with Mary Luelling, 15, and they were married. She bore a son but died, infant being adopted by Davis family. He died within two years and was buried next to mother, Mary Meek.

At wife's death William Meek headed for California gold, accompanied by brother-in-law Alfred Luelling. After small success they returned to Oregon but Meek moved to California permanently in 1860, dying there in 1890. Graves in front are for members of Hector Campbell family. Campbell was member of Convention in Salem Aug. 17, 1857 to draw up Oregon Constitution, issue of slavery overshadowing all others.

road builder Samuel Kimbrough Barlow—(see *Boot Hill*) was a member of a wagon train that left Illinois for the Oregon Country. He loaded his wagon with the best grafted tree saplings obtainable in his home state with visions of making his fortune from an orchard in the rich Willamette Valley. At Independence Rock Barlow met with a man going the other way, fresh from Oregon, who told him, "You might just as well dump out the whole works. There are already orchards at Fort Vancouver that produce all the apples anybody would want", adding that Barlow would have enough difficulty getting his wagons over the mountains without carrying trees too.

Whatever his knowledge or motives, the man's words caused William Barlow to abandon his tree project. The wagon train was lucky to have no serious difficulties on the way west and when it arrived at Fort Vancouver and Barlow found the apples only seedlings, he must have cursed his minded brothers, was born in North Carolina, April 23, 1809. At 21 he married his childhood sweetheart Elizabeth Presnell, and seven years later the couple and growing family moved to Salem, Iowa where he started his nursery business. On April 17, 1847, they left for the Oregon Country, family now including eight children, the oldest boy, Alfred, 13, the oldest girl Mary, about 11.

The Luelling wagon was trailed by another, possibly the strangest vehicle to cross the plains — a wagon with a deep box filled with a foot of good Iowa soil in which were planted 700 tiny trees, vines and shrubs. To guard the tender and valuable cargo from hungry cattle, a "fence" was built around the portable garden. As the party neared their destination, Elizabeth bore yet another child, this one named Oregon Columbia Luelling, history not stating whether the baby wore pink or blue bootees.

The party arrived at Fort Vancouver in mid-November, at Milwaukie in early February. Many of the precious trees had perished but about half were in fair condition, and to nurture them, Henderson immediately bought a land claim on the east bank of the Willamette. On this land now are located an exclusive country club, grassy golf courses, a highly restricted residential district and the Milwaukie Pioneer Cemetery.

The dormant nursery stock was carefully set out and in a few years bore fruit. Even more valuable than the fruit were the propagated trees which found a ready market at good prices. When it came into bearing, one the original cherry trees displayed large black fruit of a type never seen,

WILLIE ANTON LUELLING lies in family plot near grave of cousin Mary Meek. Photographer made numerous visits to cemetery hoping to find even lighting on this stone, finally settled for tree-spotted illumination.

before, this a natural sport. It was named for Luelling's Manchu helper Bing and is still one of the best varieties of sweet cherries.

OLD APPLE TREE from Lewelling place grows at edge of author's grounds. In spring its immense contorted limbs bear blossoms as fresh and lovely as those on any sapling.

VENERABLE APPLE TREE planted in 1824 is surely oldest in West. Planted on grounds of Fort Vancouver (then Oregon Territory, now Washington) it has suffered over years. Neglected most of time, City of Vancouver took over care in recent years, adding plot to city park system. Worst damage to tree was in Columbus Day storm which took terrific tree toll over Northwest, literally cut old seedling in half, ravaged other branches. Mayor Rudy Luepke had tree pruned back to original shape, accounting for comparative small size now. Luepke also officiated at ceremonies in 1962 dedicating descriptive plaque placed by Vancouver Historical Society.

THE PAST IS ITS FUTURE

Founded on the discovery of gold in January, 1852, by partners James Cluggage and J. R. Poole, Jacksonville grew from a tent camp into a major gold mining town. Its history was not turbulent but there were always Indian troubles, even in the very early days prior to the general war in 1855, which came to a head with two murders perpetrated within a short time.

Indian George and Tem were convicted of killing James Kyle, and Indian Thompson was judged guilty of killing one Edwards. All three were summarily executed on the gallows the day after the sketchy trial and the triple hanging, first legal execution in town, was made a gala affair attended by a huge crowd.

Not long after this two young Indian boys innocently wandered into town, perhaps out of curiosity, were seized by a few townsmen and tied together. The terrified boys protested loudly and the group of men grew to a mob with arguments for and against hanging. Then T. McF. Patton settled the matter by jumping up on a wagon and making a speech that convinced the majority that the boys should be killed. The two struggling youths were pulled to a large oak tree and hanged.

In 1855 Indian attacks on settlers in the neighborhood became general. Most of the Jacksonville men were busy with well-paying placers and mines. refusing to get excited. The women thought this outright apathetic and formed protesting societies, holding meetings in churches and hall, upbraiding their cowardly mates.

At the height of these demonstrations early risers one morning discovered a petticoat flying at half mast from a pole in front of the express office. Men gathered around to guffaw and saw women "in arms" — irate ladies with axes, one attempting to chop the staff down. Dr. Brookes quelled the riot by stepping forth and hauling down the offending banner. The next day two effigies hung from a big tree, one wearing pants and swaying in a position somewhat superior to the other in a gorgeous, if shabby, silk dress. However enraged the women were, they could not think of chopping down the tree and none dared to be so unladylike as to climb it. The figures remained, swinging in the wind and rain all winter until they disintegrated. It was all somewhat of a tempest in a teapot, the Indian disturbances never having much effect on the town itself.

Much more serious was a strange sickness in a colony of halfbreeds at the edge of town. Local physicians diagnosed the trouble as chicken pox and by the time it was found to be the dread small pox, seeds of it were planted all over town. One of the more prominent victims was Col. T'Vault (see Battle Rock story in this book) who started the first newspaper west of the Rockies in Oregon City. T'Vault was attended in his dying moments by a priest, no one else daring to come close even though the man was one of the most prominent of Oregon pioneers.

Many old structures remain today in Jacksonville but the town is geared for tourists, the one-

UNIQUE among western cemeteries is Jacksonville's, somewhat resembling an early New England graveyard. Ornate tombstones, crowded together fill Ish family plot to overflowing, patriarch Jacob Ish surrounded by descendants, in-laws, garden benches, urns, pedestals. Dark branches of cypress trees form sombre canopy.

time stores, saloons and law offices turned into art galleries and displays of such artifacts as old bitters bottles.

Jacksonville cemetery is one of the most beautiful in the country. Situated on a high hill overlooking the historic gold camp, the burial ground is densely planted with madronas, cypresses, oaks and pines. Most of the area is gently sloping, walks winding in all directions among some of the most striking monuments to be seen anywhere. The spot is a popular tourist attraction with an unusual feature — little or no evidence of vandalism, to the credit of the visitors.

TALL SHAFT marks graves of N. C. Dean and wife Anna, first white couple married in southern Oregon, says bronze plaque on left side. Husband was born in Whiteborough, N. Y., wife from New Jersey outliving husband many years. Immense stump in foreground shows typical bark pattern of very old madrona.

LOGTOWN was a small gold camp a few miles from Jacksonville, now completely disappeared. One pioneer buried in rather extensive cemetery brought out "Harrison's Yellow" rose from the East, planted it by side of cabin door. At her death cuttings were taken, planted on grave. Original bush seems to be gone but historians have started entire hedge of roses bearing a myriad of tiny double blossoms in June along cemetery fence. Marker is wooden slab in shape of state of Oregon.

JEWISH SECTION is near upper end. Horizontal sunshine of early morning penetrating dense trees and shrubbery. Standing guard is very old manzanita, tree-like here, upper branches shaggy with lichens. Red trunk resembles that of madrona but leaves are smaller, bole gnarly.

BRITT FAMILY plot. Peter Britt, whose name appears on left side of monument, was eminent pioneer photographer. He tried gold mining on Ashland Creek but in 1852, at 22, built a small house in Jacksonville, setting about to make a living as a daguerreotype artist. The area was alive with miners, supply agents, traders, drifters, prostitutes—a wild and stormy boom camp kept on edge by frequent raids by Rogue River Indians.

Peter Britt had two aims—to make the finest photographic portraits in the new Northwest and to build a fine "picture home". He succeeded in both. His work found early recognition and popularity in Oregon and California, portraits beautifully executed. The gracious Victorian mansion with spacious grounds gave him equal fame as horticulturist and landscape architect.

MADRONA TREES are most conspicuous in Jacksonville cemetery. Trunks are bright, cinnamon red, young specimens always peeling, old ones with alligator-like texture. Large leaves fall constantly, ground littered ankle deep in noisily rustling carpet. Tree is said to reach 200 feet, this one about 75.

JEWISH inscription in detail.

SKULL DUGGERY

ALDRICH was second soldier killed in retreat from Indians. On June 29, 1878, detachment of soldiers was sent out to head of Murderer's Creek, about 30 miles from Dayville, to find and destroy Indians who plundered ranch home, killed owners. Unable to find natives, troop of 14 started back, were ambushed by hundreds of Indians and tried to flee. "We could see Indians on both sides and behind us," one survivor wrote. "We had to go so fast and the ground was so rough we had to stop and rest our horses at intervals, all the time firing at the Indians to hold them back."

Aldrich and several others died, rest straggling into Canyon City in afternoon. Large pile of rocks marked Aldrich grave, buried where he lay, but parents later moved body to Roy Ziler ranch, about 5 miles east of Dayville. Howard Black, curator of Grant County Museum at Canyon City, found once neat picket fence down, stone knocked over, broken by cattle. He had monument brought to Canyon City for repairs where author photographed it. At present burial spot cannot be visited because of fences, cattle, but may be accessible later.

SKULL at left is that of Berry Way, first man hanged in Canyon City. Way killed partner Gallagher while they were taking $80,000 in gold dust to mint in The Dalles and escaped with fortune to Idaho. When Gallagher's body was discovered, Way was suspected, traced to hideout, brought back to Canyon City, summarily tried and hanged next day.

Skull in center is that of William Cain hired by one Sullivan as helper on placer claims. When Sullivan was unable or unwilling to pay wages due, hot-tempered Cain killed him with old-fashioned cap and ball pistol. After quick trial Cain joined Berry on the hill.

Identity of skull at right unknown but thought to be that of white man killed by Indians, found in brush near town. Author was given permission to arrange and photograph skulls, remainder of bones supposedly lie in rock-outlined graves in Canyon City's Boot Hill.

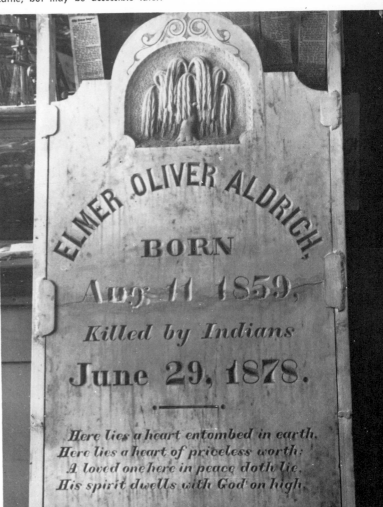

ELMER OLIVER ALDRICH,
BORN
Aug. 11 1859,
Killed by Indians
June 29, 1878.

Here lies a heart entombed in earth,
Here lies a heart of priceless worth;
A loved one here in peace doth lie,
His spirit dwells with God on high.

ORNAMENTAL CORNER POST of "pineapple" design at Mitchell, one of several towns along "Gold Trail" between Canyon City and The Dalles. Old cemetery contains many wooden fences, put together with handwrought nails. Several of them are seen here, products of craft popular a century ago, no two being exactly alike.

OUTLINED IN STONES, several graves near Canyon City Cemetery are believed to be those of early victims of hangman during turbulent, roistering days of Eastern Oregon gold mining town during Civil War.

TREACHERY AT THE TENT

The Modocs were a remnant of a once large tribe, the Lalacas. With their cousins, the Klamaths and smaller allies, they occupied the Klamath Lake basins country, homeland extending 300 miles from the Pacific into much of southern Oregon and northern California. About Revolutionary War time the Lalacas were in a great internecine struggle which separated the main tribes, the Modocs proper becoming restricted to a comparatively small area near Tule Lake.

Before the coming of the white man they found life agreeable. The lakes were full of fish, fields yielded roots and herbs, the brushy hills deer, antelope and rabbits. When immigrant wagons came grinding into the lake basins, the Modocs numbered around 600, brothers Schonchin, "Old" and "John" heading the tribe, the former as chief.

He fought the whites in early skirmishes but at the time of the Modoc War he attempted to keep peace with them while brother John remained hostile to settlers and soldiers.

While there was question of "legitimate descent" of the Schonchins from Moadocus, legendary ancestral chief of the tribes, there was no doubt of John's lineage. Born on Lost River, a member of the Moadocus family, his real name was Kientapoos but in later life was known familiarly as Captain Jack because of a fancied resemblance to a miner called that. The two would be the central figures heading up the rebellious Modoc fighting forces while Chief Schonchin kept most of the tribes in peace on the reservation.

The chief contended, with probable justification, that the war between the Modocs and whites stemmed from the latter being unable to distinguish one tribe from another. It seems thieving Snakes got away with some horses and mules of settlers passing through. Later Pitt Indians stole the animals or won them by gambling, then either lost or sold them to the Modocs. When whites recognized some of their stock, they asked no questions, slaughtered the Modocs and took back their property. The incident started hostilities and is typical of the misunderstandings.

In September of 1852, Modocs still smarting under loss of the horses and killing of their warriors, learned of an approaching wagon train bringing 65 men, women and children. They secreted themselves among the rocks the train would pass on the shores of Tule Lake and overwhelmed the party. 63 adults and children were slain and suffered unprintable tortures. One man escaped and two girls, 12 and 14, were held as prisoners, taken

as wives by warriors but later killed when jealous Modoc women threw them over a cliff.

The massacre was considered the actual start of the war, location known as Bloody Point, and caused a punitive expedition to be sent against the Indians. The group of soldiers was made up of volunteers from the Yreka, California, area and led by one Ben Wright who was reported to have packed a supply of strychnine to "fix the varmints". Upon reaching Modoc country Wright contacted missionaries and the tribes were invited to a huge barbecue. They arrived but asked the soldiers to partake of the food first. Wright ordered his men to open fire on the unprepared Modocs, the fusillade killing 40 of them.

The "Ben Wright Affair" was widely publicized. Most fair-minded whites were outraged, feeling that had Wright killed the savages in open battle he might have been a hero but his flagrant disregard

IN THIS STONE CORRAL were buried bodies of soldiers killed in skirmishes against Modocs, remains later transferred to various military cemeteries. Location is at base of prominent ridge (top right) once extending into Tule Lake, being observation point for officers watching proceedings at "peace tent".

of the white flag of truce was unforgivable. Certainly the Modocs did not forget. The incident would bear "bitter fruit" during the Modoc War twenty years later, according to historian Ray Glassley.

These dreary years were marked by fighting in sporadic bursts, in repudiated treaties, broken promises and treachery on both sides until the period when old Chief Schonchin held most of his people in peace on the reservation about six miles from Fort Klamath on the north end of Klamath Lake while Captain Jack, by this time recognized as a chief, held his band of bitter renegades on Lost River. In 1865 the white settlers of that area, feeling the menace of hostile savages so near their homes, requested Captain MacGregor, in command at the fort, to force Jack's warriors back to the reservation.

Finally, in 1869, Alfred B. Meacham, superintendent of Indian Affairs for Oregon, and O. C. Knapp, agreed to try to drive Jack and men from their stronghold. Lost River was a capricious stream, running from Clear Lake through the porous lava beds to disappear suddenly into the rock, then reappear at another point to empty into Tule Lake.

Meacham sent a courier to Captain Jack with overtures for a meeting, the messenger returning with one in effect, "Don't call me — I'll call you," and indicating that the possibility of a peaceable talk was quite remote, and any attempt to send a party of whites to Lost River for any purpose would be disastrous.

Not lacking in bravery or caution, Meacham led a party to Lost River with a guard of soldiers from Fort Klamath. In the afternoon they came

CROSS seems to be original erected at site of fatal attack on Gen. Canby, rotted base re-attached to new support several times. This was location of "peace tent", at that time almost on beach of much larger Tule Lake. Captain Jack killed Canby here and was hanged. Undoubtedly guilty, time shows extenuating circumstances. White officials, soldiers, settlers often lied to Indians or reneged on promises. During Modoc conference in lava beds Captain Jack held stoutly for peaceful settlement but savage, rebellious sub-chiefs clapped woman's hat on his head, called him coward. Only then did he join murder plot and turn bloodthirsty, insisting on personally slaying Gen. Canby. Latter was eventually buried in Crown Hills Cemetery, Indianapolis, Ind.

GENERAL E.R.S. CANBY WAS MURDERED HERE BY MODOCS APRIL 11, 1873

VIEW FROM CENTER of Captain Jack's stronghold looking north. White line in distance is Tule (for cattails) Lake, shoreline once extending to base of comparatively recent lava flow. Rocky projections (top right) were bastions from which Indians picked off advancing soldiers. "Fort" was secure against bullets but not against thirst. When attacking soldiers prevented Modocs from reaching lake shore, Indians used ice perpetually existing in deep recesses of caves, retreating when this was exhausted. Pursuing soldiers threw up temporary defense walls, remains shown in center foreground.

upon a few Modoc warriors posted on the outskirts of a renegade village. Meacham sent word to Captain Jack and prepared his men for a wakeful night keeping soldiers on watch.

When supply wagons came up a feast was prepared for the expected Modocs but Captain Jack, upon arriving at the parley grounds, merely stared at Meacham, refusing to speak. Neither would the Indians eat, reminding Meacham of the Ben Wright catastrophe. All this time the white men ate with obvious relish and the Modocs were impressed enough to begin stuffing themselves with bacon, beef, hard bread and coffee, and agreed to listen to Meacham's message.

"What do you want us to do?" Captain Jack asked. "Come back with us," Meacham answered, "and live on the reservation in peace." "And if I am not willing to do this?" "Then", the white leader told him, "we'll whip you until you are

willing." Tension at this point was running high and Winema stepped in. She was the Modoc wife of white Frank Riddle and niece of Captain Jack, and with a few English words she appealed for the sympathies of both sides and for a "cooling off" period in negotiations. Talks then proceeded until evening when the Modoc leader was given until next morning to make up his mind. Meacham and party prepared for another sleepless night, after sending a courier back for a larger contingent of soldiers, these cautioned to approach only to a point within earshot of the next morning's talks, and on no account to move in unless gunfire was heard.

Negotiations began again early the next day, both sides moving to some accord, when the company of soldiers sent for rode full tilt into camp. The men had stopped somewhere on the way and filled up on whiskey, forgetting all instructions. The

CAVE IN LAVA BEDS was hiding place of Captain Jack and family until forced to leave for lack of water.

Modocs took to the sagebrush, soldiers encircling the entire Indian camp and keeping a guard around it all that day and night. Next morning they found they had a bag of some 200 Modocs but not Captain Jack, Schonchin John and subchiefs, who had fled to the lava beds.

Relieved of their arms the captured Indians were allowed to bring up their ponies, Meacham and party ready to move everyone, including "Mary, Queen of the Modocs", a sister of Captain Jack. She was considered "very intelligent", having lived with a number of white men possessing considerable worldly goods, changing to a new one when collecting all she could. She proposed that if released she would search out her brother and try to talk him into going to the reservation with the tribesmen. The request was granted and after waiting several days, Captain Jack and Schonchin appeared to join the pack.

The cooperative mood did not last. Friction developed when Indian agents prohibited all gambling, a popular pastime which often involved the exchange of wives or daughters. Further roughness occurred with the Klamaths, blood relatives but traditional enemies. The trouble was so bad Captain Jack appealed to the authorities, getting little action, the Klamaths taking advantage of the situation to steal food and building materials from the Modocs. Still nothing was done and Captain Jack called his people together, decamping to the lava beds along Lost River.

A series of futile, highly dangerous parleys followed, none leading to any conclusion. All promises offered by the whites brought the same answer — "White man's promises worth nothing." The Modocs grew bolder and began attacking the nearby white settlers, stealing their stock and burning homes. In spite of the protest of Brigadier General E. R. S. Canby, Department Commander, cavalry came from Fort Klamath on demand of the Indian agent to move the renegade Modocs back to the reservation — "Peaceably if you can, forcibly if you must."

An attack by the cavalry resulted in several deaths on both sides, Modocs scattering, then gathering into a group solidly entrenched in an almost impregnable fortress atop a rise in the lava beds at the southern edge of Tule Lake. Not far away, also at the edge of the lake but on more level ground, the soldiers settled down to await reinforcements. By Jan. 17, 1873, the force reached about 400 men. On that day the army launched the first real attack of what was to prove the most costly of the country's Indian conflicts, the Modoc War, on which half a million dollars was spent and in which 83 whites were killed.

Commanding Officer Col. Wheaton led the initial charge. At the abrupt edge of the lava beds his men were met by withering fire from an unseen enemy, several soldiers falling at once. The fantastic jumble of caves, tunnels, piles and pinnacles seemed a chaos but the Indians used it for complete concealment and those armed with stolen rifles had ready-made loopholes in a solid rock barricade. It was easy for an Indian to remain invisible yet pick off any soldier exposing himself. This advantage enabled a force of not more than 60 of them to hold off 1,200 white soldiers for about five months. The end of the first day of open hostilities saw 39 soldiers dead without a single Indian being sighted.

By the following April the soldiers had worn themselves out chasing the invisible enemy. Gen. Canby tried another conference with the Modocs, naming Gen. Gillem, Rev. Thomas, Alfred Meacham and Leroy Dyer to go with him to the parley, Frank Riddle and wife Winema serving as interpreters. A tent was set up less than a mile from army headquarters and slightly more than a mile from Captain Jack's Stronghold — a name the rocky promontory carries to this day. At the first meeting on April 14 the Indian leader held that his tribe should have the lava beds as a permanent home, since — "No one else will ever want that ground". Meacham pointed out there was no alternative to the return of all Modocs to the reservation or a separate one if they could not get along with the Klamaths. In refuting this Captain Jack called it another promise that would be broken as soon as he gave in and bolstered this argument by citing the Ben Wright affair again. Meacham pointed to the massacre at Bloody Point and made it clear that the Modocs must not only surrender in a mass but must name the perpetrators of the massacre. This, said Captain Jack, they would not do. He would never give up his young men to be hanged.

The parley ended unsuccessfully but Meacham was sure Captain Jack would have been willing to give up had not Schonchin John and other leaders now looked upon Captain Jack as a potential traitor. Meacham sent Winema to talk to her uncle in secret, to tell him the army would give him cover if he would come to the conference tent again. At the rocky retreat, Captain Jack suspected her mission and refused to talk to her in secret, knowing she would not betray him. So she told the assembled head men only that the whites wanted another meeting. On her way back she was approached by a Modoc hiding in wait, who told her the subchiefs had held a war dance and decided to slay the whites at the next parley. This information she dutifully reported.

Next day the Modocs sent Bogus Charley of the negotiating party of leaders, to the white camp to ask for another meeting. He learned Winema had apprised the whites of the planned treachery, reported this to his own people, they sending another messenger to the whites demanding Winema go to the stronghold at once. Meacham decided she should go but sent word warning the Modocs that if she was harmed, the whole army would retaliate. After a tearful parting from her ten year old son Jeff, Winema went to the camp and was questioned as to how she knew about the plot. The spirits told her she said but finally told the truth, steadfastly refusing to name the Modoc informer. The most bellicose Indians threatened to kill her but through her tears, Winema managed to make it clear that any harm to her would bring the army down. Captain Jack stood almost alone in defending her and provided an escort for her safe return. She implored Meacham not to attend the parley.

The whites faced a dilemma. Officers who arrived after the disastrous assault on the lava fortress maintained the army could exterminate the whole band in minutes. Veterans of that fiasco wanted another meeting in spite of the danger.

"Captain Jack is ready to capitulate", they argued, as another messenger arrived from the Modocs to see Rev. Thomas alone. He was told the Indians "had changed their hearts", that they were now in complete accord with all demands of the whites and would agree to come into the reservation. But the white mediators must go to the tent unarmed to show their good faith.

The next day was Good Friday, April 11, 1873 and a Modoc messenger arrived to say Captain Jack and others were waiting impatiently at the tent. Meacham was not in favor of the meeting, saying it would mean certain suicide, but if the others were determined to go, he would too. But Winema refused to let go the bridle of his horse, sobbing out, "You no go, no go. You get killed!" Canby and Rev. Thomas were already on their way and Meacham called after them, "In my judgment we'll all be murdered!" Canby called back that

SCHONCHIN, Modoc chief, tried in vain to keep tribe together in peaceful coexistence with Klamaths on reservation. Successful with most tribesmen he could not control rebellious Captain Jack and followers. Rebels did make attempt to live on reservation, could not get along with Klamaths, took to lava beds and precipitated Modoc War so costly in lives and money. Chief is buried in Schonchin Indian Cemetery near town of Sprague River on that stream named for Capt. F. B. Sprague of Indian wars.

WINEMA'S GRAVE in Schonchin Cemetery (Chief Schonchin's grave in background left) is marked by monument placed by D.A.R., Winema Chapter. Pure blooded Modoc girl, born on Link River, was called in childhood "Nan-ook"—the strange one—because of disregard for tribal rules, taboos. Later she became Winema, to whites known as Tobey. She often accompanied father on grizzly bear hunts in nearby forests. She attracted young lover U-le-ta, encouraged him, but during visit to white man's town of Yreka, Calif., met and married Frank Riddle.

U-le-ta was insanely jealous of Riddle, followed him with rifle, watchful Winema following both. When U-le-ta raised rifle at Riddle, she shot own rifle in air. Indian boy fled to village, wandered about as if dazed for days, stole canoe and launched it into rapids of lake's outlet, jumped out and drowned. Winema lived out her days on now terminated Klamath Indian Agency, dying Feb. 30, 1920, aged 78.

Meacham was unduly cautious, "After all," he said, "there are only five Indians in the tent. When Thomas complained Meacham lacked faith in God, he gave in and as he started to mount his horse, someone slipped a Derringer pistol in his pocket. He allowed it to remain in spite of the agreement for all to go unarmed and the party proceeded with Bogus Charley as escort. The Indian was carrying a rifle.

Through binoculars the white observers noted the council fire was at the back of the tent, out of sight, and Meacham sighed, "We are doomed." With him, Gen. Canby and Rev. Thomas were Dyer, Frank Riddle and Winema. Waiting in the lava beds were Captain Jack, Schonchin John, Boston Charley, Schacknasty Jim, Hooker Jim, Ellen's Man, Bogus Charley and Black Jim.

The talking began, Riddle translating the Modoc speeches into English, his wife Winema relaying the white's talk into Modoc. The parley was rambling, no points being made, and Bogus Charley walked over to Meacham's horse, took the folded overcoat from the saddle and put it on, saying, "Now me old man Meacham." In the same spirit of jest Meacham offered Hooker Jim his hat. The Indian refused it with the surly words, "No hurry, old man. We have all soon".

At Captain Jack's signal came the Modoc war whoop. Barncho and Slolux raced a few feet to the rocks at the edge of the lava beds, retrieving several rifles hidden there. Meacham yelled, "Jack—what does this mean?" and the Indian answered by drawing a six shooter from his overcoat. He aimed it at Gen. Canby's head and pulled the trigger. There was a misfire but the second effort sent a bullet into Canby's brain. As the general fell he was pinned to the ground by Captain Jack while Ellen's Man slashed his throat and fired another bullet into his head, then stripping all clothing from the body. In the meantime Dyer and Riddle took to their heels in a hail of bullets.

As Boston Charley shot Rev. Thomas above the heart he fell to the ground, then struggling to his feet, started to run. The Indian tripped him with the words, "Next time you'll believe what a squaw tells you, won't you?" As Thomas fell dead, another rifle bullet struck his body which was immediately stripped.

Coincidental with the first signal, Schonchin John who had been delegated to kill Meacham, drew both revolver and knife. Prepared for treachery Meacham recognized the signal for what it was and aimed his Derringer at his assailant but the little pistol failed to fire, even a second time. He dropped his head the instant before John fired at it and backed away, getting his pistol fully cocked this time. He was about to fire when Winema threw herself on the Indian, crying, "Don't kill him, he is Indian's friend!" While she was grabbing John's gun, Slolux ran up and struck her on the head. Meacham jumped for the temporary safety of a pile of rocks, looked up to fire his one bullet and was staring at Schonchin John, eyeball to eyeball. Both fired, Meacham getting a bullet under his eyebrow, his own wounding John. Both fell, the white man getting two more bullets. As Indians started to strip his body

Captain Jack ordered his warriors back to the stronghold, realizing the soldiers would soon be on them. Delaying to get Meacham's scalp, Boston Charley took out a knife and started to cut the skin but Winema threw herself at him so hard he fell over against a rock. Roaring a threat to kill her if she interfered again, he had the knife on Meacham once more when Winema screamed that the soldiers were coming. The Indians took to their heels without confirming this, while the Indian girl felt for Meacham's heart beat and thinking him dead, set out for the soldiers' camp.

At the first sound of shots the soldiers started a march for the tent, meeting Riddle who confirmed their fears. They ran up to the scene of disaster and saw Meacham trying to get to his feet, partly stripped and covered with blood. One soldier took him for an Indian and was about to fire when an officer called out, "Don't fire! He's a white man."

Surgeon Cabanis first ordered a stretcher, then bent over Meacham and tried to pour a drink of brandy betwen the wounded man's lips. Teetotaler Meacham refused to swallow it but Cabanis forced him to. The stretcher bearers arrived, taking the bodies of Canby and Thomas back to camp.

On the 14th the army resumed the attack on the stronghold. Several soldiers were killed in the first onslaught and a retreat was sounded, the men getting out of firing range yet able to prevent Indians from capturing any of the wounded until the dead were removed from the field. Then the soldiers operated in shifts to keep the Indian women from getting to the lake for water.

Lack of it caused the Indians to suffer most as they even ran out of ice, semi-permanent in the lava beds. One night a young warrior dressed as a woman made his way to the lake. The soldiers allowed him to drink but as he started back his walk gave him away and he was killed. Soldiers took his scalp, cutting it ample enough to share it with comrades.

Thirst forced the Indians to move several times, one shift causing a detachment of soldiers to be cut off. One of them laughed with a boast, "Let's go out and raise some Indians". They did and 53 officers and men were killed, not one of the 24 attacking Modocs harmed. Toward the end of the slaughter Scarface Charley called out, "You fellows better go home. We don't want to kill all of you in one day."

Scouting Indians intercepted a young white settler named Hovey. They wounded him and took his scalp while he was still alive, then beat his head to a pulp with rocks. A series of pitched battles at various points followed, Modocs returning to their old stronghold. Emboldened by victories, they attacked the main body of soldiers which had been strengthened by a detachment of Warm Springs Indian scouts, led by Donald McKay, son of Thomas McKay (see *Boot Hill*). These troops possibly turned the tide, the Modocs suffering reverses new to them. Among the Indians killed was Ellen's Man, his death stirring up quarrels among the tribesmen which were crucial in ending the war. Captain Jack had been unpopular for some time, suspected of being at least a potential traitor to his

IMPRESSIVE CROSS standing almost alone in otherwise crowded burial ground on hill above old Jacksonville, Ore., marks grave of one William Boddy. Author photographed stone for distinctiveness, later found Boddy was one of settlers killed Nov. 29, 1872 by vengeful Indians after skirmishes with soldiers. Modocs told settlers, "We do not kill women and children, but you will find your husband dead in woods." Just previous to trial of Modocs several widows were invited to claim effects stolen on bloody day. Seeing Hooker Jim whom she identified as one of the attackers of her husband she lunged at him with knife, screaming "You killed my husband!" General Davis disarmed her, suffering several knife wounds.

people. Now he was accused of placing in the front line of battle those not closely related to him. A splinter group split away from his forces, the dissenters being Shacknasty Jim, Bogus Charley, Hooker Jim and Steamboat Frank. These were the leaders of a group of 14 Modocs who went to the army, offering to track down and deliver Jack and the leaders remaining faithful to him in exchange for amnesty.

The army took up the proposal which resulted in the capture of Captain Jack and a few of his warriors on June 1st, remaining members of the dwindling band taken on the 5th. All were secured in Fort Klamath where they would be tried for the murders of the Peace Commissioners.

The trial, held in military court at the fort, began July, 1873. Seated on a bench were Captain Jack and Schonchin John, shackled together in leg irons. Black Jim and Boston Charley, Barncho and Slolux lay on the floor for unexplained reasons. Among the witnesses were Frank Riddle, Winema and one who barely escaped death, A. B. Meacham. Near the open door lolled the Modocs who betrayed their former leader—Hooker Jim, Bogus Charley, Shacknasty Jim and Steamboat Frank. To observers their attitudes seemed insolent. They were not confined in any way.

The conclusion of the trial on July 9 was followed by verdicts of guilty for Captain Jack, Schonchin John, Black Jim, Boston Charley, Barncho and Slolux. The judge announced no others would be put on trial, thus saving the necks of a number of Modocs as guilty as the ones condemned. Date for the execution was set for October 3.

A long scaffold was completed the day before in an open meadow near the fort to accommodate six persons, six ropes dangling from the beam. Gen. Wheaton, in charge of the executions, and the post chaplain, Father Huegemborg, visited with the prisoners. Captain Jack complained that when he surrendered he expected to be pardoned and live out his days on the reservation, that he felt those Indians who betrayed him had won out over everybody including the U.S. Government, that he felt the execution should be delayed until the whole case could be laid before the President, who he thought, did not know who actually instigated the killing of the Peace Commissioners.

The next morning at 9:30 a guard was stationed in front of the jail, a wagon with four coffins in the bed drawing up at the door. The blacksmith cut the chains of the prisoners who then got in the wagon, perhaps wondering why there were only four coffins.

Captain Jack, Schonchin John, Black Jim and Boston Charley were made to climb the scaffold steps, Barncho and Slolux remaining below. Nooses were adjusted around the necks of the four on the platform, Captain Jack's first, then two documents read, one condemning the six to death, the second commuting the sentences of Barncho and Slolux to life imprisonment. Axes swished against the ropes and the four dead Modocs were placed in the coffins for the trip to the burial ground. Barncho and Slolux never left the wagon, sitting on the coffins of their less fortunate tribesmen.

It was said that just before the execution, Gen. Wheaton was offered $10,000 for Captain Jack's body and indignantly refused the offer. All manner of wild rumors have continued. Were the bodies

DETAIL OF BODDY STONE at Jacksonville, Oregon.

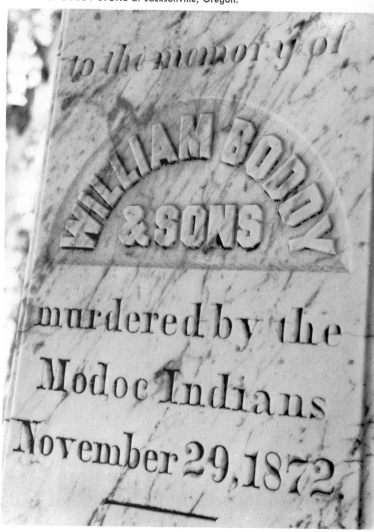

CAPTAIN JACK, Chief of the Modocs. Photo courtesy of Lava Beds National Monument.

PEACE COMMISSION TENT and stone on which Gen. Canby was seated when shot by Captain Jack. Photo courtesy Lava Beds National Monument.

CAMP OF COL. C. GILLEM, troop commander during part of Modoc Campaign spring of 1874. In middle background lower end of Tule lake, now dry at this point. In right background are lava beds where Modocs holed up. Photo courtesy of Lava Beds National Monument.

actually buried there? It was claimed they were removed and stones substituted, that the stones rattled as the coffins were tipped to the ground. Another story has Captain Jack's grave opened and the body removed. One old resident of Fort Klamath, now of Chiloquin, told this author, "Yes, some white man opened the grave, dug up the body and carried it away for a sideshow." It was also said a Col. Robert Miller, dying in Portland, Oregon, many years ago, left to the Masonic Lodge all his effects which included a box containing two skulls, one marked "Captain Jack", this being turned over to the University of Oregon. There is no truth to all this, said Mr. Shotwell of the Museum of Anthropology at the University. Later he added he had heard the Smithsonian Institution in Washington, D.C. has the skull.

And that report is a fact. After the execution army medical officers withheld all four heads. A few weeks later they were shipped by Assistant Surgeon Henry McEldery, U.S.A., to the office of the surgeon general in Washington, D.C. who placed them in the Army Medical Museum. Later the Museum turned over its entire skeletal collection to the Smithsonian Institution. Included were the skull and lower jaw of Captain Jack which became part of the Smithsonian collection Jan. 7, 1904.

THIS VIEW OF MONUMENT ROCK was made from elevation of about 7,000 feet, Mt. Hood in background, 11,245 feet. Period of greatest activity in creation of volcano was during late part of Pliocene Period, alternating lava flows and deposits of ash elevating peak to about 12,000 feet. Actual crater, visible from Timberline Lodge, is here concealed by intervening rock ridges. Of several glaciers shown, Reid Glacier starts high on mountain at left center and passes out of photo at left, is named for Prof. Harry Fielding Reid of Johns Hopkins University. This section of mountain was favorite climbing area of men who now rest in rock just below.

EAST FACE of huge rock on open slope high on Mt. Hood is monument for two long-time friends, members of The Mazamas, Portland mountain climbing club, named for mountain goat. William Hardesty was past president of club, greatly increased membership during long tenure, was 79 when he passed away in Portland. Charles Sholes reached age of 94, was member of original party which climbed Mt. Hood on July 14, 1894, and there founded the Mazamas. Sholes was nearly blind when author met him at photo salon in Mazama clubrooms in penthouse atop Pacific Building in Portland. He was nevertheless very much interested in pictures, examining them from distance of few inches. At that time he expressed wish to be buried on slopes of his beloved Mt. Hood and at his death in 1947 his ashes were placed near those of friend Hardesty in recess of immense rock. Gene Dowling, also friend of author and also deceased, made address at interment of ashes.

HOLOCAUST AT SILVER LAKE

On Christmas Eve, 1894, George Payne was sitting near the decorated tree set up for the dance hall party above his store. His view of the children's pageant on the stage was somewhat impeded and he stepped up on the bench, his head striking one of the lanterns. It was knocked to the floor and in moments the flaming "coal oil" had spread to the cotton-covered tree and gaily covered paper streamers hanging from the ceiling. The entire hall was soon ablaze and forty-three people in Silver Lake were to perish.

Silver Lake is the shrunken remnant of a once vast body of water covering much of central Oregon. In what geologist-author Phil Brogan calls the "Pluvial Days", when rain was more abundant than today, Silver, Fort Rock, Thorn, Christmas and other lakes were one large body. Through the years it drained and evaporated, the lakes dwindling to pools or disappearing, as Silver Lake likely will eventually. At the edge of what might be called its high water line lies the tiny, little known village of Silver Lake.

AFTER FATAL BLAZE citizens and ranchers sifted ashes of burned building, salvaging all human remains possible. These and victims of falling balcony were accorded community funeral, mass grave located in tiny cemetery along present Fremont Highway just south of town. Impressive monument was erected some time later, names of victims inscribed on sides. They remain legible in spite of years of cutting, scouring, sand-laden winds which whip area much of time.

HOMESTEADS were liberally scattered over eastern fringe of Oregon Cascades at time of Silver Lake's disastrous fire, precipitation and shallow wells providing sufficient water for crops and cattle. As this dried up almost all ranches and homes were abandoned, bony ruins still in evidence along entire strip. Trees in background are Ponderosa pine, important timber crop in region.

DETAIL OF COLLAPSING WALLS of old homesteader's cabin in drying rangeland. Logs of Ponderosa pine were cut, shaped by hand, possibly around 1880's.

December of 1875 saw a post office established in a log cabin nine miles east of the present town site which was homesteaded in 1884 by H. F. West and platted a few years later. Most of the fifteen blocks are still unimproved. The first Silver Lake business was a blacksmith shop, the proprietor Sam Allison. A few more small buildings were erected and formed a supply center for a vast desert area broken only by a few isolated ranches. After several years the town still numbered only about fifty persons.

The largest, most impressive building in 1894 was the two-story one housing F. M. Christman's store with auditorium dance floor upstairs and on Christmas Eve of that year, the whole place was a beehive of activity. The entire population for miles around was in town to buy supplies or attend the Christmas party in the dance hall. An outside stairway leading to a balcony was the only access to the hall. The large room had only two windows, both on the same side, and between them stood a big Christmas tree, branches heavily laden with a white burden of cotton "snow". A number of kerosene lanterns hung from the ceiling and ranged before the stage on which children were presenting the Nativity scene were several rows of benches for the audience.

Then came George Payne's accident and the quick-spreading fire.

Some escaped from the inferno by the one door which was suddenly jammed by a crush of panic-stricken children and adults. Those downstairs in the store rushed up to help, found the door blocked shut by the human barricade inside and as the load on the small balcony increased, it crashed to the ground, killing some and injuring almost all. Somebody placed a ladder against the outside wall under one of the windows but clouds of smoke poured out of the broken pane and there was little escape that way.

As the fire continued to rage Ed O'Farrell saw that many would need medical aid. The nearest doctor was a hundred miles away in Lakeview but he jumped on his horse and galloped over the wasteland, stopping at ranch houses several times to change horses and arrange for fresh mounts to be ready for the doctor. As Phil Brogan relates in his book *East of the Cascades,* "The story of Dr. Bernard Daly's ride through the lonely range land to the scene of the fire is a saga of western medical history". Dr. Day gave emergency aid to the injured and burned victims but forty-three people died, most of them unidentifiable, their bodies reduced to charred skeletons. The blaze was Oregon's worst of the times and the deaths led to the enactment of the state law requiring that doors of public buildings must open outward.

CAME THE DELUGE—AND DISASTER

On the Sunday evening of June 14, 1903 the sky above Heppner turned black and the deluge commenced, with huge raindrops drenching the wooden sidewalks, then hailstones fell so thick they piled up like snowdrifts. Yet the downpour of rain and hail was nothing as compared with the storm in the hills above the headwaters of Willow Creek and its tributary, Balm Fork. Ordinarily small enough to jump over, both streams swelled with a roar and a wall of muddy water over 12 feet high swept down on the town. This was disaster.

Like Marcus Whitman's Waiilatpu, the valley nestling at the confluence of Willow and Hinton Creeks was "a place of rye grass." In this spot, sheltered by dome-like foothills, cattlemen grazed their herds during the years before and after 1858. Settling there about that time, George W. Standsbury built a log cabin, the locality known as Standsbury Flat, level ground in a land of rolling contours.

A small town grew up around the Standsbury cabin, large enough in 1872 to support a store, which was built by partners Jackson L. Morrow and Henry Heppner and stocked with supplies brought in by ox team. With settlers came children and the need for a school and since there was no money for education, resourceful Henry Heppner jumped on his cayuse, made the rounds of all farmers and cattlemen and gathered the funds for a small school, "I think," said Standsbury, "we ought to recognize the initiative Henry displayed by naming our community for him." So the cattle-sheep-wheat center became Heppner.

By 1903 the town had several thousand people, including those on outlying ranches. It always suffered alternately from drought and flash floods but the bursts of muddy water coursing down Willow Creek were not too dangerous and the accompanying rain so welcome, the people did not worry too much about them. And then the rains did come with a vengeance.

All unaware of impending disaster on that fatal day in June, the citizens were going about their usual Sunday evening activities. Several Chinese were slaving over steaming tubs in the laundry by the creek and saloons were dispensing liquids for dry throats. But menace was coming down the creeks, flood water slowed some just above town when debris jammed against the willows along the banks. Then the great mass gave way with a great explosion, inundating the laundry and demolishing the concrete and stone building and Chinese in it.

The grinding roar alerted customers in the Belvidere, first saloon just below the laundry, and most of them escaped. One Dick Neville was reported to have clutched a beer tap and shouted, "I'll stay with her 'til Hell freezes over!" That building stood firm but the next saloon in line, Swaggart and McAtee's, was crushed to splinters.

HEPPNER, OREGON after flood waters and debris poured through main street. (Photo Oregon Historical Society).

By this time the weight of water was increased by a deadly load of timbers and small buildings which smashed down all other structures in its path, destroying virtually everything in the lower part of town. Altogether 225 people died in the waters or were killed by plunging timbers.

Young Leslie Matlock and Bruce Kelly were among those who fled the Belvidere and they realized the flood would soon reach the small towns below, Lexington and Ione. Matlock kicked in the door of the hardware store and grabbed shears to cut barbed wire while Kelly got two horses from the livery stable. They pounded across the hills in the downpour and lightning flashes, reaching Lexington as the waters did, racing on to Ione. Kelley's horse fell winded and Matlock went on, riding down the hamlet's main street shouting warnings in time for everyone to get to higher ground.

The outside world heard of the disaster from 15-year-old Guy Boyer who rode to the rail station in Echo where he was put aboard a special engine and a run made to Pendleton where he told the news to telegraph operators. Newspapers printed black headlines magnifying the horror — "FIVE HUNDRED DEAD AT HEPPNER", one

screamed. Yet several Oregon papers made humanitarian efforts to rush relief supplies to the devastated towns. Although Lexington did not receive as much damage or publicity as Heppner, there were 9-foot piles of debris and mud in the main street and 12 bodies found in them, some being washed down from Heppner.

In that town martial law was declared and the problem of quick disposal of the dead in the hot weather grew serious. Long rows of bodies lay in the Opera House and Belvidere Saloon, almost the only buildings left intact. Identification was difficult, often impossible. Embalming fluid and coffins were exhausted. In the cemetery on the hill ministers passed from one yawning grave to the next repeating the burial service.

Although 64 years have passed and most of the physical scars long since erased, "The Flood" is still the most important event in Heppner's long history. And there is always the fear of just such another, Federal plans for flood controls, dams and channels have been delayed or postponed repeatedly. Next summer or the one following another wall of water could rush down on the eastern Oregon town of Heppner and cause more death and damage than that one of terror in 1903.

HEPPNER CEMETERY contains graves of many victims of flood in which 225 people died. Author made rubbings of several typical monument inscriptions.

GRAVE OF HERO of Heppner flood — Leslie L. Matlock — in Heppner Cemetery. (Photo Heppner **Gazette**).

PRESIDENT OF CALIFORNIA

The Grand and Glorious Republic of California lasted just twenty-five days. With the raising of the "Bear Flag" William P. Ide was elected its president and the period of glory for both might have lasted longer had not the United States and Mexico become involved in actual war. As it was, on July 7, 1846, the American flag was raised over the Customs House in Sonoma, heretofore Mexican California. And two days later a contingent under Lieut. Joseph Warren Revere, grandson of famous Paul, arrived to lower the Bear Flag from the pole in the plaza, and replace it with the Stars and Stripes.

William Brown Ide was born in Rutland, Mass., March, 28, 1786. After a sketchy education for a common school grade his father trained him as a carpenter. He married in 1820 and after raising a family caught the fever that swept many to the Far West. Leaving Independence, Missouri, in 1844, for Oregon he was influenced by the glowing reports coming from California, altered his course and arrived at Sutter's Fort near Sacramento in October of the following year. Learning Ide was clever with hammer and saw, Peter Lassen hired him immediately to oversee builders at his ranch on Deer Creek in Tehama County.

HISTORIC SPOT in old Sonoma Plaza where Bear Flag was raised and William B. Ide, described as "tall, lean, ugly Yankee", was proclaimed President of New Republic of California. Monument sculptured by John McQuarrie and placed on 40-ton block of granite, was erected June 14, 1915. Battered bronze plaque on face of rock is nearly illegible.

Author made rubbing with enthusiastic help of high school girls sunning in park. "Deciphered" inscription reads: "This monument was erected by the Native Sons of the Golden West and the State of California to commemorate the raising of the Bear Flag on this spot June 14, 1846, and their declaration of the freedom of California from Mexican rule. On July 9, 1846 the Bear Flag was hauled down and the American Flag here raised in its place by Lt. Joseph W. Revere, U. S. A. who was sent to Sonoma from San Francisco by Commander John B. Montgomery of the U. S. Sloop of War **Portsmouth**, following the raising of the American Flag at Monterey July 7, 1846 by Commodore John Drake Sloat."

Ide was nicely settled in his new job a week later and while he was congratulating himself on his luck, some of Lassen's relatives arrived from the East. One claimed to be a carpenter and Ide was fired. He started ranching not far away and grew friendly with his neighbor, Henry Lewis Ford. The latter had just been on a trip south to the area around Sonoma and learned Mexicans there were resentful of American immigration, were burning houses of American ranchers and destroying stock with the intent of running every "foreign American" out of their country. Ide's patriotic nature was inflamed since he felt all California should be American.

There were others who shared the feeling and Ide, Ford with thirty-one patriots moved south. Meeting a party of Mexicans driving a herd of horses toward Santa Clara, they forcibly "borrowed" the animals and rode on to Sonoma. There they grabbed Mexican Commander General Vallejo even though he had been friendly toward the Americans and hustled him off to Sutter's Fort as a virtual prisoner.

Early in the morning of June 14, 1846, a rough looking band of gringoes made up of farmers, trappers and hunters burst into the sleepy plaza of Sonoma. Ezekial Merritt, member of the party, later wrote to Commodore Stockton, "We charged upon the Fortress of General Guadaloupe Vallejo, and captured eighteen prisoners, eight field pieces, two hundred stand of arms, a great quantity of cannon, cannister and grape shot, and little less than a hundred pounds of powder."

While this token resistance was being subdued, several men were busy designing a flag to symbol-

ADOBE HOME of William B. Ide who raised California "Bear Flag", was president of California Republic which lasted less than month. Located where California-Oregon road then crossed Sacramento River, it was constructed by carpenter Ide and hired Indian labor. Well made adobe bricks were solid enough to be used in restored structure.

Immense Valley oak, towering over house, is only slightly smaller than specimen near Chico said to be largest in world. When Calif. State Div. of Beaches and Parks took over property tree was in bad shape, now stubby, broken limbs are neatly trimmed (center left), split crotches braced with heavy metal bars (upper right).

LAST AND MOST NORTHERN of California Missions was San Francisco Solano, later known as Sonoma Mission, started in 1823. Secularized in 1880, building was turned over to state in 1903, kept in repair now as museum. This photo was made at edge of where long vanished mission cemetery is thought to be, identified by venerable cacti. Trail at rear of mission leads around cemetery and along stuccoed, tiled wall.

ize the new republic they intended to establish. The white ground carried a large grizzly bear, signifying savage resistance to attack, a red star and the words "California Republic." A four-inch stripe of red ran along the bottom edge.

Someone commandeered a woman's white petticoat, or less romantically, a flour sack, for the flag. Bear, star and stripe were cut from a man's red flannel shirt. Most historians agree Henry Lewis Ford suggested the design and William Todd, nephew of Mrs. Abraham Lincoln, sewed on the emblems, painting the letters brown. Benjamin Dowell, one of Ide's party, declared it a good job and approving the symbolism, said, "A bear stands his ground always, and as long as the stars shine we stand for our cause". The proud flag went up, hoisted on a staff in the center of the old Sonoma Plaza. The crowds of Mexicans greeted it with laughter and derision, taking the rather corpulent bear for a pig.

William Ide's brush with glory lasted only the twenty-five days. He worked his way home on a steamer going up the Sacramento River and did ranch jobs for a time, always hoping to have a piece of land of his own. The cry of "Gold!" from the Sierra foothills changed his mind. Of his nine children several sons were grown and one or more went with him to the placers, as did Lady Luck. The Ide men returned home with $25,000 with which the father bought his coveted land, a parcel on the banks of the Sacramento, 17,707 acres, which he called Rancho de la Barranca Colorado — Ranch of the Red Gully.

The house became known as the Ide Adobe, built with the aid of friendly Indians who called Ide their chief. Some time later he went east to visit relatives and returned to find his wife had died. Having no heart to live at the ranch house without her, he moved to Monroeville, seat of Colusa County. During his last illness Ide gave shelter to an unknown man who later came into town to report Ide's death from smallpox. It was strongly suspected he murdered his benefactor and took his money.

INTERIOR OF IDE ADOBE, fireplace a rarity in crude cabins of day. All relics date from period, some as a desk, actually belonging to Ide, were originally in place here.

BEAR FLAGS of California, original and present. First bear was ridiculed as pig by Mexicans at Sonoma. Native Sons of Golden West say 13 flags have successively flown over state beginning with that of Spanish Empire, and including those of England, Russia, Argentina, Mexico.

BONES OF WILLIAM B. IDE are believed to rest unmarked in this neglected, vandalized cemetery near Monroeville, in field adjoining chicken ranch. Monument shown here is base for shaft, fallen at right. Other markers, tombstones, are shattered in disarray. Only saving grace is benediction of towering Valley oak spreading branches over burial ground.

MONUMENT to William B. Ide stands short distance from ghostly Monroeville, at edge of road and about half a mile from old cemetery where Ide is believed buried.

INSCRIPTION on bronze plaque at base of obelisk, facing road.

WILLIAM B. IDE'S PUBLIC SERVICE

EARLY CALIFORNIA PIONEER
MEMBER OF ORIGINAL
BEAR FLAG PARTY
ORGANIZED JUNE 1846 IN COLUSI COUNTY SINCE CHANGED TO COLUSA.
AS FIRST AND ONLY PRESIDENT OF
"CALIFORNIA REPUBLIC"
ISSUED, ON JUNE 18, 1846,
HISTORIC PROCLAMATION.

HELD OTHER OFFICES WHICH HE ADMINISTERED WITH HONOR AND DISTINCTION
JUSTICE OF PEACE AT TEHAMA 1846; SERVED IN COLUSA COUNTY; 1851 AS DEPUTY
CLERK, ASSOCIATE JUSTICE, COURT OF SESSIONS; TREASURER, AND JUDGE IN 1852

WATERFALL admired by Pierson Reading, member of party raising Bear Flag in Sonoma, lieutenant of artillery in Fremont's battalion, who traveled extensively in present Shasta County area. After leading his men over precipitous country above Pit River Canyon, he wrote:

"In some places the top of the bank to the water must have been 1,200 feet, the stream pitching over the rocks and ledges, forming beautiful cascades, one of which has an abrupt fall of about 150 feet." Actual height of Burney Falls is 128 feet. Most of water has source in huge spring above falls supplying 200,000,000 gallons per day all year, with more added in spring freshets. Pool at base is 24 feet deep, follows slow recession of falls as cliff erodes few inches a year. Good trail reaches pool by numerous easy switchbacks and where it passes close to tumbling waters air is filled with heavy mist, welcome on hot summer days.

THE GREAT IRONY of Samuel Burney's life, spent attempting to advance cause of his Indian neighbors, was in his being killed by a party of warriors. Many places and geographical features in Shasta County, Calif., bear the Burney name.

Born in Scotland, Burney was the first white man to settle in the Shasta valley, building a log cabin, barn and corral about a half mile north of the town now bearing his name. His grave is almost at the very edge of the highway, the outermost one in a burial ground notable for its well kept lawns and flowers.

PEACE IN THE PLACE OF THE LAMB

They lived in a brush hut at first, the young pioneer and his child bride, in a swale along Bull Creek Flats which was flanked by a grove of giant redwoods on the Northern California coast. The grass was high, as were those great trees—and their hopes.

From his home in Texas two years before, Tosaldo Johnson led a party with a huge herd of cattle to the mining communities of northern California. He left behind the girl he loved, Addie Steward, and when the cattle were safely delivered, he returned to marry her, not staying in Texas as he had planned but going back to farm the homestead on Bull Creek for which he had filed earlier.

It was a problem to find logs small enough to use for a cabin but finally Johnson did build one and secured a few horses, cows and sheep. A lamb strayed from the flock one day and although pregnant with her first child, the young wife went in search of it. She crossed the creek and heard the small animal's plaintive calls, finding it in a grass-covered glade ringed with giant redwood trees. When her husband returned to the house she told him of the idyllic scene, adding, "Tosaldo, if anything ever happens to me, I think I'd like to be buried there."

Addie Johnson had her baby and then another, both girls. But with the second birth she had trouble. Lingering near death for several weeks, she succumbed and her husband placed the body in burial at the spot where she found the lamb.

In time Tosaldo had neighbors and married the daughter of one of them, Roxanna. As the community grew a burial ground was needed and since there was not sufficient space for it where Addie lay, a site was established not far from Bull Creek, named by settlers because Indians had feasted there on a bull stolen from them.

The community grew and the cemetery grew, the boundaries gradually extending near the creek. A moderate flood came so close to the burial ground the descendants were alarmed. They petitioned for removal of the graves to a higher elevation but a permit was refused.

Then in 1955 Bull Creek became a raging torrent, tearing out all but 17 of the graves. That forced permission to move the cemetery and a new site, a very beautiful one, was established much higher up the hill, far from the creek, surrounded by mountains swathed in a mantle of giant redwoods.

MRS. RUBY HAMILTON, wife of one Hamilton so numerously represented here, wrote author, "After we moved the remaining graves up to the new cemetery the ladies of the community got together and held card parties, dances and cake bakes, anything to raise money. Then we got this marble monument." Horizontal plaque lies in front of flagpole near edge of new cemetery, late afternoon sunlight slanting across darkening marble. Large acacia tree stands nearby, shedding twisted pods on marker.

PIONEER GRAVE discovered when park system was established in redwoods. Identity of woman buried there was eventually made mainly through efforts of Mrs. Grace Johnson Baxter, daughter of Roxanna Johnson, who also alerted author as to story. Park service placed new marker on grave, not disturbing trees planted by husband. Area is inaccessible now because of flood damaged roads. Park supervisors were sympathetic to author's problem, later sending man to grave for pictures, of which this is one. Photo California Division of Beaches and Parks.

CREATION IN CHAOS

His friends gave the fifteen year old boy a year to live. He stretched it to twenty-five in a life filled with torment and tragedy, tussles with the bottle and insecurity of genius. A flashing success as a popular writer, he was perpetually in debt and trouble — a man born under a dark star and dying under a darker one. This was Jack London, romantic figure in the popular notion who found romance goes under the name of Jones.

The knowledge of his illegitimate birth was to dog London all his life, a concern not so much for the fact as for an answer to his consuming curiosity to know who his father was, coupled with a burning desire to found a new line of his own. He never learned for sure who fathered him and although marrying twice, and having innumerable women, he never had a son.

Biographers think London's father was most likely "Professor" W. H. Chaney, Irish teacher of astrology, the mother, Flora Wellman, living with him during the critical month. She was no "loose woman" in the usual sense but was fond of Chaney and her excuse for being seduced was, "I was so young and he promised me a bed of roses".

London kept voluminous notes on his own life, always intending to write an autobiography entitled "Sailor On Horseback". One of his earliest references to his boyhood is of his overhearing, when he was six, of a violent quarrel between the man he supposed was his father, and his mother. He recalled the man saying, "You're nothing but a whoring bitch. No wonder you got a baby with no father to give it a name."

Flora and Chaney separated before the birth which occurred in San Francisco on January 14, 1876. She called the baby John Chaney for eight months until she married John London, widower with ten children, all grown but two. One of them, daughter Eliza, took over most of the care of the infant Jack and remained the one woman he could always lean upon, steadfast support among hundreds of paramours, casuals and two wives.

Immersed in poverty, the boy carried two newspaper routes, at times the only support of the family. In some manner he obtained a leaky boat, sailing it up and down the bay, capsizing often to the great joy of the lad with salt in his veins. At thirteen he graduated from grade school with honors but lacking a decent suit, would not attend the exercises. Instead of going to high school he swept out waterfront saloons and the small earnings went to mother, step-father and step-sisters, Jack being more interested in the oyster pirates and wads of

money they made looting private oyster beds. At a time when the family was living in a squalid shack with filthy outhouse and no running water, Jack worked in a cannery at ten cents an hour, ten hours a day, spending every spare moment at the Oakland Public Library.

A new era began with the sloop *Razzle Dazzle*, offered for sale by an oyster pirate for $300. Jack left the cannery, borrowed the money from his old colored nurse to buy the craft and at fifteen started a career of piracy. Now he realized his dream of sleeping on the water — and not alone. Mamie was the sixteen year old cabin mate of the *Razzle Dazzle*'s former owner and known as "Queen of the Oyster Pirates", and when the sloop changed hands the girl took one look at Jack's flashing smile, shock of hair, deep blue eyes and white skin and declared she went along with the boat.

The first few nights of pirating oysters allowed young London to pay off the loan from Mammy Jenny and help his family substantially. In a few months he was drinking straight rot-gut whiskey with the seasoned men of the sea, often going on such binges his friends gave him a year to live. Stumbling aboard the sloop one night, he fell into the cold water and although a strong swimmer, spent hours in the numbing bay before being picked up near Mare Island toward dawn. These months of drinking, adventure and women set a pattern for Jack London's adult life. He was a periodic drinker, going dry for a month or two then embarking on a monumental bender, falling into the steady drink habit only during his last hectic months.

Still in his teens, London worked as hand on the sealing vessel *Sophie Sutherland,* went to the Bering Sea by way of Yokohama and returned to San Francisco considerably richer. He immediately paid off all debts and turned most of the remaining funds to the Londons. He then tried to be "King of the Hoboes", always driven by the need to be top man. He rode the rods, panhandled with success aided by his boyish smile and ability to fabricate hardluck stories. He "made the bucket" often, the penitentiary once and joined the vast mob of unemployed later known as Coxey's Army in the march to Washington. Often in difficulty with the law, he became an active Socialist. The unpopular association colored his later successes.

At nineteen London tried to get a high school diploma but failed to meet the standards of Oakland High teachers and pupils. He was unkempt, his mop of hair ruffled by a habit of running his

JACK LONDON rode near this site not long before his death, telling step-sister Eliza, "When I die I want you to bury my ashes on this hill". Stone covering grave is enclosed by picket fence to discourage vandals.

hand through it, wore no tie, his open-necked shirt one of heavy wool. He chewed tobacco, frequented saloons. The fact that he had to earn a little money by sweeping the halls and scrubbing lavatories after school did not help his popularity. He was lonely. His step-sister Eliza, now married and with some funds, offered to pay for the repairing of his decayed, unsightly teeth if he would stop chewing tobacco.

But even with an improved appearance Jack realized he could not stay in school for three years and instead took a "cramming" course in Alameda, financed by the faithful Eliza. After five weeks of intensive study he went into voluntary seclusion in his room at Flora's home studying the books to earn a high school diploma. He had twelve weeks of this, then University of California entrance examinations, a sail in his boat drinking with old seaman pals, and the first days at the university.

They were also his last. He had determination, his clothes were informal but pressed and clean, hair neatly combed and he looked, said a friend, like a combination of Scandinavian sailor and Greek god. But his step-father, John London, grew too frail to work and Jack left school to lock himself in his room for a week, turning out essays, short stories and humorous items. He mailed them to various publishers with his last cent for postage and back they came like homing pigeons. Working in a laundry at $30 a week, room and board provided, he turned the money over to his mother.

Then came the cry from the Klondike and Jack London jumped at the call of adventure. Eliza Shephard's husband also caught the fever and she mortgaged her home for a thousand dollars, drew five hundred more from her savings account. In San Francisco the men bought the thousand pounds of food required by the Canadian government and sailed on the *Umatilla* for Skagway. Then came the transportation of supplies to Dyea and the back-packing of them up and over the Chilkoot Pass.

The party, made up of several friends Jack made along the way, arrived at White Horse Rapids where Jack made extra money guiding other boats on the perilous journey. Winter overtook them about where the Stewart River enters the Yukon, the party making camp in an abandoned cabin until spring. With all the other weight of necessary supplies London carried many books and read *Origin of Species* and *Paradise Lost* over and over. When the ice went out the men built a raft which took them down to Dawson City. Twenty-year-old London never did go prospecting, spending the summer talking to people, courting the loose women who swarmed the place and absorbing color, atmosphere and characterizations for the many stories he would eventually write. All this time, from the summit of Chilkoot Pass to miles beyond Dawson, London was living in Canada. Yet his biographers and reading public insist it was Alaska, the myth pervading all of London's subsequent history. When he left Dawson for the coast, his boat did enter the true Alaska but since the journey of 1900 miles required only 19 days, he saw little or none of Alaska except the stretches of beach where nights were spent.

Back in San Francisco, Jack London set himself at writing once more and almost without

TRAIL LEADS to meadow, then up to summit of small knoll where Jack London's grave is located, about a mile distant. In 1919 widow Charmaine built home for herself of fieldstone gathered on property as a memorial to her author husband, idolized by millions, victimized by "friends". Structure now serves as headquarters for Jack London Historic Park, houses museum full of artifacts connected with author's life—desk, books, items collected on cruise of **Snark**. Furniture was to have been used in never-lived-in Wolf House.

funds, became shabby, thin and generally distraught. At last a story was accepted, $7.50 promised "upon publication". When the story appeared in print he was elated but had to dun the publishers in person to get payment. Yet this was the beginning and in a few years his work was appearing regularly. Then he was lionized, women fawning over him more than ever.

He married Bessie Maddern and set to work on the book *Son of the Wolf*. It was published in 1900 and proved to be a "time bomb" in its explosive success, Jack London developing into the most popular writer of his day. He had his disappointments. Bessie presented him with a daughter instead of the hoped for son and she was again pregnant. Jack was heavily in debt, never having money enough, never waiting for funds definitely due but always spending. He took an assignment to cover the Boer War and on the train to New

York spent several nights with a woman. In England his arrangement was cancelled but before returning he went into the London slums in the guise of a poverty-stricken habitue to study living conditions.

At home he told Bessie they must go their separate ways, that he intended to marry Charmaine Kittridge. Then the Russo-Japanese War broke and he was sent to Yokohama by the Hearst chain to cover it. In Japan he and other correspondents were "confined to quarters" by a government wanting to keep affairs under wraps. London rented a junk in Korea to reach a point near the front, was there arrested as a spy and sent home, yet did manage to file the only dispatches of the war at that time.

On the Bay he bought what would be the nucleus of his vast ranch holdings in the Valley of the Moon, a 130-acre tract costing $7,000. He mar-

ONE OF PIONEER GRAVES existing on knoll before Jack London's ashes were buried there. Presumed buried close by are ashes of wife Charmaine who lived to be 84, dying in 1955, long after death of husband in 1916 at age of 40. Charmaine's grave, at her request, is unmarked.

RUINS OF WOLF HOUSE, reached from trail leading to grave. When original 130 acres of ranch land increased to peak of 1,500 acres, London began building dream house. His draft horses dragged huge boulders three miles from quarry, redwoods on property cut for beams and interior. House had 26 rooms, 9 fireplaces, courtyard with "reflection pool", seemingly large enough for swimming. Overall dimensions were 80' x 82', cost about $75,000. Just before midnight, August 22, 1913, shortly before occupation date, house went up in flames. Arson was suspected but never proved.

ried Charmaine and planned to build a vessel named the *Snark* in which he and wife would sail around the world, selling all manner of stories written about the cruise. One magazine signed a contract, advertised that it was "sending the author around the world". Costs of construction of the *Snark* zoomed, materials proved to be the poorest and delays held up the launching months beyond schedule. Once at sea, the boat began to fall apart and in the tropics Jack broke out in a rash of skin diseases, his recurring illnesses finally forcing a return home. There his doctor diagnosed the troubles as the skin being unable to withstand equatorial sun.

Expanding his ranch land, London also bought the fanciest stock — cattle, sheep, hogs and draft horses, always going deeper into debt. He tried to patronize his many "friends" in the purchase of animals and supplies, and in the erection of buildings, getting about one-fourth the value of every dollar spent and finding himself again on the verge of bankruptcy, in spite of the fact that he earned well over a million dollars during his brief writing career. Another girl baby was born and it lived only three days. Calamity piled on calamity, stock dying in epidemics, trees and grapevines succumbing to disease.

The London's dream home, "Wolf House", burned to the ground on completion, a shattering tragedy for its owner. He was growing flabby and bloated, drinking heavily, often riding down to Glen Ellen to invite the entire population into the saloon to drink with him.

One morning in 1916 the Japanese house boy reported the master could not be awakened. The doctor summoned from Santa Rosa found him in a state of "acute narcosis". On the floor of the sun porch where he slept were two bottles which had contained morphine and atropine sulphate. Jack London died that evening, opening his eyes once to mutter something like "Hello".

EVEN TEMPERED CLIMATE of Northern California coastline is kind to many members of Amaryllis tribe. Botanical ramifications of family are many, controversial and impermanent. This old favorite is variously termed Belladonna, Naked Ladies, etc. Bulbs are long established in old cemetery near Westport, north of Mendocino. Town was established as lumber shipping center by Lloyd Beal of Eastport, Maine. Cemetery is perched on extreme edge of cliffs directly above booming surf of Pacific, contains many old graves, the tiny wooden headboard on this one illegible but seeming to mark resting place of infant.

CLOSE-UP DETAIL of carving on Captain Hawkins stone.

MEN OF OLD MENDOCINO were seafaring lot, when they died it was considered fitting to ornament their tombstones with marine motifs. This stone marking grave of Captain George E. Hawkins carries striking carving full-rigged sailing vessel of type then much in use.

OLD CATHOLIC CEMETERY at Mendocino is full of beautiful novel markers. This wooden headboard is remarkable for well preserved condition, though rotted off at base. Inscription is unique, letters are cut from metal, tacked on.

OLD CATHOLIC CEMETERY at Mendocino is high on hill above town and ocean. View southwest is over crescent-shaped bay, tips of horns set with tree studded cliffs. Groves of immense Redwoods back city but do not venture near rocks where soil is shallow. Here wind-blow "bull pines" take over.

BEAUTIFULLY CARVED MARBLE tombstone is example of nearly lost art. Inscription carved on lower portion reads "William H. Tainter—Sheriff of Mendocino County—Who was drowned Oct. 20, 1863—Aged 31 yrs., 5 Mo., 7 Days—Sleep on, dear Billy, take thy rest—God hath done what he thought best—Erected by his affectionate wife Molly Tainter—As she loved him in life so she loves him in death."

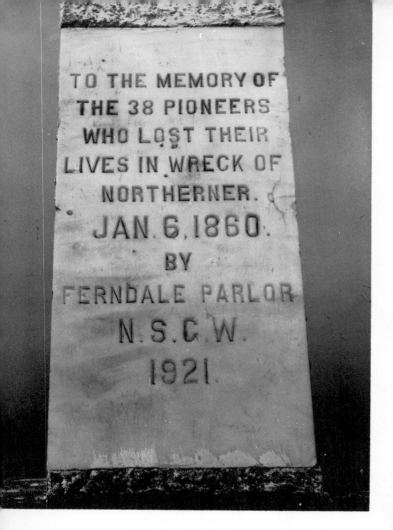

TO THE MEMORY OF
THE 38 PIONEERS
WHO LOST THEIR
LIVES IN WRECK OF
NORTHERNER.
JAN. 6, 1860.
BY
FERNDALE PARLOR
N. S. G. W.
1921.

ONE DAY OUT of her home port of San Francisco, January 6, 1860, the steamer **Northerner** struck a barely submerged rock off Cape Mendocino. Taking water badly, she listed over, spilled many passengers into surf rendered savage by storm. Vessel eventually drifted onto beach and broke up, losses listed as 17 passengers, 21 crew members. Large white cross stands near summit of ridge running parallel to ocean, plainly visible from beach.

CONCRETE CROSS bears marble plaque installed by Native Sons of the Golden West, suffering many scrawls by vandals in spite of difficult access. Centerville Beach below is frequented by fishermen who wade into surf using uniquely designed, framed nets. Nearby town of Ferndale is veritable museum of unaltered Victorian homes, well preserved.

EXPOSED ROCKS continue in scattered formation out into deeper water, there barely covered. In severe 1865 storm, sailing vessel **Brother Jonathan** attempted to find shelter in bay out of present Crescent City. Captain De Wolfe seemed unaware he was heading his ship directly into the teeth of St. George's Reef. Historian Bledsoe writes: ". . . suddenly she struck with tremendous power on a hidden rock, with such force that her foremast went through the hull, her fore-yards resting across the rails. Instantly the deck became the scene of the wildest confusion. The crash was so sudden, so unexpected, so awful, that those on board had scarcely recovered from the shock when they saw that their doom was sealed—the ship was fast sinking into the embrace of the hungry waves, and short time was left to prepare for death. Of the hundred passengers and crew aboard only one boatful was saved, between 80 and 90 being lost to the cold waters washing St. George's Reef."

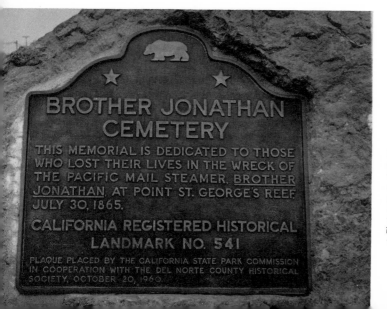

BROTHER JONATHAN CEMETERY is described in some histories as a neglected pioneer cemetery with many headstones revealing a terrible tragedy of the sea. Since then Crescent City has spread suburbs beyond graveyard, has completely reconditioned area, planting circular plot of greensward, placed salvaged grave-stones in circle, perhaps with no relation to actual graves, identification long lost. In center is flagpole, in front huge rock bearing this memorial plaque. Cemetery faces sea, encircling drive-way with parking lot directly on cliff above surf.

MARBLE HEADSTONE dedicated to memory of Polna Rowell now lies flat in well kept lawn, clean inscriptions almost illegible.

BROTHER OF POLNA? Number of bodies recovered from wreck of Brother Jonathan is unknown as is number of graves marked with permanent type headstones. Remaining now are only few of casualties.

INDIANS GOT THE BLAME FOR MURDER

Peter Lassen was a firm believer in green pastures, that the greenest lay just beyond the fence. Unrest made him leave a lucrative blacksmith trade in his native Denmark, at 29, to see the new world which was America, and the American Fur Co. gave him a chance to keep on traveling. He went west to Oregon City with a party and found a town of 75 families. From there he set sail on the *Lausanne* for California and left the vessel at the Russian settlement of Fort Ross, spending the winter at Pueblo de San Jose.

Lassen farmed for a year or more in the Santa Cruz area, moving to Sutter's Fort in 1843. Because of his friendship with General Sutter who had connections with the Mexican government, or because of persuasion and energy, Lassen soon found himself the possessor of Rancho Bosquejo, containing 26,000 acres of rich farming land. Kept from his new farm by winter floods, Lassen set up a trading post near Deer Creek on the east bank of the Sacramento River. He siphoned off whatever money and valuables Indians and settlers had and went on to his ranch about 1845.

Two years later he made ambitious plans to found a colony on his farm, hoping to build it into a city. He returned to Missouri where he had earlier made friends, among them Senator Thomas H. Benton who now helped him round up a group of settlers which he brought back to his farm. He named the new town Benton City and expected great things of it, but all his hopes went glimmering with the discovery of gold, even that of establishing a Masonic Lodge for which he had a charter. His settlers left for the placers and Benton City died aborning. The charter was taken to the booming gold camp of Shasta, May 9, 1851, the lodge established there. (For photo of Masonic Hall still standing see *Ghost Town Shadows*).

Now disillusioned with colonizing Rancho Bosquejo, Lassen began breaking it up. The first parcel went as a gift to a friend, trapper Henry Gerke, this land and most of the remainder eventually passing into the hands of Stanford University. Lassen moved from one venture to another. One was a trading post with a man named Burton, raising vegetables on the side which he sold to miners at a high profit. Another was the cutting of grindstones which he transported by muleback 20 miles to Sacramento, floating them on barges to any available market.

In June of 1854 Lassen pulled into a spot where Susanville would later be. There he found a single prospector, Isaac Roop, who was lonely and broke, having wandered over the mountains from Shasta the year before. Roop, Lassen and a few other prospectors dug a ditch for drainage, discovering gold in the process. A wild boom town grew up on the spot, Lassen and friend Isadore Meyerwitz, building a cabin in Elysian Valley, a few miles south of present Susanville, on the south side of Lassen Creek.

In the spring of 1859 Peter Lassen went prospecting with Lemericus Wyat and a man known only as Clapper. At a point some 140 miles northeast of Susanville the three made an overnight camp, Lassen and Clapper meeting their deaths here in a manner always in doubt. Wyat appeared in town with the story that all three men slept in a common bed, Clapper in the middle. About dawn Wyat heard a rifle shot and tried to waken Clapper,

GRAVE OF PETER LASSEN, trail maker, with background of open clearing in Elysian Valley, near Honey Lake (between trees and mountains). Lassen, founder of first Masonic Lodge in Calif., is well remembered by Masons. Monument on rock at turnstile gate reads, "Dedicated by Lassen Lodge No. 149 A. F. & A. M. to Peter Lassen, founder of Peter Lassen Trail". Original grave marker, also erected by Masons, is seen framed in left half of gate, second in right.

PETER LASSEN is remembered in two tombstones, one at left over actual grave. Newer marker is obelisk, right, erected 1917, reads, "In Memory of Peter Lassen who was killed by Indians April 26, 1859, aged 66 years. Erected in honor of Peter Lassen by the people of the Northern counties of the state of California." Site selected for grave was under sweeping branches of enormous pine, only stump now remaining.

then he saw he was dead, blood spurting from his temple. Lassen stood up, peering around to see the attacker and another shot brought him down. Thoroughly frightened and expecting to be the next casualty, Wyat jumped on his horse with no saddle and rode in without food or drink.

Strong doubts were cast on the story, which seemed to blame Indians. Lassen was friendly with Chief Winnemucca and his tribes in the area, the Indians calling him affectionately, "Uncle Pete". Wyat, over 60 and weighing more than 200 pounds, was described as "extremely awkward" and incapable of any such bareback ride. Moreover a party of whites inspecting the murder scene found all supplies untouched, too much to expect of Indians. Lassen was known to be carrying a map of a rich silver mine location and this was missing. No formal charges were ever made against Wyat, the two deaths being officially charged to Indians.

The victims were buried where they lay but later a party of "Honey Lakers" exhumed the bodies, returning them to a point at the edge of Honey Lake where they were reburied, Lassen under a giant pine with full Masonic honors.

ORIGINAL MONUMENT placed over Lassen grave by Masons in October of 1862, is fissuring, crumbling into decay, seeming near collapse.

LASSEN PEAK, named for trail builder, is pictured in widely distributed commercial murals. Author's photo was made inside crater, where red lava was seething in 1917, exploding in bursts of furious activity. Crater is peaceful now, though many fissures, pockets still hiss hot steam, sulphur fumes, some only inches from permanent ice and snow, as at bottom of photo.

When Lassen led a party of new settlers over crude Lassen Trail to Benton City, long and rough detour around peak caused grumbles of discontent, emigrants referring to trail as "Lassen's Folly". At one point they threatened to hang him but agreed to let him climb towering peak nearby, presumed to be this one. He saw Sacramento Valley from top, descended with glad news and party went on peaceably.

CONE OF DIGGER PINE. Some Indian tribes of California are termed "Diggers" as they lived on roots, bulbs from earth. Pines in same area, roughly along Lassen Trail, received same name. Digger pines are distinctive, trunks usually dividing, branching in manner unlike pine. Needles are sparse, grayish, droop as though wilting.

Cones like this one picked up along Lassen Trail are among largest of varieties, often reaching 10" in length, weighing several pounds when green. Cone produces abundant amounts of fragrant pitch, usually forming in glittering globules as shown here in center. Note also sharply hooked scales, painful if cone not handled carefully. A few seeds, among largest of pine nuts, still remain among scales.

NO THORNS BETWEEN HIS ROSES

California had gold and redwood trees and men came tumbling over each other to get to the mines and woods. It had seaports that brought ships from all over the world and drew men West to harvest the yield of fish from ocean depths. And it had climate, a temperate, gentle climate. But what adventurer would go to a land just for the climate? One did. He came to raise potatoes. His name was Luther Burbank.

Born in Lancaster, Mass. on March 7 of the same year that saw the great gold rush to California, 1849, Luther Burbank was educated in the local academy and then worked as a stonecutter. When the marble dust began to affect his lungs he obtained a small plot of ground for truck farming. He noted all the potatoes from a particular hill varied markedly in color and conceived a grand plan. He would plant all kinds of potatoes, tubers and seeds just to see what other types might result. As he set the plan into execution, Luther Burbank grew more kinds of improved vegetables, flowers, nuts and fruits than were ever developed by one man.

Burbank realized the world's real need was for potatoes of uniform size, smooth and reasonably free from scab. For four years he concentrated on the effort to produce them, nearly starving in the process, but developed the Burbank potato, the rights to which he sold to nurseryman Gregory for $150. With the money and ten of his own tubers — allowed him by the nursery firm — he set out for California and its milder climate where he could work at his hobby in winter too.

He first located near Los Angeles but stayed there only long enough to give the community his name. In Santa Rosa, about fifty miles north of San Francisco, he found, in 1875, an area with a mild winter yet with sufficient coolness to induce a proper dormant period in the plants he wanted to work with. The soil was rich and deep, climate temperate. In a letter sent back home to Massachusetts he wrote, "I firmly believe, that from all the places I have seen, that this is the chosen spot of all the earth . . . everything is like a beautiful spring day all the time."

But he was a stranger in a strange land, poor in health and purse. He worked in a nursery for low wages and lived in a room over the humid greenhouse. After two years, saving almost every penny he earned, he bought a tract of land in an undeveloped area where he planned to build a home and establish a small nursery. He dreamed of the place becoming world famous as the Burbank Experimental Garden. He worked as hard as his frail body would permit, almost killing himself before he discovered he had something more salable than mere muscle. He obtained an order for 20,000 prune trees to be produced in a year and Burbank, with a keen mind for publicity, saw the feat got wide notice. He was on his way to fame then, fame which put him in a class with men of great vision, associates Thomas Edison, Henry Ford, Edsel Ford and Harvey Firestone.

CEDAR OF LEBANON, planted as a small tree among others by Luther Burbank on newly acquired home property. As tree grew he placed chairs and table under drooping branches for entertaining friends, visitors. Plantsman was buried under tree, as he had requested. Now 120' tall, famous cedar is central feature of Annual Santa Rosa Christmas Celebration on Burbank grounds. Platform is erected in center of lawn, hidden spotlights arranged around tree. Few days before holiday, band mounts stand before guests. After speeches, child from orphanage or children's home presses button which turns on battery of lights. Foliage, being shiny "glaucus" or silvery blue-green, reflects light brilliantly. Band ends ceremony with Christmas music.

LOWER LIMBS of tree sheltering Burbank grave swoop to ground at location of it. General public does not know spot, only "under the tree", horizontal bronze marker covered with turf, because widow, still living in old house on property, suffering constant invasion of her privacy by people wanting to see grave, and feared vandalism of marker. Even so Mrs. Burbank places flowers on spot each Memorial Day. Supervisor of grounds pointed out spot to author, trusting publication of photo would never lead to desecration.

For two years he propagated his ten potatoes, sold seed on a large scale which brought him sales and prosperity no doubt greater than that of the nursery that bought the original rights. His business grew fast and he hired a secretary, Miss Elizabeth Waters. Association with her overcame a reluctance to marry and in 1916 she became Mrs. Burbank. During these growing years, Burbank accumulated little actual wealth. He had the true scientist's mind and often refused to consider such mundane matters as insisting on payment of money due him. This altruistic attitude was rewarded with a grant of $100,000 by the Carnegie Institute.

In 1924 this author visited Burbank's home and was told by Mrs. Burbank her husband was resting and could not see visitors. She would not know that the visitor, a shy boy passionately interested in horticulture, had hitch-hiked from Portland to San Francisco and Santa Rosa just to talk with the great Luther Burbank.

He died at his home April 11, 1926, at the age of 77. The author considers his life and work with admiration and respect, seeing him as a great scientist, his experiments often proving invaluable in inspiring and stimulating other horticulturists in their own originations and propagations.

The original Burbank potato probably had more permanent value than most of those painstakingly developed in many succeeding years. But his "spineless cactus" for cattle food, propagated in arid desert areas and wildly lauded in the press, subsequently planted in huge fields, was not successful. As time went by, the stubborn cacti tended to revert to the original form, developing sufficient prickles to discourage consumption for cattle. His famous "white blackberry" turned out to be a mere novelty, the fruit tasteless. Other berries rendered spineless by Burbank's genius had fruit of poor quality.

Yet other developers took Burbank's introductions and made them successful. His famous Shasta Daisy, huge and vigorous, now includes many garden forms, tall and short, with plain and curly, single and fully double flowers. His Crimson California Poppy, previously and appropriately golden, is now salmon, rose, burnt orange, and semi-double.

HUGE CLUMP of "spineless" variety of cactus, planted by Burbank on home grounds. Careful examination of slab at extreme right reveals small spicules, evidence of plant's persistent efforts to "go native". On many slabs in clumps beside path are four letter words carved on flat surface by visitors. Author lacks ability to understand such vulgar vandalism.

FAMED "SPINELESS" CACTUS had glamour and wide publicity never accorded more useful Burbank potato. Photo shows natural form of slabs of Opuntia Cactus plants laden with edible fruit.

A WILD IDAHO FLOWER

To the twin camps of Custer and Bonanza, Idaho, in the late summer of 1878, came the beauteous Agnes Elizabeth King, and her consort, handsome Richard King. Their marital status may have been in doubt as was their past, for the good looking pair had fled the notorious Bodie, California, flourishing camp in the Sierra Nevada, just why no one ever knew.

The fading ruins of the two gold mining camps lie on Yankee Fork of the Salmon River, about twelve miles above the main stem of the River of No Return, the camps being named for the vast wealth of gold thought located there, and for the ill-fated general. In boom days the twins shared such luxuries as church, hotel and cemetery, but each had its full quota of saloons.

Charles Franklin, founder of Bonanza, had just finished the hotel building, the Franklin House, when the Kings arrived. He took an immediate liking to Dick King, with a much deeper feeling for Lizzie, the first woman in the camp not a "soiled dove". Or was she? No one ever knew for sure but what they did know, she had a "golden beauty, the poise and grace of a queen," says Esther Yarber in her *Land of the Yankee Fork*.

Lizzie had ideas about making money. She

AMONG NATIVE SHRUBS growing near grave of Lizzie King and paramours are fine specimens of Idaho state flower, Philadelphus, with its white, fragrant blossoms.

THREE GRAVES lie inside picket enclosure of miniature Boot Hill, that of Agnes Elizabeth King in center. Better known as Lizzie, her grave is flanked on either side by her two husbands, or lover and husband as some believed.

talked her husband into buying a block of real estate from Franklin, then announced she would build a dance hall and saloon. Franklin was deeply shocked, thinking she was too much of a lady to be a saloon keeper, but the buildings went up, logs, hand-split shakes and all. All this put Lizzie and Charles Franklin on closer terms, King being busy with dabblings in real estate, starting a company with William Dillon. The two bought much property to hold for resale.

The spring of 1879 saw the simultaneous "Grand Openings" of Lizzie's two adjoining emporiums, Arcade Saloon and Yankee Fork Dance Hall, both thriving under her soft but capable hands. And Charles Franklin's admiration for her grew.

King and Dillon ran into difficulties very soon, the former becoming more interested in prospecting and hot-headed Dillon growing irritated at his partner's absences. They agreed to dissolve the partnership but quarreled over which of them owned a lot in Custer that Dillon had sold. The argument reached its head at Lizzie's bar. The lady went to get their drinks and returned to hear her husband say, "You know damned well that was my lot." Dillon drew his six shooter and without warning fired a bullet into King's spine. Lizzie cradled his head in her arms as he moaned, "Lizzie, he killed me." He lived a few days, until July 14, 1879. No charges were pressed against Dillon but he was advised to leave town, and was never heard from again.

Now Charles Franklin asserted himself, comforting Lizzie in every way he thought of. He had a coffin built for Dick King, planning to bury the body in the new Bonanza Cemetery until citizens demurred, saying there was some doubt as to King's respectability. Franklin then fenced off a separate plot with room for only three graves. He and Lizzie stood by the palings after her mate's burial, agreeing that they would also be buried there when the time came.

Everybody assumed the two would be married until dashing Robert Hawthorne came to town and overwhelmed Lizzie into marriage. Left out in the cold, Franklin watched Hawthorne closely, the newcomer seeming to have little money yet dressing well and putting on a prosperous front. After the wedding Lizzie asked Franklin's forgiveness, saying she did not want to hurt him. He assured her everything would go on just the same. It didn't.

Lizzie ordered a freight wagon full of new furniture, wanting to redecorate her new house for her new husband. When it arrived she told the driver to tie his horses, to go over to her saloon and have a drink on her. She went into the house for her bridegroom of a week, wanting to show him the surprise.

A small boy walking past the house heard two shots and ran in the house to see the bodies of Lizzie and Robert Hawthorne on the floor, both oozing blood. He screamed, ran out to tell the nearest passerby, Joseph Boggs, who tried to find Charles Franklin but could not immediately. Search of the house revealed no gun and another mystery developed. Franklin coolly ordered coffins made for the two and saw them buried beside Richard King in the tiny Boot Hill on the pineclad rise.

GRAVES are inside picket fence Charles Franklin built.

Franklin became withdrawn, seldom speaking to the townspeople. He quit his real estate business, at length loaded a wagon with his belongings and retired to a small claim he owned not far away. About three years later two prospectors knocked on the cabin door and getting no answer, broke in to find Franklin's dead body on the bed, hand clutching a gold locket with small photo of Lizzie King in it. Decomposition was far advanced, the strangers gathering the corners of the blanket and burying everything a few feet from the lonely cabin, seven miles from the three graves of the woman he loved and the two men of her own heart.

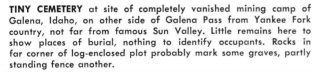

TINY CEMETERY at site of completely vanished mining camp of Galena, Idaho, on other side of Galena Pass from Yankee Fork country, not far from famous Sun Valley. Little remains here to show places of burial, nothing to identify occupants. Rocks in far corner of log-enclosed plot probably mark some graves, partly standing fence another.

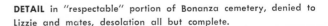

DETAIL in "respectable" portion of Bonanza cemetery, denied to Lizzie and mates, desolation all but complete.

A RESCUE MISSION

During the height of the Nez Perce War in Idaho, some of the most vital skirmishes took place near Mt. Idaho (see *Ghost Town Treasures*). One of the battles involved a party of 17 volunteers under Capt. D. B. Randall, traveling from Mt. Idaho to Cottonwood. Almost within sight of the destination a number of mounted Indians appeared suddenly and the volunteers, not equipped to carry on a major battle, set off for Cottonwood at full speed. Immediately the woods and fields were swarming with hostiles, at least 100 of them.

Randall saw the Indians would intercept his men and cut them off from safety. He ordered his force to head for a small knoll but the Indians swerved to head them off. Randall and his men charged them directly, the surprise tactic resulting in hand-to-hand combat which ended quickly with the Nez Perce retreating. One of the volunteers was killed and Randall received wounds that proved fatal. Several volunteers were wounded less seriously and many Indians killed.

The battle was so close to the Cottonwood garrison soldiers there could see and hear the action. They were eager to go to the defense of the volunteers but Col. David Perry held them back, believing it impossible to get through the Indian lines. However, as soon as the Nez Perce began their retreat, Perry's soldiers went to the knoll and brought back the survivors and dead.

Shortly after this, on Independence Day, 1877, scout William Foster, 24, and Charles Blewett, 19, attached to Gen. Howard's command, were sent to locate the Indians. Almost immediately they ran into an ambush and were separated. Foster shouted to Blewett that they must slip capture somehow and do it speedily, but with youthful bravado, Blewett called back something like, "Not until I get me an Indian," according to Foster's story back at the garrison.

Blewett got off his horse to get a better shot at his Indian but was crippled by a wound in the leg. His mount stampeded and although Foster tried to intercept the animal, it got away. He then called to Blewett to try to make it to a dense thicket nearby and that he would go for aid. He last saw his chum limping toward the brush along the creek.

In camp Foster urged Perry to send a detachment to save Blewett and the whole force volunteered. He sent a force of 10, including Foster and led by Lt. Sevier M. Rains, to attempt the rescue. The men went only a short distance when they were suddenly surrounded by screaming savages. Every man was killed, Foster the last to die as he ran from the mount shot out from under him.

All were buried on the spot and later the soldiers' bodies were removed to Walla Walla, Foster's remaining. Blewett's body was discovered two and a half months later and buried at Cottonwood House, and subsequently transferred to Walla Walla. Following the funeral there the Walla Walla *Union Bulletin* reported "On a September Sunday, the First Cavalry band led the cortege from the First Presbyterian Church to the cemetery. Members of the garrison followed on foot and each dropped an evergreen on the coffin at the graveside . . ."

GRAVE OF SCOUT William Foster, near Cottonwood, Idaho. (Photo from **Here Rolled The Covered Wagons** by Albert and Jane Salisbury).

IN A WAGON BOX TO ETERNITY

The Oregon Trail saw a host of traumas and tragedies, few of them as pathetic as the mass murder of a family seeking a new life in the West, at Little Spring Creek near the present town of Soda Springs in Idaho.

The wagon train pulled away from the creek in the morning after a night's camp, leaving one family behind. Their horses were lost and the father would not go on without them. On the following morning three men saw the lone wagon standing by the creek. Curious, the men, George Goodheart, Bill Wilburn and John Taung, went to investigate and found the father, mother and five children had been murdered.

"They had made their beds on the ground by the wagon," George Goodheart later told Abraham C. Anderson. "I think the murderers came up when they were sound asleep and killed the father. It looked like the mother had grabbed the baby and started to run. I think her screams woke the children. She was found dead with her feet on the bed and her body on the ground, her baby in her arms. The oldest boy was about a rod from the wagon. The next oldest boy was around behind the wagon . . . with a broken arrow in his back. . . The girl was lying about three feet from her mother at the foot of the bed. . . The boy next to the baby was in bed with his throat cut. . . The mother was stabbed in the breast. It looked like the baby had been stabbed above the ear. . . It may have been done for revenge.

"I think the Indians had stolen his horses and had them cached . . . the emigrants told us that the man was very brave. I think that when he found the horses cached he must have taken a shot at the Indians and taken his horses by force. And the Indians followed them up and murdered them while they were all asleep."

Goodheart and his party took the bodies to the place of burial and dug a grave. They laid the father and mother side by side, the baby in its mother's arms, and the rest of the children around their parents in the same wagon box the family lived and traveled in for so many miles to the lonely knoll at Soda Springs.

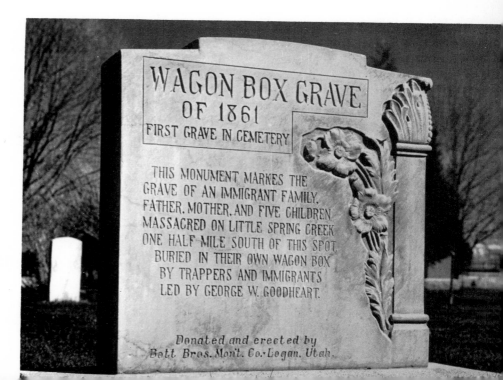

WAGON BOX GRAVE was journey's end for family of 7 killed by Indians at Little Spring Creek near Soda Springs, Idaho.

IN MASSACRE ROCKS
WAS THE GATE OF DEATH

On the Oregon Trail near the present American Falls, Idaho, is a barricade of rocks which presented an obstacle to traveling pioneers. They saw the passage between the rocks was narrow but avoiding them entirely involved many extra miles. Chancing the small opening meant the possibility of encountering enemy Indians hiding there in ambush. The Oregon Trailers took the chances . . . and the rocks became known as Gate of Death, Devil's Gate, Massacre Rocks and Massacre Gate.

The first known incident ocurred in 1851. A group of emigrants led by a Virginian named Miller were attacked by Indians as they passed through the narrow opening. One man was killed and one of Miller's daughters wounded, but the party escaped further trouble. Later the same year Hudson Clark and his family from Illinois were assailed. Traveling in a light wagon somewhat ahead of the main train, the Clarks were allowed to go through the gap. As they emerged Indians attacked, killing Clark's mother and brother. His sister was wounded, dragged from the wagon and

GATE OF DEATH — Massacre Rocks from the west. The Oregon Trail came through the gap following the same course as this present road.

FLAT FACE of rock conveniently near Rock Creek Camp is well preserved register, some signatures very clear. History gives aura to scribblings that would be regarded today as vandalism. Fence protects collection from latter day additions such as "Kilroy was here." The date Aug. 20, 1862 is just a couple of days after the massacre at the rocks, undoubtedly put there by one of the party who participated.

raped. Still later in 1851 a wagon train led by a man named Harpool fought a two-hour battle with the Indians at the opening before repulsing them.

A large train of 52 wagons carrying 88 men and 46 women drew near the rocks on August 10, 1862. It was divided into three sections and Snake Indians concealed among the rocks allowed one section to pass, the second attacked as it went through. One man was killed and a woman shot in the neck. The horses were run off and wagons pillaged, feather beds ripped open and bloody feathers caught by wind added confusion to the scene. Simultaneously, the first section four miles further on suffered a like fate. Two men were killed, several wounded, most of the livestock saved.

The third and last section of the train made noon camp some miles back up the trail. Warned of the attack by a messenger from the second section, it moved up warily. "We . . . found quite a quantity of blood," wrote John C. Hilman, a member of the party, "and fragments of such things as emigrants usually carry with them. It was evident that the Indians had done their hellish deeds in a

hasty manner and left. . . We were obliged to camp on the very ground which the Indians had a few hours previous, made to ring with their pandemonium-like shouts, and red with blood of innocent men and women. . . We hoped the night would be a short one."

The following day an expedition was organized to attempt the recovery of the stolen stock. Indians were encountered and when fired upon, immediately attacked. The outnumbered emigrants defended themselves as best they could in a running battle of three miles, three white men being killed and scalped, several wounded before the Indians gave up the chase.

In the three attacks the dead were George Adams, George Shepard, A. J. Winter, Charles Bullwinkle, William Motes, Thomas Newman, Maesmo Lepi and an unidentified Italian, Elizabeth Adams dying later of her wounds. All the victims were buried along the trail, most of them at the rocks, Elizabeth Adams at Raft River, a few miles farther on.

SILENCE IS GOLDEN?

The Silent City of Rocks, early wayfarers called the land covering about 25 square miles and lying south of Oakley, Idaho. California-bound Oregon Trailers, using the Hudspeth Cut-off, found the high mountain meadow with a stream running through it a good stopover point. Adventurers, explorers, emigrants rested here to repair wagons while the women cooked a meal. Horses and oxen gathered strength to face the strenuous pull through the mountains. And Indians made the rocks resound with war whoops and blood cries.

At Twin Sisters Rocks, in 1863, a group of seven wagons of returning Californians was attacked by Indians. Chief Pocatello and his Bannock warriors tomahawked and clubbed to death every man, woman and child in the party. After looting and burning the wagons, they drove off the stock.

The Silent City of Rocks stage station was three miles east of the rocks. When a Kelton-Boise stage was held up, legend has it that $90,000 in gold was taken. One of the robbers was killed, the other dying in prison, claimed he hid the gold in a clump of trees in the Silent City. Eager searchers have never found it.

OLD WAGON ROAD led from Silent City of Rocks to bright horizon and California.

ALMO IDAHO
DEDICATED TO THE MEMORY
OF THOSE WHO LOST THEIR LIVES IN A MOST
HORRIBLE INDIAN MASSACRE 1861.
THREE HUNDRED IMMIGRANTS WEST BOUND
ONLY FIVE ESCAPED.
ERECTED BY S & D OF IDAHO PIONEERS
1938

STATE-SHAPED MONUMENT erected by State of Idaho to the emigrants who died near Silent City of Rocks.

INSCRIPTION daubed on with "wagon dope" as emigrants called axle grease. Smooth faces of rocks along old Oregon Trail bear signatures of many who passed that way from 1842 on. Sand-laden winds have scoured away more of uncovered rock than letters, leaving impression more enduring than hands that wrote them.

INDIAN EMISSARY WITHOUT PORTFOLIO

Whenever there was a tough job to do for his Indian people it was Chief Tendoy who was called upon to do it. Could the tribesmen be restrained from killing whites? Could the Mormon colonists be assured the Indians meant no harm? Could the U.S. Government be talked into a fairer distribution of food and supplies? Let Tendoy do it. And Tendoy usually did it.

He was a Shoshone, born in the Boise Valley, given the name Un-tin-doip which sounded like Tendoy to the whites. As a youth he left his tribe to move in with his uncle, Chief Snagg, and the mixed Shoshones and Bannocks living along the Lemhi River in Idaho. River, valley and town were named for a character in the Book of Mormon.

Brigham Young's orders to the advance guard of settlers were to convert the Indians and establish colonies in the valley. Although Snagg and his warriors were friendly to the missionaries, other unattached renegades bitterly resented what they called "invasion" of their camping and hunting grounds, and they killed several Mormons. When news of the disaster reached Brigham Young, the colonists were recalled and Mormon settlement of the valley ended.

In 1863, while visiting near Grasshopper Creek near Bannack, Montana, Chief Snagg was killed by outlaw Buck Stenson — the man later hanged with Henry Plummer and Ned Ray at Bannack. Tendoy was chosen as the new chief, a judicious decision since he held family ties and was ably suited to head the band.

His first job was to try to placate his tribesmen who were enraged over the wanton murder of Snagg, and to do it quick. In full chief's regalia he rode his war pony to Bannack where he talked with the whites and drew an apology for the incident on threat of general war. Returning to his home village, he held a big pow-wow, convincing the Indians they should remain at peace with the whites. These coups, brought off through a masterly handling of the Shoshone language, started Tendoy on a long career of diplomacy.

Although his band had adopted the name Lemhi and was friendly to the whites, some splinter groups of renegade Shoshones roaming the Salmon and Lemhi Valleys were not, plundering and killing settlers. Tendoy and his braves took out after them, persuaded them to join his people on the Lemhi and lead peaceful lives.

10-FOOT MONUMENT over grave of Shoshone Chief Tendoy on open hillside above his ranch, visible from Highway 28, half-mile below. He was of great influence in protecting white settlers from marauding Tukuarikas, Sheepeaters and other hostile tribes. Inscription on stone reads, "Chief Tendoy Died May 10, 1907 Aged 73 Years Erected By His White Friends." (Photo Byron Larson—Portland).

OLD TENDOY STORE still stands, though precariously, about 6 miles south of present town of Tendoy, now consisting of little more than combination filling station - store. Early Indian tribes along Lemhi River practiced cave burial and huge rock here serves as "monument" to extensive burial caves, rock itself and cliff almost directly above.

Viola Anglin, postmistress of Tendoy, reports, "When I was a girl in 1938 I went up there with a group. We found human bones scattered around from graves that had been opened, possibly by animals. We looked in some of the caves and saw more bones, also such things as saddles and other things buried along with the bodies." Asked if bones were removed for burial elsewhere, she said, "I don't think so. I believe someone did shovel dirt over the exposed ones." (Photo Byron Larson—Portland).

Recognizing his value as an emissary of peace, the chief traveled up the canyon and over the divide to Dillon, Bannack and other Montana towns, and down the Lemhi to its junction with the Salmon at Salmon City. And he could listen as well as talk. He learned other Indian tribes were receiving food and supplies from Uncle Sam and to see his own people sharing in these benefits, he set out on a long journey to Washington in 1879.

He gained audience with the head of Indian affairs and got results. The next spring government officials surveyed an area ten miles square at the junction of Hayden Creek and the Lemhi, land then set aside as the domain of Tendoy's band. A school and hospital were built there as well as house for a permanent agent and depots for distributing clothing and food. The government also installed a doctor and nurses for the hospital, white teachers for the school. Tendoy himself was awarded a lifetime pension of $15 per month — this at the instigation of Senator Shoup.

In succeeding years the chief stood firm against all appeals by neighboring tribes to join them on the warpath. One of these was headed by Buffalo Horn who served as scout under Gen. Howard in the Nez Perce War and was familiar with army

OLD LOG STRUCTURES used by Chief Tendoy remain in fair condition on his ranch. Part of this building likely served as Indian chief's home. (Photo Byron Larson—Portland).

tactics. Unable to gain the support of Tendoy's Lemhis, Buffalo Horn joined other Indian bands in attacking settlers on Camas Prairie, and was later killed in a short but bloody battle with troops.

The lands allotted to the Lemhi tribe were not desirable for agriculture, the altitude and rough terrain almost precluding productive farming. In spite of this Tendoy and the Lemhis wanted to stay there and not go to Fort Hall where the government wanted to send them. It was characteristic of the chief's ability to present a case that he gained his choice of location, the stipulation being the tribe would move to Fort Hall if and when they thought it best to go.

Chief Tendoy never lost his love of roaming the neighboring mountains on his cayuse. During the winter of 1906-7 the passes were choked with snow until early in May. The 73-year-old Tendoy, restive from a long winter's confinement, but in ill health,

set out to visit the Copper Queen Mine in the canyon above the agency. On the return he fell from his horse while crossing Agency Creek. He managed to reach the bank but unable to crawl, froze to death. The body was discovered by some of his tribesmen alarmed at his long absence.

Members of the band dressed the body in full chief's regalia, war bonnet and all, and placed it in a lifelike sitting position under an especially built wickiup. More than a hundred of Tendoy's white friends passed it in single file, each stopping to pay respects to the dead chief. Then they were asked to go away so the Indians could conclude the funeral ceremony in their own fashion.

With their beloved leader dead, the Lemhis were desolate. Two years later, in 1909, the 474 tribesmen remaining made a decision to move to the richer lands around Fort Hall.

DEATH TRAP ON THE RIVER

Heat, dust and thirst dogged the pioneers on the Oregon Trail over the rough, barren country from the Raft River to the Snake . . . and there the walls of the canyon were so steep in many places the coveted water could not be reached, or if they got to it and tried to cross, it often meant tragedy.

"While watering, some of their cattle swam over the river," said Mrs. Elizabeth Smith, relating what happened to her party September 7, 1847. "One of the men swam after them but before he got across sank to rise no more. He left a wife and three children . . . the man that owned the cattle however, took the horse and swam after them and while coming back . . . got off the horse and sank and was seen no more. He left a wife and six children. It is supposed there is a whirlpool at the bottom of the river."

The emigrants had to cross to the north side of the river at Three Island Crossing or Island Ford. Always dangerous, it was sometimes necessary to block the wagon beds and float them over. At times Indians lay in wait and ambushed the pioneers as they crossed. Later a ferry was established.

Bannock Indian Chief Buffalo Horn and his band of 200 warriors raided Glenns Ferry on June 2, 1878. Commandeering the ferry, they maneuvered themselves and their horses across the river, plundering several wagon loads of merchandise which were waiting to cross. Finding quantities of liquor in one they had an all-night orgy on the river bank and moving down river in the morning, met John Bascom and two other men, killing all three and taking their horses.

DANGER LAY IN WAIT at this Three Island Crossing. Wagons were "rough locked" so wheels would not turn, skidded down steep hill. Then teams were fastened together, weakest in middle. A single horseman carrying one end of a rope, swam to first island. Guided by rope, others on horseback followed until enough were across to pull teams over, process repeated on each island until north bank was reached.

ROUGH STONE MONUMENT to pioneers killed by Indians morning after drunken orgy. Bannock Chief Buffalo Horn and band of 200 raided Glenns Ferry, Idaho, plundered several wagons waiting to cross Snake River, one of these containing liquor.

THE MILLS OF MONTANA GROUND SLOWLY BUT EXCEEDINGLY COARSE

In 1841 Father De Smet with five priests and lay brothers founded the mission of St. Mary's near the "Traveler's Rest" of Lewis and Clark, now called Lolo. The original chapel was built of lumber whip-sawn on the spot, structure held together with pegs whittled from scraps of wood.

De Smet and party brought with them a plow, symbol of their purpose, to teach the Indians how to till the land, the effort signaling the start of agriculture in what would be Montana. Also brought in were oxen, seed wheat and potatoes but no milk cows until the next year when several were driven from Colville.

Four years later there was wheat enough for flour and then a new priest arrived with a pair of mill stones to grind the grain, these shipped to Fort Vancouver from Antwerp, Belgium, and hauled overland. The new priest was Father Anthony Ravalli who helped De Smet erect the grist mill and took over so the founder could be on his way to the Flathead Valley to establish St. Ignatius Mission.

Father Ravalli was a man of almost unlimited talents. Skilled in medicine he administered to the Indian's bodies as well as their souls. As artist, he painted the backdrop for the altar and carved wooden images to flank it. His skill at the forge made new farm tools possible and repairing of the old ones. The mission prospered and the Indians were industrious.

The area became a center for traders and trappers who found the climate to their liking, braves eager for whiskey, the Indian women easy to seduce. When they were upbraided by the priests they incited the Indians against their "tyrants" and when the cooperation and friendliness of the natives failed, the mission did too, forced to close after only a few years of service.

Father Ravalli departed sadly to take up duties at other places, returning to visit the old St. Mary's site in 1866. By this time Fort Owen was established nearby and order among Indians and trappers restored. Two years before a sobering incident ended most outlawry there. "Whiskey Bill" Graves had hidden out at Fort Owen for the winter but vigilantes tracked him down. At pistol point Graves was bound hand and foot, then mounted on a horse behind one of the vigilantes. A rope was tossed over

GRAVE of Father Ravalli, who died Oct. 2, 1884, in cemetery behind the church.

MISSION CHURCH of St. Mary's, near Stevensville, Mont., Old structure still shelters many mementos of pioneer period, including art objects painted and sculptured by Father Ravalli.

a convenient tree limb, the noose adjusted around his neck. The man in front called out, "Goodbye, Bill" as he suddenly spurred his horse. Whiskey Bill was left dangling and jerking — an example to himself and other brigands.

When Father Ravalli came back to the old place he felt the improved atmosphere of security warranted the re-establishing of the mission. The old buildings were gone to Fort Owens but he erected a new church of logs with boards to finish the entry and steeple. There he served Indians and whites until his death in 1884.

CHICORY was one of the comforts introduced by priests establishing missions in Montana and the West. With coffee non-existent or rare; welcome substitute was found in dried, roasted and ground root of **Cichorium.** When coffee became more available chicory was used as adulterant or flavoring depending on amount used, practice continuing today. Plant is scraggly, unattractive, but daily produces wealth of beautiful sky blue flowers which unfurl before dawn, shrivel in afternoon. Plant escaped cultivation in early days, is now so widely distributed as to seem native.

FINDERS NOT KEEPERS
LOSERS NOT WEEPERS

You could discover gold almost anywhere. It might be an outcropping in a rocky cliff or a lost burro might kick out a gleaming nugget or a wounded bird fan dust away from a chunk of jewelry ore. But at Alder Gulch, Montana, 100 million dollars worth of gold was found because Crow Indians captured Bill Fairweather and some friends.

Early in February of 1863 Fairweather and a party of goldseekers were on their way to the Big Horn Mountains in the hope of finding a good deposit there and establishing a town. But on May 2 a war party of Crows surrounded them, took away their horses and marched them into their camp. One of the white men, Henry Edgar, later wrote, "I don't know why it was but a rattlesnake would never bite Bill. When he saw one he would always grab it up and carry it along a ways. They never seemed to resent anything he would do, and he never killed one. As we were going toward this Indian village he picked up a rattlesnake and just at the outskirts he picked up another. When the Indians saw him coming with a rattlesnake on each arm, they were awed. He put the snakes in his bosom and Simmons told the Indians he was the great medicine man of the whites."

The men were taken into the lodge with a bush in the center, the Indians circling it time and again. Fairweather, always an impatient and impetuous man, said with pique, if they marched around the bush just once more he would pull it up. They did and he did, whacking their medicine man over the head with it. The six prospectors then lined up, three to three, back to back, holding their guns

DISCOVERER of wealth in gravels of Alder Gulch died a pauper, having literally flung away the nuggets he scooped up there. Grave is in Virginia City Boot Hill on brow of hill at edge of town.

which they had refused to give up, ready to fight off the enraged Crows who were held back by their chief with a whip.

After a parley which lasted from noon to midnight, the Indians gave their captives a choice — give up their horses and be set free, or simply be killed. While Henry Edgar called this "Hobson's Choice" there seemed to be a definite advantage in living. So they gave up the horses, receiving in exchange several sorry nags, blind or crippled or both. Also exchanged were such supplies as three Oregon blankets for one mangy buffalo robe. But the prospectors did get away, leaving Simmons as hostage.

Gone now was any idea of getting to the Big Horn country. Instead the men moved toward Bannack as fast as they could, encountering and dodging Indians most of the way. On May 26, 1863, they came to a stream in a valley that would later be called Alder Gulch for the trees fringing it, and made camp about 4 in the afternoon. With Fairweather posted as guard the men scattered for a little prospecting before fixing supper. Bill took the horses across the creek to picket them for the night and noticed a portion of rimrock jutting up from the bed and called to Edgar, "What do you make of that?" Edgar wrote that he replied he would get a shovel and pan, "Then we'll see."

Handing the shovel to Bill he held out his pan for the first scoop of gravel. "Dump it in", he said. Bill started to work with the remark, "I hope we can get enough dust to buy some tobacco in Bannack". The pair worked quietly for a while, then Fairweather shouted as he saw gold gleaming in his shovel, "I've found a scad!" Almost at the same time Edgar shouted back, "If you have, I've found a thousand." Bill's scad was a nugget worth $4.80, the dust in the first pan $1.25, the next $1.75, then $4.40 and so on. The next day the diggings yielded a total of $180 but by evening their meager provisions were exhausted. They staked out their claims, each man marking for his own two holdings 100 feet wide, extending from rim to rim. Edgar wrote the posting notices and they went to Bannack.

Like many another prospector Bill Fairweather sought gold for the thrill of finding it. The pick and shovel work was something else. So his share of the $100 million was not too large and he tossed it into the air in Virginia City just to see people scramble for it or threw it over the bar for whiskey — and girls. Love, like gold, was where you found it.

PRESENT DAY VIRGINIA CITY is actually a museum relic, many buildings standing on dirt streets and wooden sidewalks looking much as they did when hangings were staged on wholesale scale. Historic town was in near ruin when Montana ghost town buff and one time state senator, Charles Bovey, visited place in 1946. Excited at wealth of Montana mining relics, Bovey was dismayed when he came to one old building going down under wrecker's hammer. He bought what remained of it on the spot and had it put back together. This was start of extensive restoration program. Where buildings had vanished they were replaced by other authentic relics from other locations.

BAD ENOUGH TO GET A GOOD HANGING

A row of sturdy boxes was placed under the improvised gallows. The condemned men were made to step up on them and nooses were adjusted on their necks. Each man faced death in his own fashion. Gallagher alternately cursed, grinned and cried. He asked for a slug of Valley Tan, Virginia City's most popular whiskey. The fiery drink down he showed his usual bravado with a flip query, "How do I look in this necktie, boys?" Helm was at first silent but just before the end he shouted, "Every man for his own principles! Hurrah for Jeff Davis! Let her rip!" Then someone called out, "Boys, do your duty!" The boxes were yanked out from under the hapless men one by one, and each dropped to his death.

Virginia City, Montana, may well hold the record for mining camp lawlessness and vigilante violence in attempts to control it. With the hanging of the Plummer gang at Bannack, the similar fates of George Ives at Nevada City and several more criminals and road agents, most of those selected by vigilantes for quick exit were disposed of.

But there were six bad ones left and on January 13, 1864 they were marked for capture. One, Bill Hunter, played a hunch and departed via a drainage ditch. The escape was futile however as he was later tracked down and hanged in Gallatin Valley.

Vigilante Thomas Dimsdale later wrote of the others. "Frank Parrish was brought in first. He was arrested without trouble in a store and seemed to expect death. . . Club-Foot George was arrested at Dance and Stuart's. . . Boone Helm was brought in next. He had been arrested in front of the Virginia Hotel. . . He quietly sat down on a bench, and being made acquainted with his doom, he declared his entire innocence. . . Helm was the most hardened, cool and deliberate scoundrel of the whole band . . . murder was a mere pastime with him. He called repeatedly for whiskey and had to be reprimanded for his unseemly conduct several times.

Jack Gallagher was found in a gambling room, rolled up in bedding with his shotgun and revolver beside him. . . . Lyons had come back to a miner's cabin on the west side of the gulch above town. . . The leader threw open the door and bringing down his revolver said, "Throw up your hands." Lyons had a piece of hot slapjack on his fork but dropped it instantly and obeyed the order. Although Lyons was graciously given permission to finish his breakfast, he declined, saying, "I lost my appetite."

At the "trial" all five strongly protested their innocence but the evidence of crimes committed was overwhelming, Helm's offenses even including cannibalism. All were condemned to death by hanging, a foregone conclusion. Justice was carried out promptly for fear some or all of the prisoners might escape with help from sympathizers. There being no time for the erection of a suitable scaffold, ropes were strung from a handy beam in an unfinished

BEAM in then unfinished building on Wallace Street at Van Buren in Virginia City where unholy five were hanged, still displays rope scars.

PLAIN WOODEN HEADBOARDS mark burial places of road agents hanged at Virginia City. (Photo Bryon Larson, Portland).

building on Wallace Street and Van Buren, the hangings performed as given above. When all ceased jerking they were cut down and laid in a row in the street. Then the friends who would have freed them were given the chance to claim the bodies which were buried on a small knoll above town. No one bothered to put up any kind of identifying markers.

Some time later two of the men who handled the executions, Wilbur Saunders and Ariel Davis, got into an argument about the exact location of the burial places. Up on the hill they dug into the earth until they came to a partially decomposed body, the feet exposed. One was clubbed, identifying the corpse as that of George Lane — "Club-foot George". When all were located the earth was replaced and pine headboards erected. George was re-interred without his club foot which was used for display in a saloon, later finding its way to a Virginia City museum.

119

WYOMING WILL BE YOUR NEW HOME

The following account by W. W. Morrison is reprinted from Casper (Wyoming) *Tribune* of March 6, 1949:

Near the center of the "Big Muddy" oil field, and a few feet from the old Parkerton station site, is the grave of "Ada Magill," an immigrant girl, who died and was buried there in 1864. A crude headstone marks her eternal resting place; kind hands of some thoughtful person have placed a row of edged brick around it; and an assortment of lilies from our yard bloom above it. A trail marker stands close by.

It was with a touch of sadness that we looked upon this little grave for the first time; that was in the summer of '41, and there was installed in our hearts, always, a longing to return. In the years that followed we never failed to turn aside and visit the hallowed spot whenever passing there. In the summer of '45, our letters began reaching relatives of the little girl, and within a year a file of nearly a hundred letters from them unfolded the heartbreaking story of her life and death. I only wish that my pen might be let free to convey the fullness of their pages; but sometimes it is wise to remain silent of much. Let us go back for a little while to that July day in 1864.

The morning sun was an hour up in the heavens when the long wagon train began to stretch, and wind away from the night's camping place at Deer Creek (now Glenrock). At two miles an hour the ox-drawn wagons lumbered along over the sandy trail. The sun beat hotter after the first hours of morning, lowing cattle plaintively called across the wild sagebrush desert; blinding, choking dust billowed about the panting oxen and hung suspended over the white-topped wagons. Tired, travel-worn men plodded wearily on; hope and care marked the faces of women. Over the single-wire Pacific Telegraph line that very hour winged the news of General Jubal Early leading his Confederate forces down the Shenandoah Valley—it was July 2, 1864.

* * *

In a covered wagon midway of the train, a child lay feebly moaning; she had taken down with dysentery shortly after leaving the fort on the Laramie; and now, there were times when she never recognized anyone. Her mother, Nancy Magill, held the sick child's head on her lap, and she watched and prayed and waited. Outside, a father's strong heart lost courage as he walked along; small wonder that a tear dropped now and then from the eyes of Caleb Magill, for the immigrants were men and women with hearts to feel, and tears to flow, and they knew that the hand of death was waiting for the hour to come. The train proceeded slowly, toiling laboriously up the beaten trail.

The child grew constantly weaker and because of this it was decided that the whole wagon train would go into camp. They traveled a little less than six miles from their last camping place, when they pulled to one side. The sorrowing parents worked, watched and waited by the side of the little sufferer; the afternoon waned; evening came, and darkness crept over the valley of the Platte. A great yellow moon rose out of the east and climbed steadily in a star-lit sky.

July 3, 1864. In the silent, lonely hours of morning, the flame of life burned low for Ada Magill, for the dark angel hovered near. Came a moment in the hour before dawn when the tiny flame flickered feebly, then vanished suddenly, and her suffering had ceased; and all was peace and quiet and darkness. Her spirit drifted gently over the threshold of its strange pilgrimage out into the great beyond where there is no longitude nor latitude—returned to God who gave it.

A tiny calico dress, her "Sunday's best," served to clothe the remains of "Little Ada," and a wagon box was cut up for to make her a coffin. A grave was dug on a small rise of ground a few feet north of the trail, and there on the afternoon of July 3, 1864, a funeral was held out on the wind-swept desert of Nebraska Territory. Of her people who were present, and who witnessed her burial, were her father and mother and five brothers and sisters.

The wooden casket was put deep into the ground and a layer of flat stones was placed above it, and when the grave was filled in, they carried rocks and heaped above it. A crude marker was put there at the time bearing this inscription, "Ada, the daughter of C. W. and N. G. Magill, died July 3, 1864, aged 3 years, 5 month and 27 days." On the morning of July 4, the Oregon-bound train took up its westward march.

The Magill family reached Oregon and the months and the seasons and the years went on. In 1888, a railroad built its line from Glenrock to Casper, and it ran close to the little grave. It was called "The Wyoming Central Railroad," was superseded by "The Fremont, Elkhorn and Missouri Valley Railroad," which in turn was consolidated by the North Western.

In the summer of 1912 a young engineer (L. C. Bishop, my friend, and grand man of the trails) was helping push a survey westward for a new highway, and he watched the lines pass directly over the little grave. It touched the young man's heart, and out of kindness and sympathy he made arrangements to move the place of interment 30 feet to the north. And when the grave had been moved to its new location he placed therein the original marker, face down to preserve it, and covered it over. He fashioned another headstone to take its place, leaving there something to inspire the minds and hearts of people for generations to come.

NATURAL GRAVEN IMAGE

FOSSIL FISH—Excellent specimen found south of Old Oregon Trail near western edge of Wyoming. State has many well preserved fossils, most beds difficult of access, buried in hard slate and calcite 35 feet thick. Parts of protective rock have been blasted away by fossil hunters who have discovered such rarities as 13-foot alligator-like creature. Author's collection includes this fish which swam immense inland sea 650,000,000 years ago.

MARKER ON GRAVE of Ada Magill would seem to be second one, made, fashioned by L. C. Bishop, it lacks final line of original, "aged 3 years, 5 months and 27 days."—Photo Wyoming State Archives and Historic Dept.

LONELY GRAVE of Mary Holmsley, not far from Fort Laramie, beside Old Oregon Trail. In spring of 1852 young blacksmith Benjamin Holmsley, wife and two daughters, set out for Oregon. On June 10 Mrs. Holmsley died of measles. The party stopped only long enough for husband to hack grave in rocky soil, bury body wrapped in blankets.

Holmsley scratched wife's name on piece of sandstone, placed it on mound of dirt for marker. Years later grave was discovered by local settlers and Mary Holmsley became symbol of all those pioneer women who died on trail. On Memorial Day of 1926 they erected this monument, ever since placing flowers around it. Photo Wyoming state Archives and Historical Dept.

PUZZLE OF THE CLIFF CARVING

Most of the Unthank family were Quakers living along the Indiana-Ohio border, and Fountain City, Indiana, was the home town of Alvah. He left there for the gold fields of California March 30, 1850, in a party of at least 26 men, many of them relatives.

Arriving at the sandstone cliff near what is now Glenrock, the men carved their names and Unthank family records present a confusing point. They state Alvah contracted cholera, dying a week after leaving his name on the rock. Yet his grave is half a mile east of the cliff. Was he ill at the time he scratched his name, the party going back to the last campsite to wait until the 19 year old youth died?

An item on the fly leaf of the Unthank family bible reads, "Alvah H. Unthank was born on the 2nd of the 1st month, 1831." Below it is the entry, "Alvah H. Unthank died on the second day of July, 1850, in the Black Hills 100 miles beyond Fort Laramie on the road to California."

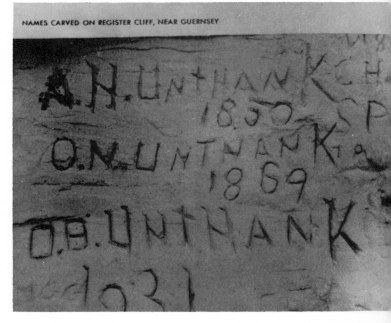

NAMES CARVED ON REGISTER CLIFF, NEAR GUERNSEY

GRAVE OF ALVAH H. UNTHANK has long been protected by fence of iron pipe. Crudely lettered sandstone slab is original one cut and placed at time of youth's death from cholera. Photo as below.

SANDSTONE CLIFF bears many signatures of pioneers who traveled Oregon Trail on way to Oregon Country or California gold fields. Alvah H. Unthank's signature was made one week before his death. His cousin O. N. Unthank served as telegraph operator at old Fort Laramie from 1869 to 1874. Knowing of his kinsman's name on rock he added the year he served at fort. He acquired intense interest in history of pioneer relatives and western history in general, accumulated vast store of papers, telegraph orders and letters. His son, O. B. Unthank of Sheridan visited cliff in 1931, adding his name. (Photo Wyoming State Archives and Hist. Dept. American Guide Series).

GRAVE of 9 year old Joel Hembree on George Powell ranch, near Douglas, Wyo. Stones were discovered in 1961 by Glen Edwards, ranch owner who through efforts of Lyle Hildebrandt, Oregon Trail researcher, turned up story of boys death from old newspaper clippings in hands of Mr. and Mrs. Paul Henderson, Bridgeport, Nebr.

Young Hembree was member of large wagon train called "Cow Column" because of its driving so many milk cows. Dr. Marcus Whitman traveled with the 150 wagons returning to his mission at Waiilatpu. In the Wyoming country Joel Hembree fell from a wagon tongue and two wheels ran over him. He died in night, his first burial of the long journey.—**Condensed from account by Paul Henderson in Annals of Wyoming, October, 1963.** Photo state Archives and Historical Dept.

PRINCESS DOOMED TO PERISH

She spent days on end sitting on a bench near the sutler's store where she could watch the soldiers on parade and dress mount on the central grounds. Major Wood, post commander of Fort Laramie, always saw to it the officer of the day wore full regalia for her benefit — bright red silk sash, ostrich plumes and all. She never spoke to the soldiers and they had strict orders not to talk to her. Perhaps they felt sorry for her, this Falling Leaf who was a stranger in her own tribe, an alien in the white man's world.

In 1820 a French trapper named Jacques La Ramie was killed by Indians on the banks of a river later named for him, Laramie. In 1834 Robert Campbell and William L. Sublette founding a trad-

ing post on the river, calling it Fort William. Next year they sold it to a trapping syndicate which in turn disposed of the buildings to the American Fur Co. It practically rebuilt the fort, adding bastions, blockhouses with loopholes. Honoring an officer, John B. Sarpy, the establishment was renamed Fort John. For a time supplies destined for the sutler were addressed to "Fort John on the Laramie" but when a careless clerk wrote simply "Fort Laramie", the simplicity appealed to the people and the name became official.

In 1849 Fort Laramie was widely known as a major stopping place on transcontinental trails to the West, a central point in the vast expanse of mountains and plains. On Gen. Freeman's recom-

GRAVE OF FALLING LEAF, Brule Sioux Chief Spotted Tail's daughter at old Fort Laramie in 1880. At funeral Indians killed girl's two white ponies, cut off heads and tails, mounted them on poles so she would have transportation to Happy Hunting Ground. Bones at extreme right could well be skulls of slain ponies. Not long after photo was taken Spotted Tail came to fort cemetery, removed daughter's bones, took them to be reburied in cemetery at Rosebud Indian Agency in South Dakota. He was buried beside her.

Labeled legendary is story of young army doctor just out of medical school and stationed at Fort Laramie, who removed Falling Leaf's bones to quarters for study. When Spotted Tail came for them, he was detained long enough for medic to replace them. Photo Wyoming state Archives and Historical Dept.

OLD FORT LARAMIE was first permanent fur trading post to be established in what is now Wyoming. First structure on Laramie River, it was built by Robert Campbell and William Sublette about 1½ miles above junction with North Platte. In 1849 post was turned into fort with garrison to protect emigrants from Indians. Many original units of fort remain, are maintained by State of Wyoming.

mendation the government bought and garrisoned the fort and during its first years of occupancy by U.S. soldiers bison roamed about it in immense herds. It is said an officer fired a six pounder among them, killing 30 animals with that shot.

Also during those years the fort was a rendezvous for swarms of Indians. Often more than 100 lodges were strewn along the nearby ridge, braves and squaws making themselves at home within the post confines. The only individual Indian to gain any special notice was a beautiful princess named Ah-ho-appa, daughter of famed Brule Sioux Chief Spotted Tail and his squaw. The girl was called in English Falling Leaf.

It could be true as romance has it that she was hopelessly in love with one of the young officers at the fort, hopelessly because of her exalted station in the tribe. Spotted Tail saw she was unhappy and tried to make her forget the soldier, if this was the reason for her lassitude, by removing

his lodge to the Powder River. But even there the girl continued to droop and finally took to her blankets in the lodge. It was now obvious she was dying of tuberculosis.

After "two grasses and two snows" at the Powder River village, Falling Leaf faded away to a shadow. She told Spotted Tail she would die soon and asked him to bury her near the fort where she had enjoyed watching the white soldiers. Did she really mean she watched only one? When she died the people broke into loud wailing that lasted two days. They treated a soft deerskin in the smoke of a sacred fire and wrapped it about the body of the dead princess. Falling Leaf's two white ponies were tied together, a basket cradle fashioned between them to carry her to Fort Laramie, a week's trip over frozen fields of snow. The people carried food but the horses had to subsist on bark from the willows along the ice-bound creeks.

Young officer Eugene Ware who was present

at burial ceremonies at the fort, later wrote, "When within 15 miles of the fort, a runner announced to Col. Maynarier the approach of the procession. Col. Maynarier was natural prince, a good soldier and a judge of Indian character. . . A consultation was held among the officers, an ambulance dispatched, guarded by a company of cavalry in full uniform, followed by two twelve pound mountain howitzers. The body was placed in the ambulance, and behind it were led the girl's two white ponies.

"When the cavalcade had reached the river a couple of miles from the post, the garrison turned out, and with Col. Maynarier at the head, met and escorted it to the post, and the party was assigned quarters. The next day a scaffold was erected near the grave of Old Smoke. It was made of tent poles 12 feet long, imbedded in the ground and fastened with thongs over which a buffalo robe was laid and on which the coffin was to be placed.

"To the poles of the scaffold were nailed the heads and tails of the two white ponies so that Ah-ho-appa could ride through the fair hunting ground of the skies. A coffin was made and lavishly decorated. The body was not unbound from its deerskin shroud, but was draped in a bright red blanket and placed in the coffin, mounted on the wheels of an artillery caisson. After the coffin came a 12 pound howitzer and the whole was followed to the cemetery by the entire garrison in full uniform. The tempestuous and chilling weather moderated somewhat. Mr. Wright, post chaplain suggested an elaborate burial service, Chief Spotted Tail was consulted. He wanted his daughter buried Indian fashion so she would not go where the white man went, but where the red people went.

"Every request of Spotted Tail was met by Col. Maynarier with a hearty and satisfactory 'yes'. The chief was silent for a long time. Then he stepped forward and gave Mr. Wright the little Episcopal prayer book which General Harney had given her mother many years ago. . . Mr. Wright deposited it in the coffin. Col. Maynarier stepped forward and deposited a pair of white kid gauntlet cavalry gloves to keep her hands warm while she was making the journey. The soldiers formed a large hollow square, within which the Indians formed a large ring, and on the four sides of the coffin stood Col. Maynarier, Major O'Brien, Spotted Tail and the chaplain." The burial services read, a procession of the Indians filed by the casket." Each one placed some little remembrance in the coffin, a little looking glass, a string of beads, a pine cone with some sort of embroidery on it. The lid was placed on it and the women took the coffin and raised it and placed it on the scaffold. The men stood mutely and stolidly around looking on, and none of them moved a muscle or tendered any help. A fresh buffalo skin was laid over the coffin and laced down with thongs. . . . The sky grew leaden and stormy and it began to sleet and grow dark. At the word of command the soldiers faced forward and fired three volleys in rapid succession. They and their visitors marched back to the post. The howitzer squad remained and built a large fire of pinewood and fired the gun every half hour all night through the sleet, until daybreak."

PIONEERS generally built homes of whatever material was at hand. Those in arid sections made use of juniper and nut-pine logs though these were small, rough and often crooked.

THE GREATEST RIDE IN WYOMING HISTORY

This account by Francis A. Barrett is reprinted from *Annals of Wyoming,* October, 1966, with footnotes omitted.

The winter of 1866 was full of bitter days for the garrison at Fort Phil Kearney. This outpost on the Little Piney in northern Wyoming was isolated by blizzards and embattled by the Sioux nation.

The department commander in Omaha, Gen. Philip St. George Cooke, advocated an open battle with the Indians during the winter. Although the Commander at Phil Kearney, Col. Henry B. Carrington, was a cautious man, he none the less intended to employ this strategy of "surprise and extermination" as soon as reinforcements arrived.

Among the newly arrived officers at Kearney was young Colonel William J. Fetterman. He, along with many of the other less experienced officers and enlisted men, was full of recklessness and bravado.

Although the Sioux were fighting with their lives to preserve their hunting grounds, Fetterman was known for his confident assertion that "with 80 men, I could ride through the Sioux nation."

Thus, on a cold, clear day, December 21, 1866, a detachment of 81 men under Fetterman's command left Fort Kearney with clear orders to "give support" to a wood train under Indian attack and to return to the fort. There was an additional order from Col. Carrington: "Under no circumstances must you cross Lodge Trail ridge." For there, the colonel was certain, Indians had been gathering for attack or ambush.

Two Moons, a Cheyenne at the scene, described the Indian strategy: "The Indians attacked the wood train and then, when Fetterman's command came out, they sent a few Indians, mounted on their best ponies, to decoy them into the hills." Among

REPLICA of Fort Phil Kearney's stockade on the site of the original fort.

the individual Sioux and Cheyenne warriors who risked their lives to lure the soldiers into the trap were several who, during the next decade, would become famous chiefs: Crazy Horse, Dull Knife, Black Shield, Big Nose, White Bull. Fetterman followed up the crest of Lodge Trail ridge and nearly 2,000 Indians swarmed in from all sides, including Cheyennes, Arapahoes, Sioux, Ogalalas. Under Red Cloud, they attacked with ferocity.

In thirty minutes, the firing was over, the battlefield indescribable with not a living man or animal. Most of the men were taken alive and tortured to death - only six killed by bullet. At the end, the Fetterman Disaster stood as one of three battles in American history from which came no survivors. (The others: Custer on the Little Big Horn 1876; Crockett at the Alamo 1836)".

For those left at Fort Kearney, the outlook was bleak. Indian attack in overwhelming numbers was likely; the remaining defenders were reduced to 20 rounds of ammunition per man; a blizzard was

JOHN "PORTUGEE" PHILLIPS, who made history with his famous ride from Fort Phil Kearny to Fort Laramie, is buried in Lakeview, Cemetery, Cheyenne. Engraved inscription of tombstone reads, "Until the day breaks and the shadows flee away." Metal plaque was later attached to monument by Wyoming Historical Landmarks Commission. Four of Phillips' children are buried in family plot. (Photo Wyo. State Archives and Historical Dept.).

storming in from the Big Horns; the nearest help was Fort Laramie, 236 miles away.

Col. Carrington made known the desperate problem at hand and the necessity of someone riding to Fort Laramie for help. John "Portugee" Phillips volunteered. As a matter of fact, he was reported to be the only volunteer.

John Phillips, born on the isle of Fayal in the Azores, of Portuguese parentage, landed on the Pacific Coast as an immigrant and worked his way east as a prospector. He with several others had come to Fort Phil Kearney as employees of contractors and the Post Quartermaster. On the morning of the disaster, he had been operating a water wagon.

As later related by Col. Carrington, "John Phillips, used to frontier life, the wiles of the Indians and convinced that utter destruction awaited the command unless relief were promptly obtained, volunteered his services as 'despatch bearer' to Ft. Laramie." The "despatch" from Col. Carrington was as follows:

FORT PHIL KEARNEY, D.T., Dec. 21, 1866 — (By courier to Fort Laramie) — Do send me reinforcements forthwith. Expedition now with my force is impossible. I risk everything but the post and its store. I venture as much as anyone can, but I have had a fight today unexampled in Indian warfare. My loss is ninety-four, 81 killed. I have recovered forty-nine bodies and thirty-two more are to be brought in in the morning that have been found. Among the killed are Brevet Lieutenant-Colonel Fetterman, Captain F. H. Brown and Lieutenant Grummond.

The Indians engaged were nearly three thousand, being apparently the force reported as on Tongue River in my dispatches of the 5th of November and subsequent thereto. This line, so important, can and must be held. It will take four times the force in the spring to reopen if it be broken up this winter. I hear nothing of my arms that left Fort Leavenworth September 15; additional cavalry ordered to join have not reported their arrival; would have saved as much loss today: the Indians lost beyond all precedent; I need prompt reinforcements and repeating arms. I am sure to have, as before reported, an active winter, and must have men and arms; every officer of this battalion should join it today. I have every teamster on duty, and, at best, one hundred and nineteen left at the post. I hardly need urge this matter; it speaks for itself. Give me two companies of cavalry, at least, forthwith, well armed, or four companies of infantry, exclusive of what I need at Reno and Fort Smith. I did not overestimate my early application; a single company, promptly, will save the line; but our killed show that any remissness will result in mutilation and butchery beyond precedent. No such mutilation as that today on record. Depend on it that this post will be held so long as a round or a man is left, promptness is the vital thing. Give me officers and men. Only the new Spencer arms should be sent. The Indians desperate and they spare none.

HENRY B. CARRINGTON,
Colonel Eighteenth Infantry, commanding

Before agreeing to the ride, John Phillips made one condition; that he be allowed the pick of any horse at the fort. He chose a thoroughbred belonging to the commanding officer, Col. Carrington. Accounts differ as to how the colonel took this selection. Some reports indicated that Col. Carrington was bitter over the selection of his favorite animal. George Lathrop, a government teamster at the post said "the old man got pretty sore when Phillips insisted on taking his horse." However, another eyewitness recorded that the colonel "quickly complied" with Phillips' wish.

Frances Grummond was also at the Fort. She, the bereaved widow of Lt. George Grummond, killed that very day in the Fetterman Disaster, had an interesting visit from John Phillips before his departure on the "ride." He brought her his wolf skin robe, paid his respects and although he had never met her before, said, "For your sake I am going to attempt to bring relief from Laramie. I may not get through the Indian lines, but in case I fail, I want you to keep this robe as a slight remembrance of me." Perhaps he felt it his duty to protect Mrs. Grummond and her unborn baby.

So John (Portugee) Phillips made his preparations; biscuits for himself, a quarter sack of oats for the horse. John C. Brough, an enlisted man in the Second U.S. Cavalry, was walking the beat: "Pretty soon we saw two men walking toward us, their heads close together, seemingly in earnest conversation and one of them leading a horse. When they got within twenty or twenty-five feet, I put myself in position and prepared to challenge, when the sergeant said 'Attention! It's the Commanding Officer!' Colonel Carrington interrupted and said, 'Never mind, sergeant, open the gate!'" According to Brough's account, following the conversation, one man mounted the horse and the other, Colonel

BRONZE PLAQUE gives facts of slaughter—details are these: Sioux attacked wagon train of wood being brought to Fort Phil Kearney for fuel. Rescue squad of 79 soldiers, 2 civilians, under Major James Powell, were ordered out but pompous Brevet Lt. William J. Fetterman claimed command by right of seniority and replaced Powell.
Col. H. B. Carrington instructed Fetterman to proceed directly to train and keep in sight of fort. Ignorant of Indian strategy Fetterman used his own ideas and when Sioux leader Red Cloud sent decoy party over ridge, Fetterman contemptuously ordered men in in pursuit. All were completely annihilated by main Sioux forces on flanks.

Carrington, took his hand and said "May God help you."

As John (Portugee) Phillips and his horse left Fort Phil Kearney, those at the post listened to the quickly disappearing hoofbeats. Colonel Carrington remarked, "Good! He has taken softer ground at the side of the trail." Thus began the greatest ride in Wyoming history.

It was a ride of 236 miles, through snow and bitter cold, over territory endangered with Indians. How did he do it? It was, according to Frances Grummond Carrington, "intensely simple" as was later related to her and others by John Phillips. He rode parallel to the Bozeman Trail. Later, when asked if he stuck close to the trail, John replied: "Hell no! More'n once I was more'n ten miles off the trail." In a talk with Capt. Proctor at Fort

Reno, he said he left the trail at Buffalo Wallows and "came around" five miles south of the "Forks" (Crazy Woman's) and then to Fort Reno.

He usually traveled at night and hid with his horse in the thickets from dawn to dusk in order to escape the notice of the Indians. He fed his horse oats and tree bark and ate biscuits himself. He passed through Fort Reno alone, stopping to rest himself and his horse. His immediate destination was Horseshoe Telegraph Station some 190 miles south of Fort Kearney. Just before arriving, he was pursued by Indians but with his strong horse, he rode a "high hill" where he stayed all night. At dawn he "made a run for it" and arrived at Horseshoe Christmas morning.

At the Horseshoe Station, where he reputedly arrived with George Dillon and William Bailey, he gave the operator, John C. Friend, two dispatches, one to the department commander in Omaha, the second to the post commander at Fort Laramie. Because there was no assurance that these messages would "get through" and because he had promised Col. Carrington that he would deliver his message to the commander at Fort Laramie, John Phillips continued his ride to his final destination, Fort Laramie.

The final 40 miles to Fort Laramie were ridden over blinding white snow during the day and falling, freezing snow at night. He arrived near midnight of Christmas Day at Fort Laramie and stopped in front of Old Bedlam, the post headquarters and ballroom. Here a full-dress garrison ball was in progress.

Lieutenant Herman Haas, the Officer of the Guard, asked the rider his name—but he was too weak to answer. He was taken inside, where a "huge form dressed in buffalo overcoat, pants, gauntlets, and a cap, accompanied by an orderly, desired to see the commanding officer." The message from Col. Carrington was the first word to reach the world outside the Dakota Territory of the Fetterman Disaster.

Phillips collapsed from exhaustion and frostbite. His horse dropped to the ground in front of "Old Bedlam," and later was moved to the stables where he soon died despite the efforts of the post veterinarians.

And so ended a four-day, 236-mile ride through deep snow and bitter cold, accompanied by danger at every turn, with most of the riding under cover of night with the barest supplies—Wyoming's greatest ride.

KILLING IS HABIT FORMING

Known in his early Western life as the man who caught Geronimo and talked him into surrendering, he became more famous after he was hung. Or was he hung? Scout, stage driver, cowboy, rancher, soldier and mankiller, he could blame whiskey and a glib tongue for his being packed into perdition. Wyoming saw few men more accomplished with gun and bottle than Tom Horn.

Born near Memphis, Scotland County, Missouri, in 1861, Tom Horn spent more time playing hookey than he did at school and that meant hunting in the woods around his farm home. He learned little from books and a lot about handling a squirrel rifle which skill he put to good use later shooting skunks and upright men. His father got him a job and when he was fired for not showing up for work several times, the elder Horn beat him within an inch of his life. Young Tom ran away and a few years later turned up at Santa Fe, New Mexico, as a stage driver.

Following the open road he drove a team of mules to the Verde River area in Arizona where he showed such fluency with the Spanish tongue that scout Al Sieber, whom Tom met in California and at Fort Whipple (later Prescott), got him placed as a government interpreter. With Sieber he went to the San Carlos Agency where he stayed 14 years, being "loaned" to army officers Chaffee, Crook, Miles and others as interpreter or guide. Horn was big and tough, over 6 feet tall, he and Sieber making a formidable pair, the latter over 6 feet and weighing 190 pounds. It was during this period Tom Horn became a friend of Apache Chief Geronimo.

When Sieber was badly wounded by the Apache Kid, Horn held Geronimo responsible and trailed him hundreds of miles. When he caught up with the old medicine man he was able to persuade him to surrender to Gen. Miles. Horn's autobiography, presumably written during his long and final imprisonment, although sometimes called "posthumous", gives Horn full credit for the feat. It is true that Miles called him his "Chief of Scouts".

With the close of the Apache wars, Horn turned to mining for a time, then ranching. He scorned "dirt farming" but practiced roping until he became top hand, and in 1888 at Globe, Arizona, won many prizes and was considered the star of the rodeo there. For a change of pace he joined the Pinkerton Agency in Denver in 1890, and four years later became a stock detective for the Swan Land and

Cattle Agency in Wyoming. He left to join Shafter's Army in the Philippines, serving as packmaster in the Battle of San Juan Hill. Returning home with a severe attack of "Cuban Fever", Horn was forced to remain quiet for a time.

Expert rifleman Horn had stayed on the side of the law all this time, an honest, upright scout, rancher, cowboy, soldier. Now he turned man-killer for profit. At a reputed $500 per head he eliminated any man unfriendly to his powerful cattle baron bosses. Victims included rustlers and those who rightly or wrongly claimed ranch land already in use by the cattlemen. When Horn appeared in the lawless area called Hole-In-The-Wall, there were dead men found along the trails, a small rock under each head by way of a trademark. Between forays in the red rock country, he was often seen in the company of cattle barons relaxing over liquor and cards.

It was said Tom Horn took great pride in his trade, making sure a single shot would be adequate for extermination. After at least a dozen men had been murdered, 14 year old Willie Nickell, son of an Iron Mountain rancher who had been running sheep in cattle country, was found dead. The case aroused wide public indignation but for some time the law could not prove Horn guilty. Then Joe Lefors, deputy U.S. Marshal was put on the trail of the former Pinkerton detective. Horn had become a heavy drinker with the wealthy cattlemen and welcomed Lefors as a convivial companion over a bottle. Loose-tongued under the influence, he bragged of his many killings including that of the Nickell boy. He was arrested. Lefors had witnesses concealed and the blabbings written down.

In that day a confession meant a sentence of guilty and although Horn denied he made one, he was found guilty and sentenced to hang. The verdict threw the state of Wyoming and much of the country into a furor of protest. Horn's record as honest citizen and war hero being better known than his deeds in the Hole-In-The-Wall. He escaped from jail, presumably aided by cattlemen but was recaptured. All this time there was a mounting tide of high feeling between cattle and sheep men coalitions in Cheyenne, scene of the trial and im-

HERO-TURNED-KILLER Tom Horn was officially hanged at Cheyenne after trial in old courthouse on present site of City and County Building, then buried in cemetery. Many believed law was bought, that convicted scout-rancher-gunman was somehow smuggled away to freedom before day of hanging, that perhaps another prisoner was hanged in his place. (Photo Wyoming State Archives and Historical Dept).

prisonment. Among rumors was one that the cattlemen would so arrange matters that Horn would be secretly released at the last moment, another that sheep men would attack the jailers, remove Horn and lynch him.

What did happen almost at the last moment was the discovery of a plot to dynamite the side of the jail and release the prisoner. It was thwarted and on the appointed day, after the militia was called to patrol Cheyenne streets, Tom Horn mounted the gallows and the trap was sprung. The lower part of the gibbet structure was carefully shielded, a not unusual precaution, and when Horn's coffin was brought out, Nickell, father of the slain boy, stepped up to it and demanded the lid be removed so he could see the body. The county attorney refused on the basis he feared a riot.

For years many claimed the whole affair to be a sham, that in some fashion Horn was spirited away, a tall dummy boosted to the noose, coffin filled with rocks and sand bags. It was later reported in various newspapers that Horn was sighted in several parts of Wyoming and the West.

THE COWHAND WAS A CLOWN

In 1886 the Fremont, Elkhorn and Missouri Valley Railroad announced it would extend its lines westward from Chadron, Nebraska, up the North Platte River. Men of foresight established themselves at several Wyoming points where they were sure steel would come. Three of them pitched tents on the Platte just north of its confluence with Antelope Creek. One housed a general merchandise store owned by C. H. King and Co., another a restaurant, the third naturally a saloon. Ranchers from far places took to stopping there, as did footloose travelers, some of them staying to put up tents of their own. The collection of canvas became known as Tent Town.

Two theological students held the first church services in the saloon in May, the altar a card table and most of the bottles covered up. Tent Town soon had three streets and boasted a newspaper, *Bill Barlow's Budget,* edited by Merris Clark Barrow who wrote under the name "Bill Barlow" and gained some fame with his humorous prose.

In June came the news that the site of the new railroad station would be some 10 miles east of Fetterman on the opposite side of the Platte. In a matter of days the Pioneer Townsite Company was laying out a new town there and it took only three more for complete removal of Tent Town to trackside. The site, at about the intersection of the Bozeman and Texas Trails, and the historic paths traveled by Robert Stuart, Captain Bonneville and General Fremont, was named Douglas City. More permanent buildings of log and frame rose up, one of them a saloon, one of its first patrons a curious character named George W. Pike.

Pike was called cattle rustler, thief, unruly, clownish, crude, but never a killer. On his first visit to the new Douglas saloon he had drinks at the bar and sat at the gambling table for a friendly game of stud. He could not understand why he was losing consistently in a game where he never came out less than even, until he saw the dealer cleverly palm a few kings and aces. Had Pike stood up, drawn his gun and blazed away at the crooked dealer he would have been known as just another dime-a-dozen gunman. Instead he simply paid his chips and walked out.

In his room Pike changed into his dirtiest rags. Pulling his hat low over his face he went back to the saloon, held his gun against the proprietor's ribs, demanding all the money in the till. He got it — some $2,500. He walked out, changed back to his better clothes in his room. Back in the saloon he asked the excited owner what the trouble was and told what had happened, he offered his sympathy and bought a drink.

George W. Pike was famous on the range as a top cowhand who believed in the principle, "What's thine is mine". This tendency, with his roping skill, often allowed him to come up with a stray dogie, and mother too, if she came close enough. Cattle outfits competed for his services, figuring it better to pay him good wages and keep him on their side. It was said no outfit employing him ever lost a cow or any money. But maybe the other side did.

GEORGE W. PIKE

Underneath this stone in eternal rest
Sleeps the wildest one of the wayward west
He was gambler and sport and cowboy too
And he led the pace in an outlaw crew
He was sure on the trigger and staid to the end
But he was never known to quit on a friend
In the relations of death all mankind is alike
But in life there was only one George W. Pike

ELABORATE TOMBSTONE in Douglas Park cemetery, erected by large cattle concern once employing George W. Pike. It was said the company gained hundreds of head from other owners while he was on payroll. Photo Wyoming State Archives and Historical Dept.

INDEPENDENCE ROCK
"REGISTRY OF THE DESERT"

Rising from the vast, stark emptiness of Wyoming prairie, on the Sweetwater River, is a mammoth lump of grayish brown granite. With the rounded haunches of some great bear-like animal, the monolith averages about 175 feet in height and 2,000 feet in length. This is Independence Rock, no doubt the largest name registry known to man. After the glaciers ground harder rocks against it as they passed over, leaving pronounced striations of the ice age, primitive peoples and latter day Indians left their markings on the rock, many of them since eroded away.

Robert Stuart camped near the rock in 1812 and John K. Townsend stopped there in 1834. He estimated the rise of the rock as about 50 feet. While it isn't known just which Independence Day somebody visited and named the rock, it must have been before 1840. That year Father P. J. De Smet referred to it as the "famous rock Independence . . . that might possibly be called the greatest registry of the desert, for on it may be read in large characters the names of several travelers who have visited the Rocky Mountains."

The ubiquitous Fremont also camped at the base of the monolith and described it as "well inscribed with the names of travelers." He did not sign his name but reported, "I engraved on this rock of the far West a symbol of the Christian faith . . a large cross, which I covered with a black preparation of Indian rubber well calculated to resist the influence of wind and rain." But this effort was unavailing as the cross has completely vanished. It may have been destroyed on July 4, 1847, when a gathering of more than 1,000 emigrants set off a keg of gunpowder. And Fremont's cross may in turn have destroyed his chance for the presidency by influencing voters against him.

The first party of Mormon emigrants under Brigham Young also stayed at the rock in 1847. One of them carried a set of stone cutting tools for use at some future home and offered to do a professional job of name carving at $1 to $5 a name depending on the number of letters needed. Altogether it is estimated some 50,000 signatures have been chiseled, hacked, scratched or otherwise inscribed on the face of Independence Rock.

Roving bands of Indians were well aware of the good water stop for travelers at the rock, sometimes ambushing and killing them near the area, particularly in the narrow pass called Devil's Gate. A white party might make a prolonged stay while an ill member rested or died and bodies were carried to Independence Rock for burial. A sizable cemetery developed, most markers being of temporary nature but enough remaining to indicate that there may possibly be hundreds buried at the foot of the big hump, making it a fitting monument to all those pioneers whose hope died there.

HUGE BULK of Independence Rock in Wyoming marked halfway point for travelers to Oregon Country. For many the well watered and marked campground was end of trail, numerous deaths occurring among emigrants too weary or ill to continue. Exact number and identity will never be known. Several graves clearly shown here at base of rock toward left.

THE UTES OF UTAH

On April 10, 1865, Barney Ward and another Utah settler, James P. Anderson, were driving some livestock rounded up on their pastures in the canyon. Clouds of dust prevented their seeing a band of seventy-five marauding Indians coming up with stock animals stolen from ranchers. The braves let loose a swarm of arrows, several finding Ward and Anderson. The Indians jumped on them, finished them off with tomahawks, stripped them naked and mutilated the bodies in the atrocious, unprintable manner then popular with the tribes. Ward left an Indian wife and two children.

The wife's story begins with an early fight between Shoshone Indians and a company of U.S. Cavalry at Battle Creek, Wyoming, which resulted in the extermination of the Indian band. Or so it seemed, until a young soldier noted movement in the robes wrapped around one of the slain squaws. Lifting a corner he found a girl baby trying to nurse at the mother's breast.

He picked up the tiny papoose and fed her some milk, keeping her alive until he could get back to his home in St. Louis where she was raised under the name of Sally. Reaching young womanhood, she ran away to search out her own people and at Fort Laramie met a stalwart young brave named Battice Everid. They were married, traveled on an extended honeymoon over Utah and Wyoming. The Everids had two children when the husband came down with spotted fever and died. Sally returned to her people with daughters Polly and Louisa.

Not long after this she met Elijah Ward, called "Barney", a settler in the area who found the Indians, especially Sally, very interesting. The two became friendly while he was acting as interpreter and guide. After a swift courtship they were married, settling down in the Salina Canyon country of Sevier County, Utah.

Then he was killed and Sally returned to her tribe for the second time, occasionally taking her little girls to visit Barney Ward's relatives. After a year or two the visits ceased, Sally, Polly and Louisa vanishing completely, never to be heard from again.

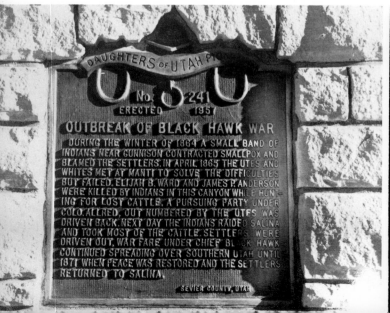

PLAQUE was placed on monument beside Highway 10 near Salida, Sevier County, Utah, by Daughters of Utah Pioneers. Story, cast in bronze, necessarily omits poignant details.

STRANGE ROCK, about 10" in length, found by author in neighborhood of Ute attacks. Has puzzled rock hounds, geologists.

VALLEY where Ward and Anderson were killed by Utes. Two days after attack Col. Alfred of Spring Valley took party of men through here to find Indians but a number of them waited in ambush, killed two whites, routed remainder. The mutilated bodies of Henry Kearns of Gunnison and James Sorenson of Ephraim lay in field three days before recovery was possible. By then elderly sheepherder and 18 year old cowherder were killed and scalped by Utes.

PATCH OF DRIED MUD in Nevada, photographed by author in desert between White Pine and Butte Mountains. Note similarity of pattern to that of rock in photo, tracks of cattle and birds. Fossilized mud often shows tracks (of contemporary dinosaurs) and identical cracks. Could Utah rock be fossil mud cracks?

INDIANS ALONG THE VIRGIN

The Mormon settlements at Salt Lake City were just established when Brigham Young sent out the word that frontiers must be extended. Many church members selected for this missionary work, men and women who had struggled to get a foothold in the desert wilderness beside the Wasatch Mountains, were reluctant to pull up stakes and move again. Still they complied without making trouble.

The first line of settlements included Logan, Provo, Ogden, all close to Salt Lake. Other families were sent to southern Utah, then termed "Dixie" since one objective was to generate cotton industries. Of these villages, some like St. George have survived and flourished, and others like Grafton shriveled up and are now almost forgotten.

Two factors contributed to Grafton's demise — unremitting attacks by Indians and periodic, raging floods of the Virgin River. Indians along the river, which they called the Pahroos, were made up of rather compact tribes, branches of the Paiute nation.

At first they did not trouble the settlers. They were cliff dwellers, traces of their houses remaining today, and there were plenty of lizards to eat, especially that called "chuckawalla". The small reptile would scurry into a crevice, wedge itself in tight by puffing up with air. The Indians got them out by jabbing a sharp stick into their lungs and deflating them.

So with lizards, insects and bulbs dug out of the earth, the natives were content until they saw the settler's cattle and sheep would make better eating. And when these animals began to disappear, the settlers began killing Indians and a war was soon going along the Pahroos. The villages were attacked more frequently, with fatalities on both sides.

With the outbreak of the widespread Black Hawk War in 1866, the military declared a state of martial law, ordering all small settlements to group at least 150 families together for self-protection. This meant all families along the Virgin must move to Rockville, two miles from Grafton. Some settlers built new cabins, some made shelters of brush under the trees, some dismantled cabins and assembled them on the new sites.

Then Rockville was judged unsafe and the brethren were forced to move enmasse to Toquerville. When Indians endangered this area, a move was made to the town of Virgin. James Jepson, son of one of the beleaguered, said in an interview at Hurricane in 1933, that his father had to move five times and said often, "I got so I just threw the logs in the new yard. They were so used to being put back together, they quickly fitted themselves where they belonged." During this time crops had to be attended to and settlers worked from one field to another in armed groups of ten to thirty men.

When the Black Hawk struggle ended in 1867, restrictions on smaller communities were relaxed,

CRYPTIC INSCRIPTION on board in Grafton cemetery may indicate burial place of Indian killed by Tom Flanigan in 1869. No greensward gentles burial ground here, sun-cracked barren clay typical of old graveyards in much of Southwest.

many farmers having already relocated. Not all returned to their former homes and the resulting shuffle changed census roles in most areas, Grafton losing many families because of the flood danger.

For years peace remained uneasy with Indians creating local disturbances. In February, 1869, Sam Green and Tom Flanigan were carrying a load of express out of Rockville. In the half-dusk of evening they suddenly came upon two Indians walking along the road and the jittery Flanigan fired at them. One was wounded and taken back to Rockville where he died.

Paiutes in the Virgin River area had a strict code of reprisal. When a member of one tribe killed one of another, the killer was required to produce a tribesman to be tortured and killed for satisfaction, the one given up for savage vengeance usually being aged, blind, crippled or otherwise expendable.

Now the relatives and fellow tribesmen of the slain Indian demanded the whites turn the slayer over to them, this Tom Flanigan. They would tie him to a stake, build a fire at his feet and stab him with spears until he died. Then they could be friends with the white man again. This apparently was a tongue-in-cheek demand for the savages settled for a butchered ox.

GEORGE WASHINGTON GIBBS, native of Union County, South Carolina, was one of last to be buried in Grafton cemetery, just before town was deserted.

ZION NATIONAL PARK, whose outer walls tower directly above old Grafton cemetery, carries Mormon term for Heaven. Zion was ancient name of loftiest hill on which Jerusalem was built. Settlers along Virgin termed vast canyon Zion until reproved by leader Brigham Young, who said mountains and valley were not Zion. Then, for a while, farmers called spectacular area "Not Zion".

Travelers rounding Mount Kinesava and entering stupendous canyon soon come face to face with Great White Throne, 6,744 feet high, of white sandstone. Monolith is seldom climbed successfully. Story is told that first climber was man who bragged of many Alpine ascents, set off alone to assault huge rock. That night his campfire was seen on summit but he did not return and was never heard from again. Presumably his bones lie caught in some lofty crevice on near vertical sides.

MANY VICTIMS of Indian raids rest here in shadow of Zion National Park, one huge rampart, Mount Kinesava, forming background here. Virgin River flows between cemetery and mountains, is usually peaceful but often turning into raging torrent estimated to carry 180 carloads of ground rock daily from Zion Canyon.

YOUNG JOSEPH BERRY was one of the last residents of Grafton, Utah, to be killed by marauding Indians before martial law forced removal of settlers. Several other victims in Berry family are buried in same plot enclosed in picket fence—well preserved for 100 years in dry Utah climate.

JOSEPH S. BERRY
BORN
DEC. 9. 1843.
KILLED BY INDIANS
APR. 2. 1866.

MOUNTAIN MEADOWS MASSACRE

With 1854 came the great expansion of the original Mormon community at Salt Lake City. Such nearby towns as Logan, Bountiful, Ogden and Provo were established around central temples or churches and Brigham Young began the colonization of the southern fringe of Utah, the country to be called Dixie, supported by vast fields of cotton. One of the colonies was Parowan and missionaries were sent to convert the Indians around it, John Doyle Lee in charge of the whole plan. Young stressed the importance of making allies of the Indians, that they must be constantly reminded of the great gulf between their Mormon friends and the "Mericats" who would drive their cattle over pastures, the herds eating all the grass and leaving desolation — people who would shoot at them just to see them jump.

In 1857 word came to Salt Lake that the U.S. Army was on its way to subdue all Mormons, prevent further expansion and discourage the custom of polygamy. Brigham Young sent orders to all outposts to make no new friends among the Gentiles, to refuse wheat or corn to all travelers not brethren of the church. The order was harsh but brought on by the severe persecution the church had suffered from its inception. In one outrage alone, at Nauvoo, Ill., leader Joseph Smith was assassinated with many other members. They were accused of everything from theft to murder of non-Mormons, theirs a religious order whose only sin was in remaining aloof from Gentiles. Now in Utah any such gesture as the Christ-like turning of the other cheek would be tantamount to suicide. So the Mormon colonists could not afford to be humble

and forgiving. They were to "take a tough line" to all emigrants, soldiers and citizens. In addition various companies of Mormon Militia were organized as a protective measure, in Parowan citizens drilling with a company based at Cedar City. All were on edge, the more warlike even eager for action.

One of the first emigrant parties to experience trouble was the wagon train led by Charles Fancher. It was a loosely knit group made up of several parties banded together for protection. Fancher had crossed the country earlier, located a rich tract of land in California, then returned to Arkansas to recruit settlers. He organized the train with eleven families — sixty-five people including twenty-nine children in the eleven wagons. Also attached was a group of single men of dubious respectability calling themselves the "Missouri Wildcats". Fancher was reported to have with him $4,000 to pay for his land.

Knowing of the terrible fate of the Donner party the year before, Fancher chose the southern route by way of the Spanish Trail which passed not far from Parowan. The party was joyful on reaching Salt Lake City but their expectations of buying food for themselves, hay and grain for the cattle and horses, changed to black dismay. All requests were refused. And as the emigrants proceeded they received the same treatment, growing more disturbed and more truculent by the mile.

There now began a series of ugly incidents between them and the Mormons, some real, some fancied. Several Mormon cattle were found dead beside a spring after the Fancher party passed. Spring and cattle were poisoned, the Mormons said. Not so, retorted the emigrants. The cattle died from eating loco weed. They were people who would not poison any spring, they said. The Missouri Wildcats swore they would come back from California with an army and decimate the Mormons.

All this made John D. Lee seethe and when Fancher and his people approached Parowan he made plans for what he thought would be justifiable reprisal. The emigrants passed through town and they saw every man watching them as an enemy— every man but one. Young William Leany recog-

MONUMENT is difficult to locate, Forest Service signs on highway at intersection of gravel road being torn down. Once turn off is found going is easy on road leading down into canyon, then around edge of meadow. This plaque is placed on north end of stone marker for mass grave.

JOHN D. LEE sits on coffin edge before execution. When somber execution party reached scene of massacre, selected for Lee's payment of death penalty, cold wind was blowing. Lee wore heavy overcoat, muffler and sat on coffin. As photographer James Tennemore busied himself taking pictures Lee requested copies to be given to his three favorite wives, Rachel, Sarah and Emma. Told executioners were ready, Lee stood up, made short speech with refrain, "I studied to make Brigham Young's will my pleasure for thirty years. See now what I have come to this day." He removed coat, hat and muffler, asking that executioners not mangle his body. "Let them put the bullets through my heart." Handkerchief was tied over his eyes, shots fired and Lee's body fell back on coffin. (Photo by Tennemore from Utah State Historical Society.)

nized a friend among the travelers and ran out to them with an armful of vegetables from his garden. The party passed on and Mormon police called Leany out of his house, struck him down for rendering aid and comfort to strangers, and left him for dead. Leany regained consciousness but never fully recovered.

Lee held a conference with leaders of the colony trying to get support for a move on the emigrants, arresting all and holding them for prosecution. One faction went even further, arguing that Fancher and his people had money, horses, supplies, and it would be better to kill them all and use their belongings to further God's Will. This was the kind of talk Lee wanted to hear and he agreed to carry out such a plan.

By this time the travelers were desperately short of food and perhaps the reports of stealing and taking food by force are true. They were exhausted and on a beautiful Sunday in September of 1857 their train was halted in a lush green field at the lower end of Mountain Meadows where they hoped

to rest for several weeks to prepare for the arduous journey ahead. They chose the meadow because, being in the open it afforded no cover for hostile Indians. This caution was justified as Indians were spoiling to attack them and well aware of the Mormon attitude toward the wagon train, tried to get Lee to help them raid the camp. He told them he needed more guns and ammunition and would be ready the next day.

Early that morning the Indians sprang a surprise attack, not waiting for Lee. Several emigrants were killed, the Indians also losing men and retreating to wait for Lee. He came on Wednesday, with Militia Captains Dame, Higbee, Haight and civilian Jacob Hamblin, and found the Indians greatly excited. "We fight for Mormon God," they said. "Bullets not hurt us." And here facts become diffused. The most acceptable version is, Lee told them to hide near Fancher's camp. Then he walked to a point near the camp carrying a white flag. Three men came out to meet him and Lee told them that if all the emigrants who had committed offenses at Parowan and elsewhere were returned there for trial, he would guarantee their safe passage by restraining the Indians. In order to show their good faith the men of the party must give up their arms. This bargain was agreed to by the Missourians. It has been assumed Fancher was killed in the Indian attack as he would probably not have assented to such a plan.

All weapons, mostly Kentucky rifles, were loaded in one wagon and all children under ten except babes in arms were put in with them. Another wagon took the sick and injured, and both moved slowly away, Lee walking between them. Women and children came next in the procession, followed by men in single file, each with a Mormon "guard" beside him.

At Lee's sudden cry, "Do your duty!", Indians hidden in the brush fell upon the women, splitting their heads with tomahawks and stones. Each emigrant man was slain by his assigned guard and Lee killed all in the wagon containing the sick and injured. While the Indians were mutilating and stripping the bodies of the women, the wagonload of small children was driven to the Hamblin ranch to be cared for.

Lee, Higbee and others at the bloody massacre

ground formed a tight circle and solemnly swore secrecy, agreeing that, "We have done our duty, in helping to defend Zion and to protect our own families and firesides. God has been with us and helped out for His purposes." The bodies of the men were searched for valuables and money — nothing reported then or later about Fancher's $4,000. Clothing was removed, shoes tied in pairs and neatly stacked in a pile. The bodies remained where they lay while Lee and his men went to Hamblin's to spend the night.

After breakfast the next morning they returned to the meadows where Lee, Higbee and Dame set the other men to enlarging the rifle pits the emigrants had excavated. The bodies were dumped in them, barely covered with rocks and soil, each man going to the spring to wash hands, arms, face and neck.

Lee drove one of the wagons home, beside him little Charlie Fancher to whom he had taken a fancy. He turned the boy over to his wife Caroline, one of seventeen wives who mothered Lee's seventy-two children. The other surviving children of the Fancher party were distributed to various women in the town to be brought up as Mormons. Colony personnel washed the bloody clothing and placed all articles on commissary shelves for sale. Lee soon left for Salt Lake to report to Brigham Young. While there he met attractive Emma Bachelor, courted, dined and danced her, the romance culminating in Brigham's own sealing room.

Although it seemed at first Brigham Young condoned, even approved Lee's actions at Mountain Meadows, he later excluded Lee from the Mormon Church, leading many to believe he had not reported his part in the massacre accurately, Young learning the truth later. Now generally discredited, Lee moved from one place to another, finally settling on a point on the Colorado River where he operated a ferry. United States authorities made many attempts to pin blame for the massacre on Lee but failed to get anything like a conviction, all Mormons maintaining silence.

It was not until July 12, 1875 that Lee was dragged out of his hiding place in his hog pen at Lee's Ferry and brought to trial. No witnesses were available but Lee made a full confession, implicating Higbee, Dame, Haight and others but refused to incriminate Brigham Young or the church. The

LEE'S BODY placed in crude pine board coffin by sons. They drove all night to Panguitch where family, knowing of Lee's desire to be buried in temple robes, removed lid, redressed body in robes as shown here. (Photo from Utah State Historical Society.)

jury failed to agree and a second trial was held in Beaver City Sept. 13. This time Brigham Young appeared to testify, admitting that he had made what was considered a threat to Capt. Van Fleet on the 9th of September. Van Fleet told Young to refrain from interfering in any way with emigrants and Young replied, according to Utah historian Juanita Brooks, "You may tell the government to stop all emigration across the country, for the Indians will kill all who attempt it. I shall not hold the Indians by the wrist any longer". To those who maintained this was a direct threat against the Fancher party, he pointed out the remark was made only two days before the massacre. Any word could not possibly have reached Lee before the slaughter took place. Further, he said, when Lee made his report of the incident, he said the Indians alone were responsible, making no mention of his ordering salvaging of the clothing.

Jacob Hamblin testified that Lee told him of

SCENE OF MOUNTAIN MEADOWS MASSACRE supports scant vegetation but provides ample sustenance to Datura, plant asking little. White trumpets, tinged with lavendar on outside, open in evening, close when sun gets hot in day. Plant flourishes near massacre scene where these specimens were photographed. All parts of Datura are dangerously narcotic.

two young girls who escaped the slaughter by hiding in the brush. They were discovered and brought in by a Ute chief who asked Lee what to do with them. Lee answered, "They must be killed. They are too old to be spared, as they will talk." The chief said they were too pretty to be killed but Lee was adamant. The Indian shot one while Lee threw the other to the ground and cut her throat.

Dame and the others were released from custody, John Doyle Lee convicted of murder in the first degree and choosing to be shot. Then he made another "confession", throwing the entire blame on Dame, Higbee and Haight, and claiming that all was done under full orders of Brigham Young. As to the emigrants, he claimed, "I used my utmost endeavors to save them from their sad fate. I know that I will have my reward in heaven. My conscience does not accuse me." Two days later he was taken to the Meadows and shot to death.

GRAVE of John Doyle Lee at Panguitch, Utah. (Photo from Utah State Historical Society.)

BODIES BURIED in own rifle pits were barely covered, predatory animals digging them up, tooth marks found on widely scattered bones. They were gathered and buried in common grave, marked by this square enclosure of field stones. A lush, grassy meadow at the time of the massacre, it was described by an eye-witness 20 years later as a plague area. "Over that spot," he said, "the curse of the Almighty seemed to have fallen. The luxuriant vegetation that had clothed it 20 years before had disappeared, the springs were dry and wasted, and now there was neither grass nor any green thing, here and there a corpse of sagebrush or scrub oak. Around the cairn that marks their grave, still flit, as some have related, the phantoms of the murdered emigrants, and nightly re-enact in ghostly pantomine the scene of the hideous tragedy." 109 years after massacre area still fits this description.

COLORADO?
COLOR IT SILVER

FIRST FAINT RAYS of morning sunlight reach summits, nearly full but waning moon still brilliant, and near to setting as seen from edge of Animas River just below old cemetery.

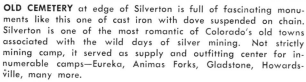

OLD CEMETERY at edge of Silverton is full of fascinating monuments like this one of cast iron with dove suspended on chain. Silverton is one of the most romantic of Colorado's old towns associated with the wild days of silver mining. Not strictly mining camp, it served as supply and outfitting center for innumerable camps—Eureka, Animas Forks, Gladstone, Howardsville, many more.

MILLION DOLLAR HIGHWAY from lookout point, so called because of gold-bearing gravels used in surfacing. Presence of high grade "colors" was discovered when someone panned sample of gravel near end of road completion. Highway winds steeply upward from Ouray to this point looking roughly south and following one of toll routes hacked out by pioneer road builder Otto Mears. Building is abandoned mill, common in Colorado, clinging to side of mountain more securely than some, seeming glued against almost perpendicular cliffs. In center background is approximate spot where Rev. Hudson's car was brushed off road by avalanche of snow and rocks.

OLD WOODEN CROSS, inscription partially decipherable, shown in dramatic contrast to mountain background. Peak is part of Sultan Mountain complex containing hundreds of once fiercely active silver mines, all long since abandoned although slender prospects of renewed activity breathe faint life into some.

BRONZE MEMORIAL PLAQUE and three white crosses placed beside Million Dollar Highway at point near spot where Hudson car was swept off road.

THIS MARKER IN MEMORY OF
REV. MARVIN HUDSON
HIS DAUGHTERS
AMELIA & PAULINE
WHO WERE SWEPT TO THEIR DEATHS 1000 FEET NORTH OF THIS
MARKER IN THE EAST RIVERSIDE SLIDE SUNDAY MARCH 3, 1963
WHILE ANSWERING THE CALL TO CHRISTIAN DUTY OF HIS
PASTORATE IN SILVERTON, COLORADO
IN HONOR
OF THE MANY FRIENDS & NEIGHBORS WHO RISKED THEIR LIVES
TO SAVE THEM AND RECOVER THEIR BODIES
A SYMBOL
OF THE CHRISTIAN FAITH THAT UNITES MEN IN CHRISTIAN LOVE
IN TIMES LIKE THESE
ERECTED BY THE CHURCHES OF
SILVERTON   OURAY   RIDGWAY
AND THE MEN, WOMEN, AND CHILDREN
WHO LOVE THESE MOUNTAINS

TELLURIDE CEMETERY was laid out, many burials made, when avalanche of mud swept down on graves, burying them 6 feet deep, headboards and all. New burials continued on top of old. Included among graves are several in mass burials, victims of snow avalanches. One of these was followed by second which buried rescuers attempting to save victims of first avalanche. Some of the multi-burial graves are shown here in foreground, enclosed in curbings. Much of old Telluride is shown in background, courthouse built before any place of worship and often used for church services, weddings, funerals.

TYPICAL INSCRIPTION for groups killed by avalanches.

JOHN BARTHEL, at 27, died in miner and strike breaker struggle at Smuggler Mine, July 3, 1901. At turn of century most of Colorado's silver mines were worked on old Cornish "fathom system", miner paid by fathom, six feet of ore, no matter how wide silver deposit might be. In Telluride mines, particularly, veins ran wide and miners had difficulty making livings. They protested system but Smuggler Company held fast and miner's union struck on May 2, 1901. Mine officials employed non-union men who were attacked by union members on July 3, battle ending with 3 men dead and 6 wounded. Next November new pay schedules were worked out and strike was settled.

In spectacular background is cascading Ingram Falls. Heart-stopping road climbs 3600 feet by sharp switch-backs to old Black Bear Mine, its stamp mill shown on ledge at upper end of road. In busy days incredibly heavy mine machinery was hauled up heavily traveled road. Heavy two-wheeled wooden carts had tongue at each end, horses changing ends at switch-backs, avoiding impossible turn. Snow clogs road at upper levels in late June, where in old days it had no chance to accumulate. Tailings at lower right are from still operating Idarado Mills, reclaiming copper, some zinc, lead, silver and gold. Enough of latter is recovered to pay for operation. In 1965 several thousand dollars in amalgams were stolen.

OURAY'S OLD CEMETERY is located several miles from town which is situated in tiny level pocket hemmed in by towering peaks rising steeply. Burial ground is full of many interesting graves and monuments, this marker unique, resembling infant's bassinet. Paper roses shown were probably left from Memorial Day.

BURIAL TOMB of Chipeta, wife of great Ute Chief Ouray, four miles from Montrose, Colo., in Ouray-Chipeta Park. For many years Ouray worked diligently to hold down friction between his people and whites. He failed at times as during conference with subchiefs Colorow, Douglas and Captain Jack when plans were made to kill Meeker and associates at agency.

In 1859 Ouray took beautiful maiden of Tabeguache Ute tribe as wife, lived peacefully for some years until 7 year old son was carried away by Kiowas. Toward end of life Ouray became embittered by often faithless whites, swore tribe to secrecy as to his burial place. When Chipeta died in 1924, 43 years later, whereabouts of Ouray's remains was revealed and they were reburied in Ute Cemetery at Ignacio, Colo.

IMMENSE COTTONWOOD once shaded Ute and allied tribes holding council near Delta, Colo. Sign beside highway US 50 indicates tree as nearby, largest in area, bearing identifying plaque.

WILD WEST SYMBOL—BUFFALO BILL

William Cody, far better known as Buffalo Bill, was born at Le Claire, Iowa. The house of his nativity stands in Cody, Wyoming, moved there from the land of tall corn. The boy had little formal education, was subjected unwillingly to some sketchy, spasmodic book learning and released from it when his father took "gold fever" and started for California in 1857. Neither father nor son got there, the elder Cody dying in Kansas City, the stranded boy finding a job cleaning out stables.

Almost immediately showing a rapport with horses, a talent that would mold his life, William was put to driving freight wagons. The next year he was on the road to Salt Lake City with a herd of beef for federal soldiers and with the outbreak of the Civil War he served as Union Army scout. After that he contracted with the Kansas Pacific Railroad to supply buffalo meat to feed construction crews and during the next 18 months killed 4,280 head contributing with other buffalo hunters to Indian hostilities toward the white man who was destroying their main food supply. It was during this period of slaughter he acquired the nickname "Buffalo Bill".

About this time Ned Buntline, pseudonym of Edward Z. C. Judson, came west in search of "blood and thunder" material on which to base a series of wild west tales. In Cody he found the prototype he sought for the highly colored "true" stories which began appearing in the *New York Weekly* and on the newsstands as dime and nickel novels, among the first of the "paperbacks". Cody's experiences were buried in a mass of "guns and gore" but the stories achieved enormous success and naturally shed a glowing aura of glory on the great Indian fighter Buffalo Bill who had actually killed one Indian while scouting on the Platte. With dramatic gusto, Fred Meader put together a hair-raising stage play titled *Buffalo Bill, King of the Border Men* which started a successful run at the Bowery Theater in New York. Buffalo Bill was made.

In 1872 Buntline dressed his hero in fancy, long-fringed buckskins, beaded and braided boots and starred him in *Scouts of the Plains,* his own version of the Broadway play. Later the author introduced such characters as Wild Bill Hickok and other publicized western heroes. This led into *Buffalo Bill's Original Wild West Show* which was produced for 30 years.

During this long period Cody made a lot of money and spent a lot of money on luxurious living. With the fading of an era and the ending of his show, he fell on evil times. Penniless and alone, he died in Denver during World War I.

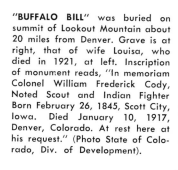

"BUFFALO BILL" was buried on summit of Lookout Mountain about 20 miles from Denver. Grave is at right, that of wife Louisa, who died in 1921, at left. Inscription of monument reads, "In memoriam Colonel William Frederick Cody, Noted Scout and Indian Fighter Born February 26, 1845, Scott City, Iowa. Died January 10, 1917, Denver, Colorado. At rest here at his request." (Photo State of Colorado, Div. of Development).

NOT A MEEKER MASSACRE

Nathan C. Meeker was agriculture editor of the powerful New York *Tribune*. In 1869 editor and publisher Horace ("Go west, young man") Greeley conceived the idea of an agricultural colony in South Park, Colorado with Meeker at its head. Fortunately for all concerned William N. Byers, editor of Denver's *Rocky Mountain News* pointed out the unsuitability of the high, cold area with frosts in summer and the location was changed to a site on the Cache la Poudre in the South Platte Valley. The success of the colony and its subsequent growth into the thriving town of Greeley impressed the government. It decided Meeker was a good organizer and appointed him Indian agent.

Apparently it was clear to everybody except Meeker and the government that this was a tragic mistake. He attempted to rule the Utes with an iron hand. Accustomed to roaming the country at will, hunting and fishing, they were forced at once by Meeker into an agricultural life. Originally they were lured to live on the reservation in peace by glowing promises of money, goods and ample food. Meeker said it would be foolish to lavish these luxuries on savages unless absolutely necessary. He was deaf to the mutterings and growls of discontent.

Then he started digging a network of ditches for a badly needed irrigation system. He showed his knowledge of agricultural methods in planning drainages and water storage areas, and his appalling ignorance of the Indians' feelings, when he ran one of the ditches directly across the ground allotted them for the exercise of their horses. This brought on such Indian hostility toward Meeker he applied for military protection.

A force headed by Major Thornburg was sent to the agency but in Red Canyon the troops were all but annihilated by a Ute war party. Meeker, knowing the soldiers were on their way but unaware of their fate, sent a message to Thornburg. "Everything is quiet here. We have been on guard here, and will be tonight, not that we expect any trouble, but because there might be." An hour after the letter was written a party of painted Ute warriors swooped down on the unprepared agency, killing every man. Meeker's wife, daughter Josephine, another woman and her children were taken as hostages. Chief Douglas claimed Josephine Meeker as his personal slave, forcing her to watch as he stripped and scalped her father's body. He sang "Swing Low, Sweet Chariot" at the grisly task, asking the girl if she thought he had a fine voice.

After Thornburg's death and that of his men, and the slaughter of Meeker and his employees, the Utes seemed satisfied, suing for peace while holding the women. U.S. Government officials tamely negotiated for the captives, paid the required ransom and allowed the chiefs responsible for the atrocities to go unpunished.

SCENE OF MEEKER MASSACRE at edge of meadow forward from grove of trees. Monument is tiny speck above letter T in first word "This" on sign. Telephoto lens was used, area sealed off by four stiffly strung barbed wire fences. Location is little known northwestern corner of Colorado in White River Valley, Rio Blanco County, river and valley names anglicized, county retaining original Spanish. State Road continues many lonely miles toward Utah through spectacular rocky scenery, past a few isolated ranches.

OLD OPHIR in 1883 was busy mining town with many miners, mill workers and families. Mail came from Silverton by carrier on snowshoes hiking over pass. Swen Nilson was mailman one year and he started from Silverton on Dec. 23 with Christmas mail for Ophir. Well aware of danger in heavy snow storm, he ignored attempts to stop him. Swen never reached destination, body being found in early summer, mailbags strapped to back. He was buried with honors in Ophir Cemetery, possibly in this grave among millions of golden dandelion blooms, sapling aspens, towering snow peaks.

CEMETERY OF OPHIRS, Old and New, in Colorado's silver mining days. Distinction between the two camps has long ago lost all meaning. New Ophir is on main road, Old Ophir some distance above in mountains on gravel road. Still higher, at 10,000 feet, is cemetery, partly overgrown with aspen trees, shown here, barely leafing out in pale chartreuse shades, in late June.

FREQUENT AVALANCHES in Colorado's San Juan mountains brought death and disaster to high altitude silver camps. This one in Telluride-Ophir are has overwhelmed offices, boarding and cook houses. Huge masses of snow accumulate on steep slopes until bulk overbalances "angle of repose". Snow is set in motion by often trivial vibration such as gunshot. Thousands of tons slide down cliffs with thundering roar, gathering momentum to extent that wave rolls up and against opposite slope. Carrying everything such as rocks, buildings along with it. Photo Courtesy American West.

ROLLING BONES IN THE DAKOTAS

Upon demand of the Indian police Sitting Bull came out of his house, half-dressed. Lt. Bull Head held one of his arms, Sgt. Red Tomahawk the other. Bull Head assured the old medicine man-chief of their protection but fixing them with a withering stare, Sitting Bull said, "I will go. I will ride on my gray horse." He referred to the trick circus horse he rode with Buffalo Bill's Wild West Show, presented to him when he left the troupe, unable to endure longer the jibes thrust at him as the murderer of General Custer. Sitting Bull started for the horse, stopped by the face of his handsome 17-year-old son and the bitter tone of his speech.

"You call yourself a chief, but you permit these metal-breasted dogs to drag you from your bed. What will your people think now of the mighty Sitting Bull?" Clarence Grey Eagle, watching the drama from the copse, saw Bull Head's mortal enemy Catch The Bear poise his rifle at the ready and push nearer the police guard. A brave drew the gray horse nearer and Bull Head offered the chief

the reins. Then Sitting Bull said. "No. I am not going". And those were his last words.

* * *

The years following the Battle of the Little Big Horn brought humiliation and submission to most of the Indians on the northern plains, including the valiant Sioux tribes. Many of them had deteriorated to become almost entirely dependent upon the white man but Sitting Bull and his followers were not among them. Standing tall, the great warrior and leader said with fire in his eye, "God Almighty never made an agency Indian. I will never be one."

Late in the year 1890 a new yeast began fermenting within the Sioux camps. A "prophet" named Wovoka had appeared among the Paiute tribes in Nevada. In his prayer circle on a mountain top this glorified medicine man had a vision in which the Great Spirit revealed to him a picture of the earth's opening to swallow all the hated white men and the ground once again turning black with herds of buffalo. All departed loved ones

CABIN OF SITTING BULL on day after he was killed in front of it. (Photo South Dakota State Historical Society).

GRAVE OF SITTING BULL at Fort Yates, N.D. photographed probably in late '40s, site now buried under Bureau of Reclamation dike. Rock cairn was erected in late '30s. Possibility exists that bones removed by party from Mobridge (see story) were not Sitting Bull's but miscellaneous ones at upper level of grave. (Photo State Historical Society of North Dakota).

would then descend from their burial platforms to return to their tipis and brush huts. All that was necessary to bring this about, Wovoka proclaimed was for tribesmen to sing and perform the "ghost dance" in the manner he prescribed.

Roving into Nevada, Sioux Kicking Bear saw and heard Indians going ecstatic over these prophecies and he conferred with the great prophet himself. On his return disciple Kicking Bear spread the news to all the Sioux, the tribes showing an enthusiasm that alarmed white authorities. Would the Sioux unite against them? No, it was concluded — there was no real danger as long as powerful Sitting Bull remained aloof from the craze. But in early December word reached them that the veteran Sioux leader was preparing to leave his camp just north of the Grand River, tributary of the Missouri. It was believed he was going to the Pine Ridge Reservation to join in mass ghost dance demonstrations as directed by Kicking Bear.

In the darkness before dawn of December 15,

1890, 39 Sioux policemen and 4 volunteers assembled in the log cabin of Indian Offenses Judge Gabriel Grey Eagle, just south of Sitting Bull's camp, and planned to put him under restraint at daybreak. Listening to the details was Clarence Grey Eagle, son of Gabriel and one of Sitting Bull's sisters, and the thought of his father about to arrest his uncle filled him with horror. When the force departed for Sitting Bull's camp, the boy snatched up a buffalo robe, jumped on the bare back of his pony and followed them, becoming an observer of the events that transpired, events that brought Sitting Bull's death, set off the infamous Wounded Knee Massacre and ended with the final subjugation of the Sioux.

The young Grey Eagle trailed the arresting party at a discreet distance and crossed the iced-over Grand River. In a copse of brushy young cottonwoods near his uncle's house, the boy slid off his pony and watched his father enter the house, the Indian police, hated badge-wearing "metal

156

breasts" following. He saw Sioux tribesmen gather into a knot of 150 and push against the police who held them back at port arms. And he saw the drama of Sitting Bull's last minute decision to resist the officers.

When the old medicine man refused the horse his followers raised a shout. One of them, Catch The Bear, put a bullet into the body of Bull Head but not before the lieutenant emptied his pistol into Sitting Bull's breast. Yet the old stalwart did not fall until Red Tomahawk fired a close range ball into the back of his skull. A policeman grabbed Catch The Bear's rifle and smashed his skull with it, then shot him. A confused melee followed, a bloody fight between Sitting Bull's warriors and Indian police.

In an open space, with bullets whizzing all around him, the old gray horse was sitting on his haunches, pawing with alternating front feet, head arching up and down, exactly as he performed when the stage coach was attacked in the sham holdup in the Wild West Show. Then a policeman jumped on him and rode safely out of the struggle, heading for help at the fort. Still concealed, Clarence Grey Eagle saw the reinforcements arrive and heard the sounds of shells falling in a scene of carnage. In the confusion soldiers were shelling the Indian

police, the Sioux band having fled beyond the river. A policeman waved a torn white window curtain and quiet fell.

Sitting Bull's two wives, Pretty Feather and Her Brown Robe, were weeping over his body when the "Blue Coats" came with a spring wagon to haul it away. As four soldiers picked up the body, the women cried, "Don't take him away, he belongs to us!" But the inert Sitting Bull was thrown into the wagon, a dead policeman on top of him and the 45 mile trip made to Fort Yates at the edge of Standing Rock Agency. And Her Brown Robe trudged every mile behind it.

When she returned she told Clarence Grey Eagle of how a funeral had been held for the 6 dead policemen, how they were buried in the Standing Rock Agency Cemetery and three volleys fired over them. Then the body of her husband was taken out of the death-house, sewed in a canvas wrapper and put in a wooden box. The soldiers hauled it to the Missouri River some three miles south, made prisoners dig a hole for the coffin and shovel dirt over it. Her story cut deep into Clarence Grey Eagle. He believed the miserable burial of his hero uncle far from his people was all wrong and vowed to dedicate his life to bringing the remains back to the old man's home. The youth would be a year

DESCENDANTS of Sitting Bull mourn at graveside day after remains were reinterred at Mobridge. Man at right bears striking resemblance to Sitting Bull. (Photo Mobridge **Tribune**).

short of 80 before this was accomplished.

The terrible tragedy of the Wounded Knee Massacre, two weeks after Sitting Bull's death, put a definite end to the old way of life for the Indians. Clarence Grey Eagle and all other tribesmen gave up any hope of ever returning to it. Such events as the coming of the iron horse meant little and for Clarence Grey Eagle there was nothing to live for except to bring home the bones of Sitting Bull.

He resigned himself to eking out a living from the plot of earth assigned to him by the government. He visited the grave of his uncle regularly and just as regularly pleaded with the agency people, finding sympathetic ears but inactive hands. When he was 34, in 1908, he heard a disconcerting rumor that a movement was on foot in Bismarck, North Dakota, to have the remains removed to that city as a tourist attraction.

Leading a delegation of his kinsmen to the State Historical Society of South Dakota at Pierre, Grey Eagle appealed to Executive Secretary Doane Robinson who was successful in stopping the removal plans and sponsored a bill in Congress to provide transfer of Sitting Bull's coffin to his old Grand River home and funds for a suitable memorial. The bill failed to pass and year after

year Grey Eagle made annual pilgrimages to the grave, pleading with the agency to at least remove weeds and rubbish from around the crude, flat concrete slab in the lonely, neglected site. Again nothing was accomplished.

At last, in 1953, a small ray of hope came to the faithful but aging nephew. The Army Corps of Engineers were building the fourth and last of the giant dams on the Missouri River. This one, at Pierre, would back up the muddy waters into North Dakota and ultimately cover Sitting Bull's grave. Surely, thought Grey Eagle, the U.S. Government would not allow this. He went to his friend Walter Tuntland, once storekeeper at Fort Yates and now president of the Mobridge Chamber of Commerce. Tuntland was agreeable to the idea of moving the bones near that city, thinking perhaps it would not hurt tourism to have the grave nearby.

Grey Eagle was given full power of attorney to claim the body, the papers needing only signatures of Sitting Bull's next of kin, daughters of Pretty Feather and Her Brown Robe. While he was getting them Tuntland organized the Dakota Memorial Association and obtained authorization to erect a monument carved by famous Black Hills sculptor Korczak Ziolkowski.

CONTROVERSIAL GRAVE of Sitting Bull at Mooridge, S. D.

On March 20, 1953, mortician Ray Miles and Grey Eagle went to Bismarck for the disinterment permit and matters proceeded well until someone recognized the name Tatanka Iyotonka on the pages as the Indian name of Sitting Bull. Arrangements then bogged down. Authorities had allowed the grave to be neglected but refused removal of remains. The question was put to Russel Reid, North Dakota State Historian, and his answer was, "What you ask is completely out of the question. Sitting Bull is a national figure. North Dakota will never give up the body." And the two Dakotas began a bitter controversy over the bones of the Indian earlier regarded as a sinister villain, a dangerous renegade.

Involved in the quarrel were governors and historical societies of both states, the U.S. military and Department of the Interior and out of it all the newspapers made hay. The military bowed out, Indian authorities ruled that descendants had full rights to the remains yet they did not wish to go against the wishes of North Dakota. Emboldened, Grey Eagle and a party of tribesmen went to the grave to remove the bones unobserved but found a guard posted and were turned away.

The waters of the Missouri rose higher and 7 Dakota towns competed for the remains if and when they should be removed from flood danger. Then Tuntland received news that the Department of the Interior would raise no objection if heirs agreed on disinterment.

A new grave was readied across the rising waters from Mobridge at a site not far from the camp where Sitting Bull lived and died. On the night of April 8, 1953, Grey Eagle rode with Ray Miles in a hearse to the Fort Yates site, followed by a truck full of Indian diggers. Arriving at dawn they attached a chain to the slab over the grave and the truck pulled the cover off. Diggers reached traces of nearly decomposed bones and those recovered were carefully placed in a blanket, the hole refilled, bundle placed in the hearse and the party hastened home. At the new grave concrete was poured around steel rails as the bones were quickly reburied and securely covered without formal ceremony.

Serious differences still remain between the sister states. Will G. Robinson, Secretary of South Dakota State Historical Society, writes the author:

"We have your letter of the 1st of December.

There is no question that the bones that were in the grave where Sitting Bull was originally buried after his death in 1890, were removed and taken to a site on a High Bluff adjacent to US 12 at the top of the Hill leading from the Highway Bridge west of Mobridge. They were taken to another place on the Standing Rock Reservation with the consent of the Superintendent of the Reservation. The North Dakota Board of Health believed that they had authority to stop such removal and did refuse a permit for removal to his next of kin. However, the next of kin under both North and South Dakota Law have the only claim to remains that will be entertained by anyone. No prosecution came out of this removal and they were placed in a grave with a huge concrete slab atop and that slab also had a shaft on which the Ziolkowski carving of Sitting Bull was placed. Both the remains and the monument are still there."

Another communication comes from Craig Gannon, Librarian of the State Historical Society of North Dakota:

"Your letter refers to two graves of Sitting Bull. In case you have included the Mobridge, South Dakota, site in your reckoning, I feel obliged to observe that excavation indicates that the remains of Sitting Bull, if any, were not touched at the time of the Mobridge episode."

PART OF OUTDOOR STUDIO of Black Hills sculptor Korczak Ziolkowski rests upon planked platform, figure in work that of Indian Chief Crazy Horse. This wood sculpture is open to question since no authenticated likeness of Crazy Horse is known to exist. Author made photo while gathering material in Black Hills in 1962 for **Ghost Town Trails.**

THE LADY KNOWN AS LEWD

Whoever would be picked for the male lead in dramas of the Old West, Calamity Jane would most certainly be the leading lady — and that in name only. She was no lady, this angular, broad-shouldered, rough and ready character. Somehow nature got mixed up when Calamity was made, endowing her with impulses that made her love the crack of a bull whip, the creak of leather and antics like riding a bull through the streets of Rapid City, South Dakota. And that was what made her news. The name of Calamity Jane springs up in history because she drank in dimly lit bars with men, used strong language and wore outlandish clothes, in a country where color was common.

Her early life is vague but it appears she was born in Princeton, Missouri, about 1848. Her un-disciplined childhood put her into close contact with equally uninhibited boys and men. Drifting west, she was supposed to have married M. E. Burke and lived for a time in Virginia City and Alder Gulch, Montana. By about 1869 in Cheyenne, she was showing the traits she carried until her death. She wore men's clothes, chewed tobacco, drank heavily and had a brilliant vocabulary never learned at her mother's knee. She was conspicuous in Abilene, Miles City, Gilt Edge and many other cow towns and mining camps but always would be associated with Deadwood, South Dakota.

Romantic tales of Calamity's life there have her closely associated with Wild Bill Hickok but this is hard to prove. It is true that the two once rode into Deadwood, whooping and hollering in their white Stetsons, new fringed buckskins and clean boots. It was the kind of thing Deadwood loved as did Jane and Wild Bill. That summer the pair were seen frequently in bars and since Wild Bill was already well known, his prestige no doubt added to the aura that would always be Calamity Jane's. When Bill was shot and killed by Jack McCall, Jane was disconsolate. She staggered from one saloon to another, crying in her beer.

Toward the end of her career, in May of 1900, the editor of the Livingston *Post* heard she was in town and thought a series of stories on this famous character would be good copy. Being apprised of her habits, he went straight to the town's largest redlight establishment and found her cavorting drunkenly with the girls. He got her back to some semblance of sobriety and health, and had no trouble getting his material, Jane always willing to talk of her most intimate life and not bothering to stay too close to the truth.

CALAMITY JANE visits grave of Wild Bill Hickok. Photo is dated 1903, same year she died. Fence enclosing grave seems to be same one standing today.

ORIGINAL MONUMENT over grave of Calamity Jane seems to have been type to stand on greensward of some Victorian home, its surmounting pot filled with geraniums.

As one result of the articles, the Pan-American Exposition hired her to appear in a sideshow and to celebrate the event in typical fashion, Jane went on a bender. Only the sad ending of the affair is known. Having shot up a bar and blacked the eyes of two policemen, she was hauled off to jail and the show went on without her. She was next spotted in Billings, Montana, and a year or later in Yellowstone. Her next and last stop was in Terry, South Dakota, a short distance from her old haunts in Deadwood.

Nobody knows why Calamity Jane got on the train and rode there but it is known she headed for the first saloon, already high on Dakota Dynamite. This time the drink did not agree with her saturated system and she became violently sick, being then carried to the Calloway Hotel and put under the care of Dr. Richards. She lapsed into a coma during the final days of July, 1903, and on August 2, it is said, she opened her eyes and asked the date. When someone told her, she said, "It's the 27th anniversary of Bill's death. Bury me next to Bill."

Deadwood's undertaker, "Charlie" Robinson, went to Terry, picked up Calamity's body, and brought it to the town that had been as near as any a home for her. John Sohn, old-time shoe repair man of Deadwood, is quoted as relating, "Charley Robinson . . . had her in his shop, and just like I said, there was an awful lot of people in there. I seen the picture they took and they had her propped up in a kinda sitting position. She looked pretty good, old Calamity Jane did. And would you believe it they went to work and they cut off her hair. The women they would come in there with shears and cut her hair off. And one fellow that was there, it was Smokey Tom. I remember Smokey Tom, he took some wire and made a screen over her.

"And one thing about it, they give her a good funeral, and the band played like it always did for a funeral. It was a fine day and it was a fine funeral, some say the biggest funeral they ever had in Deadwood."

As a final touch, it was said that this same Charley Robinson who had closed the eyes of Calamity Jane, and then the lid of her coffin, was a little boy when a smallpox epidemic laid Deadwood low. His nurse was Calamity Jane, who was no more afraid to attend smallpox victims than she had been of anything else.

INDESTRUCTIBLE PILE of boulders and plaque replacing first monument which was chipped away by vandal souvenir hunters.

HE HELD A DEAD MAN'S HAND

Called the "Prince of Pistoleers" and one of the handsomest men on the frontier, James Butler Hickok was born in Illinois about 1836. Kit Carson was his boyhood hero and in an effort to emulate him, the boy went west while still an adolescent. He became in succession freighter, hunter, trapper, stage driver and scout in the Union Army. He penetrated Confederate lines three times, it was said, each in a different disguise.

During the period of rail building in Kansas, each town at the end of steel became a haven for bandits, gamblers and prostitutes. Wild Bill served as town marshal of several of them and was generally credited with finishing off 27 men, although he himself kept the matter vague.

Considerable doubt is cast on his "nerves of steel". On what proved to be his last job as marshal in Abilene, Hickok shot it out with several badmen and was barely holding his own, when his right hand man, Deputy Mike Williams came into view, rushing to aid him. Wild Bill, not so "icy calm", unaccountably shot and killed Williams.

Dismissed from the job, Wild Bill wandered from one place to another and for a brief period was an actor in Buffalo Bill's show *Scouts of the Plains*. Cody fired him and later said, "When he went on the stage before an audience, it was almost impossible for him to utter a word." The words he

was supposed to utter could well have choked a strong man — "Fear not, fair maid, you are safe at last with Wild Bill, who is ready to risk his life and die if need be in the defense of weak and helpless womanhood."

Several years later, in 1876, Bill married a Mrs. Agnes Thatcher Lake but after a time he became more fascinated by the gold rush to the Black Hills in South Dakota. So he told his bride he would make a fortune and send for her, and headed for Deadwood. He knew he would not be dirtying his own elegant hands at mining but would flick the picture cards in games with those who had dug the yellow metal and gently disengage it from them.

In Deadwood Wild Bill was almost 40 years old and lonely for his bride, writing her many letters about setting up a home soon. His eyes were giving him trouble and he feared blindness. Unaware of this but fully aware of his reputation and 27 victims, the gamblers, madames and saloon keepers had no intention of seeing him made marshal. So they hired whiskey-soaked Jack McCall to kill him, promising him $300 which did not include a tour of the saloons to lap up the courage.

Sufficiently braced, McCall located Hickock having a friendly game of cards at the No. 10 saloon. Luck was on his side. Wild Bill sat with his back to the door and when shot, fell dead across the table. Somebody thought to look at the cards he held. They were aces and eights, a hand known from then on throughout the West as the "Dead man's hand."

McCall fled the scene. Although captured and tried by the Miner's Court for the murder, he escaped the noose with a verdict of "Not Guilty". Not feeling safe in Deadwood, McCall took his blood money to Cheyenne, where he predictably got drunk and bragged of his exploit. Again arrested for murder, he was taken to Yankton and again tried. This time his luck ran out. He was convicted and hanged despite a plea of "double jeopardy."

STANDING TALL

In spite of disease, noxious insect bites, bad water, unfriendly Indians, dangerous accidents in rivers and on land, the Lewis and Clark Expedition suffered only one casualty—Sergeant Charles Floyd of the U.S. Army. In contrast the man who replaced him, Private Patrick Gass, would live longer than any other member of the heroic company.

Although rigorously trained by Captain Clark and Sergeant Ordway during the winter previous to the start of the journey, the men could not be protected from all tribulations. Boils and dysentery, among other afflictions, became almost intolerable burdens, especially under the blazing summer sun.

More dangerous was the "Biliose Chorlic", as Clark recorded it, which laid him low. On July 31, 1804, Floyd wrote in his journal, "I am very sick and has been for some time, but have recovered my health again." Historian Bernard De Voto suggests the strong possibility that Floyd's illness was due to an infected appendix which became acute and perforated.

Leader Clark was less optimistic about Floyd's recovery. He wrote, "Sergeant is taken very bad all at once . . . we attempt to relieve him without success as yet, he gets worse and we are much alarmed at his Situation, all attention to him."

Lying in the bottom of the boat as the party moved up the Missouri River, Floyd suffered from spasms of vomiting and his pulse grew steadily weaker. When it became obvious that the young sergeant was near death the boats were ordered ashore. On August 20 he whispered weakly, "I am going away", and died moments later.

His body was carried across the river and to the top of a bluff overlooking the Missouri and he was buried with military honors. Clark wrote that Floyd was "much lamented" and a cedar post inscribed, "Sgt. C. Floyd Died here 20th of August 1804."

As the expedition went to the Pacific Ocean and returned, the men did not forget Sergeant Floyd. More than two years later they came abreast of the place where he died, Clark recording on Sept. 4, 1806, ". . . at 11 a.m. passed the Enterence to the big Sieoux River which is low, and at meridian we came to Floyd's Bluff below the Enterance of Floyd's river and climbed the hill, with Captain Lewis and Several men, found the grave had been opened by the natives and left half covered. We had this grave completely filled up, and returned to the canoes. . ."

As the years rolled by the municipality of Sioux City was founded near this site and expanded to the very edges of Floyd's Bluff. Time and the elements had eroded the slope where Floyd was buried and reburied until his bones were again exposed. Aware of his importance to history, citizens formed a committee to relocate the grave on higher ground and when this was done men were lowered on ropes to collect all recoverable bones, these reburied safely out of reach of the hungry river.

TALLEST TOMBSTONE in the West, it is said, pierces sky from bluff near Sioux City, Iowa. Although Lewis and Clark Expedition was accomplished only in face of unimaginable physical hardships, only man to succumb was young Sergeant Charles Floyd, his death apparently due to perforated appendix.

THE PREACHER WASN'T SCALPED

"Reverend Weston Smith", wrote S. Goodale Price in his book *Ghosts of Golconda,* "was one preacher lucky enough to have a monument built in his memory after a Sioux arrow took his life on the trail between Deadwood and Crook City."

It was never Reverend, but Preacher Smith. Born January 10, 1827, in Ellington, Connecticut, he came to Deadwood with a wagon train led by freighter Capt. G. V. Gardner who also brought the first gold mining equipment to the Black Hills. Smith was loved by the people there, both whites and Indians who proved their regard by not scalp-ing him after putting several arrows through his body.

On a Sunday afternoon in August, 1876, Preacher Smith held services at Deadwood and then as was his custom, took the trail to nearby Crook City where another congregation awaited him. It waited a long time, then set out to learn why he did not appear. The search party found him lying in the dust beside the trail, dead but unscalped. A wagon came along and Preacher Smith's body was laid on the hay and taken to Deadwood.

REV. HENRY WESTON SMITH is buried in Mount Moriah Cemetery on ridge directly overlooking once wild and woolly Deadwood, South Dakota. Soft sandstone shows considerable deterioration, more the result of natural weathering than because of souvenir hunting tourists who concentrate on graves of Calamity Jane and Wild Bill Hickok nearby.
Another historic grave here is Seth Bullock's. Originally a cowboy, he organized Theodore Roosevelt's Rough Riders, was immediately appointed captain. After becoming president, Roosevelt made him U.S. Marshal for South Dakota and he held position many years. On his deathbed he requested gravesite be within view of monument erected to his here Rough Rider.

NEVADA'S HAVEN FROM HEAVEN

Bartender Faddiman had been warned often enough. Friends told him, "Don't take that job at Pioche." . . . "You're as good as dead if you go to work in Pioche" . . . "No bartender ever lasted longer than a year there." Not one of Faddiman's well wishers wanted to see him go to certain disaster but his reason was simple, his need urgent. "I need a job and I don't care where it is. I can take care of myself". He did go to the most notorious camp in Nevada — and stayed there. In his second week a drunk ordered a drink. "You don't need an-other drink", Faddiman told him — and those were his last words. The customer objected to them, simple and straightforward as they were, took out his six shooter and Faddiman set up no more drinks.

The killer walked calmly behind the bar, stepped over the barkeep's body and stripped the till. Then he went next door to the butcher shop of buxom "Nigger Liza" and for variation, slit her throat with his knife. He emptied her till too but by this time the sheriff knew about the bartender's slaying and met the murderer at Liza's door with a

LONG ROWS OF GRAVES, barely discernible, makes up famous Murderer's Row at edge of Pioche's Boot Hill. Nearly 100 killers of all types lie here in area fenced off from more respectable occupants of cemetery. During heyday of large mining town, tramline was run over Row, ore buckets clanging constantly. They now hang immobile, except as they sway in often violent winds.

PIONEER BURIED HERE lies in anonymity like many others in Pioche cemetery. Headboard inscription has long since faded away, unusual condition since most painted lettering preserves wood to some extent, outlasting unpainted surface. Perhaps this one was carved, allowing moisture, abrasive sand to erode lettering or could inscription have been chiseled away for some reason? Note horizontal marks.

rattle of lead. And this was the way the single row of unmarked graves in Pioche's Boot Hill grew so long, so fast.

Piochee, pronounced Pee-oche with accent on the last syllable, was developed by Frenchman F. L. A. Pioche, although original deposits of lead-gold-silver ore were discovered by William Hamblin in 1863. Hambin had it easy. Instead of spending years at prospecting, his Paiute Indian friends led him to the highly colored ledges that were to produce $40 million in ore. Hamblin had little money for developing and later sold the claims to the French banker from San Francisco.

By 1870 the camp was considered the wildest in the West, the gun being the only law. The climate was fine enough to keep people from dying of natural causes, unnatural being most popular, the first 75 deaths being from "lead in the head" or violence of some sort. Not only did bad men drift into town to bully and shoot residents but mine owners imported their own bad men at the rate of 20 a day to fight encroachments. Death rate of these assassins was high and they got the camp's Boot Hill off to a good start, with special sections for various categories.

In Murderers' Row are two desperadoes convicted of the wanton slaying of an old prospector for his money. The sheriff's deputy in charge of their execution was the tidy sort and not wishing to dirty his hands unnecessarily or cause extra work, forced the two hapless killers to stand at graves dug at the end of the row when he shot them.

In 1871 a young lawyer, William W. Bishop, came from Illinois to spend a few hours in Pioche. He later attained some fame by defending John Doyle Lee in the notorious Mountain Meadows Massacre. Bishop brought his bride with him and as they stepped down from the stage, a shot sounded from around the corner, another across the street. By the time they got to the hotel room, says the story, a deputy shot and killed three bad guys on three different corners and the newlyweds had had it, heading back to civilization.

Legend departs from tales of violence to relate that during the Independence Day celebration of

WILLIAM L. McKEE must have been one of the solid citizens judging by his grave in Pioche cemetery.

ERODED WOODEN HEADBOARD is carved in distinct manner and message raises questions. Was spinster's given name meant to be Malinda or Matilda? Was she born in Virginia? The board was "mobile". Did whimsical ghosts move it about in some macabre game?

167

THE CATHEDRAL, standing majestically few miles below Pioche. That haphazard erosion in chalky clay could produce near perfect replica of European cathedral seems fantastic and could well have inspired composer of "The Cathedral", title song in album named Cathedral Gorge. Cathedral State Park contains many beautiful shapes like this, none as aptly shaped.

1876 the town bell was kept clanging constantly for hours by drunken miners. The people could stand it but not the bell, and it cracked. Dismayed, the townsmen declared another holiday to melt enough metal for a bell that could really take it. A melting pot was fired up at the smelter and a procession of citizens filed by, each contributing dollars or silver bars or jewelry until there was enough mass for a pour. It is said that the new bell had a sweeter tone than any other in the country but no mention is made of its fortitude.

Today Pioche is no longer wild. Many relics of the old days remain, such as the Lincoln County Courthouse. Built of brick in the late 1860s, it cost more than half a million, was condemned as unsafe in 1933, three years before it was paid for.

WALK A MILE AND REST AWHILE WE'RE NINETY NINE MILES FROM HOME

He walked a hundred miles to his mining claim near the Johnnie Mine and his burden was not a duffle bag or a bundle of prospecting tools. It was a body, the body of a dog — Paddy. He performed the burial and settled down to make the occasion memorable, to create a memorial. How long was he there at the grave? A week? A month? There is no record. The man faded into complete obscurity.

The Johnnie Mine gave rise to the town beside State Highway 16 in the Las Vegas area, the mine workings high on the mountain. Johnnie Town is easily accessible, a very dead ghost, harboring not a single inhabitant. Johnnie Mine is very hard to reach, a rough and rocky road going part way, the rest foot work. From a distance the mine camp seems to be a living village but all the buildings are empty, houses vacant, streets weedgrown.

In 1891 an 8-foot ledge was discovered on the mountain side, an outcropping with gold nuggets sticking out "like plums in a pudding". This and other finds generated wild excitement, prospectors and miners flocking to the district to stake claims all over the steep slopes, the accompanying town built several miles below, where the ground was level.

The following years saw several periods of boom and bust. In 1945 after a lean spell when the government closed all gold mines, Johnnie's workings were reactivated and about then Mrs. Kathryn West, now of Chula Vista, moved to the mountain, her engineer husband hired by a group of Hollywood investors to restore Johnnie Mine to its former glory.

Kathryn West often went for long walks over the brush and cacti covered hills for rewarding vistas of the valley far below. She discovered the grave of a dog and began probing into the story of a miner and the pet he loved.

The unknown miner was a veteran of World War II who suffered a disability and recuperated at the U.S. Veterans' Hospital in California. He took up wood carving and regained a measure of health, being discharged and cautioned to remain in a dry climate. The veteran had some money and prospects of a regular government check.

PADDY'S GRAVE fascinated Kathryn West, photo made by her husband in middle 1940's when grave was nearly intact. Kathryn writes, "Our own little dog acted very strangely, staying well back while we were taking the picture."

He turned miner in a small way, buying a small claim near Johnnie Mine and working it as much as his health would permit. Somewhat of a loner, he had one faithful companion, a dog named Paddy, who never left his master's side, sleeping at his feet and sitting on a pile of rocks to watch the excavation. The claim proved disappointing and when the man was offered a job he could handle at Searchlight, Nevada, he and Paddy went there to work. The pair had hardly settled into their new life when Paddy died.

The owner wrapped his pet in its small blanket and set out on foot for the only plot of ground he owned, a place he felt would suit Paddy, the claim on the mountain near Johnnie Mine. It was a long slow traverse with that burden in the blanket.

At the claim the man built a finely-worked coffin and Paddy was laid in it, still in the blanket, his collar on top. The man covered the coffin with a sheet of heavy glass and built a crypt of ore, petrified wood and colorful rocks, leaving the glass exposed. Then he set to work carving an amazing collection of wooden ornaments, placing them around the crypt, surmounting the whole with a carved replica of Paddy himself. Where he saw any space available, he filled it with purpled glass and other objects. Several crevices were filled with soil and planted with cacti. This was the memorial to a faithful friend. It lies there in the Nevada sun but the man disappeared.

LEVEL GROUND at Johnnie Mine workings was scant, augmented by fills against rock retaining walls. "Veranda" of building where Kathryn West and engineer husband camped is supported on wall. During heydey of camp miners attempted some measure of homelike landscaping, planted grove of ornamental trees around houses, screened porches with vines. Some trees still survived while Wests were there but lack of water has killed all but scant native growth.

TEN O'CLOCK
SCHOLAR?

THOMAS S. DILLARD is, as of now, saved from anonymity by good quality of paint used for lettering inscription and by carving letters before painting — both making identification last longer that that on nearby boards.

NO GREEN LAWNS temper harsh aspect of Wadsworth's old Boot Hill, relieved only by few scanty clumps of wiry desert grass. Town was once most important railroad terminal in Nevada. Wagons took railroad freight into vast empty spaces of desert for isolated mining camps in need of machinery, supplies. Wadsworth was nearest settlement to scene of disastrous battle between Paiutes and soldiers sent to subdue them. Indian revolt was stirred by incident at Williams Station when two men seduced pair of squaws. (See **Boot Hill**).

FAMOUS OLD COAL CAMP of Madrid, some 30 miles from Santa Fe, N. M., was one of many of its kind in the state. But it could boast of its annual all-out Christmas celebration when streets, houses, buildings and encircling hills were decorated for the holidays. Town is now very much a ghost except for garage and inevitable tavern.

Old cemetery is even more ghostly with memories of many miners who died in dark shafts. Accidents were frequent, accepted as fate, as were shooting scrapes, all helping populate cemetery on hill high above town. Miners were largely Mexican, Spanish names predominating on headboards that can be read. Burial ground is shambles, walking in it a hazard with rolling rocks and nails standing up in fallen pickets.

GOLDEN AGE OF NEW MEXICO

In the 1830s a gold fever was gripping the Ortiz and San Pedro Range, during which period the little church was built to serve the boom town of Golden. It faded when prosperity did and was almost in ruins when Golden was revived by new discoveries. By 1900, when Golden had a population of 3,000, a new bank, theater and even a stock exchange, little money was expended on the old church, worshippers attending mass in a drafty, leaking structure. When walls began to cave in, about 1918, a tin roof was placed on the church.

Forty years later, in one of Golden's sudden wind storms, the tin roof sailed off into infinity. High church authorities commissioned Fray Angelico Chavez, O.F.M. to restore the dilapidated building in entirety and fortunately Fray Chavez was an artist. When workmen, proud of their ability to square off a corner, began "truing up" edges of the adobe-plastered walls, the good Father told them to round off corners and edges, as old walls, he said, must continue to have the appearance of age, although newly plastered. Built primarily of the plentiful native stone, the walls must retain the irregular lines given them by the original builders who lacked modern tools. The result is an old-new church with an unadulterated aura of an aged structure.

Through all the years the church was active, the little burial ground, characteristically in front of the door, was filling with deceased citizens of Golden. Many of the deaths were the sudden kind as befitted miners of hot-tempered, Latin ancestry who lost inhibitions after a few glasses of Taos Lightning and pulled guns on each other or slipped knives into ribs. It is said by several of the dozen or more inhabitants of the hills around town that half the graves in the church cemetery hold victims of violence. If so, they likely lie in the many graves unmarked except by piles of stones.

LITTLE CHURCH of St. Francis de Assisi and graveyard are located at edge of old gold mining camp of Golden, not far from once huge coal town of Madrid. Although all graves are old, they are not all forgotten. Artificial wreaths and several with very modern styrofoam frames are scattered about graveyard.

Area is noted locally for sudden, violent wind storms, attested to by author and Dr. Mason. Each made just one photo when air was suddenly filled with dust. Cameras were hastily hustled into camper, made secure against grit by inserting them in plastic bags. In moments camper was swaying, rain pelting heavily.

RUSSIAN BILL and Sandy King were hung in Shakespeare (see **Ghost Town Shadows**), their bodies cut down, hauled in wagon to burial ground some distance from town. Both were unceremoniously dumped into one grave at outside edge of cemetery. Grave remained unmarked for many years until historian and one-time resident Emma M. Muir arranged to have stone marker placed over historic spot.

GRANT HOUSE, hostelry in Shakespeare where dual hanging of horse thieves took place. Bodies were left swinging from ceiling as object lesson to prospective guests arriving on next stage.

IN ARIZONA'S DUNGEONS DARK AND HOT

The reputation of the Old Yuma Territorial Prison was so widespread that a man sentenced to spend a term there felt he might be better off hanged. It is possible that he felt a gleam of hope at first sight of the grim fortress-like structure. The walls were of adobe! Surely, with patience he might be able to peck an opening in the sunbaked mud walls. Final incarceration, though, blasted this plan as being premature, the inner cell blocks having walls of stone.

In 1867 Congress started a move to authorize construction of a prison in territorial Arizona. Someone sent a congressman a clipping from an Arizona newspaper of the time, hoping to spur construction. The item was plaintive, reading "We wish that a few of our citizens could be permitted to live until they die a natural death so as to show the world what a magnificent and healthy country this is."

At any rate, Congress did appropriate $25,000 for the job. Red tape being tangled, actual construction didn't begin until 1876. Once under way, the people of the territory were so eager to put it to use that they sent a prisoner even before the new hoosegow was ready. He was William H. Hall who had been convicted of murder in Tucson. He was placed in the county jail from which he promptly made good his escape. Captured as promptly, Hall was put in irons while finishing touches were put on the prison.

The structure was built with security in mind. Outside adobe walls were 8 feet thick at the base, 4 at their tops 18 feet from the ground. There was a watch tower at each corner. Over the main gate was the water tank and on top of this the central watch tower from which guards could quickly aim their Gatling guns at an escaping prisoner.

The completed structure celebrated its Grand

VIEW OF MAIN CELL BLOCK from north gate. Each cell measures 9 x 8 feet, contains two tiers of 18 inches wide, steel-latticed bunks. Thin tick only was provided, a galvanized bucket served as toilet for all six men, it was emptied once each day. Now open to sky, block was originally roofed over and surmounted by hospital building.

YEARS OF CLOSE CONFINEMENT under unsanitary conditions encouraged heavy incidence of tuberculosis among prisoners, particularly in those of Indian extraction. Here shown is block of cells for sufferers from pulmonary disorders, cells are constructed of adobe, considered strong enough to resist feeble escape attempts of sick prisoners. Comparatively small effects of erosion attest tiny amount of rainfall annually allotted Yuma area.

Opening with closing doors for 7 shackled men. By 1885 there were 169 inmates more or less controlled by 17 guards. At one time there were 376 men in durance. The end of the notorious prison came in 1909 when Florence succeeded Yuma as the site for the territorial prison.

At the time of maximum population the 9x9 cells meant for 2 were jammed with 6, each of whom was chained to the floor at night. Instead of toilets there was a wooden pail. With summer temperatures often soaring well over 100 and cooling little at night, these airless cells were as much like hell as any man confined there was likely to ever experience.

There were special sections. One group of cells was for tuberculars, these confined in the same fashion as the others, only being segregated. The violently insane had privacy in a 3x5 hole closed by a heavy door facing into the sun most of the day.

Any man protesting his lot was confined to the Dungeon Block, locally referred to as the Snake Den. It was about 15 feet square and equipped with rings chained to the floor, these effectively separating violent men who could otherwise vent their frustrated fury upon each other.

Not surprising is the number of men who attempted to escape this desert Devil's Island. Although some did get out, most eventually returned, a few voluntarily. The site is surrounded by inhospitable deserts extending hundreds of miles in every direction. No man could get far without water. If he did make it a short distance away from the prison he was sure to meet with Indians who would be glad to return the weakened man for the proffered reward of $25. One man did get clear away, his name — Martinez, but 64 died in the attempt.

There were several concerted efforts at mass breaks. Nearest to succeeding was one occurring on October 27, 1887. Seven convicts suddenly grabbed Warden Thomas Gates for a hostage. A spokesman demanded that the gate be opened and fire withheld, otherwise Gates would be killed. The group was plainly exposed to view of guard B. F. Hartlee in the main tower. Hartlee began firing. When 4 felons had dropped one by one, those remaining realized their situation was hopeless. One of those remaining then plunged a butcher knife deep into Gates' neck, then into his chest. At this juncture one Barney Riggs pulled out a pistol and shot the man attacking Gates. The would-be jail break was finished, adding 5 bodies to the cemetery on the bluff.

Some time after the bloody episode, Riggs was

pardoned for saving Gates and released. Only then was it discovered that he had deliberately planned the whole thing. Freedom for Riggs was ephemeral. He soon got into an argument in a saloon, slew his antagonist and was returned to prison, this time with no hope for a pardon. As for the subsequent history of hostage Gates, he survived the attack, living on in misery for a time. Unable to endure his sufferings he finally committed suicide.

Pearl Hart was only 17 and supposedly innocent when she came to Arizona. Her escort was a young gambler named Dan Bandman. Dan soon "broke in" the girl to the ways of life in the raw western frontier, giving her a full education in gambling, and several other arts. When he tired of her he went on his way. Pearl soon picked up another consort, this one a highwayman named Joe Boot. The two planned a happy life in which they would make a lot of money the easy way. Misadventure was to be their lot, though. They were soon apprehended red-handed while holding up a stage. Boot got 7 years in Yuma Penitentiary, his female sidekick only 5. As it turned out Pearl was to get out sooner than that. After a couple of years in the pen she was found to be pregnant.

Prison officials took their unique problem to the governor, Alexander Brodie. Brodie could see nothing but embarrassment if events were allowed to take their inevitable course inside the prison walls. The outcome was that the grim prison gates were swung wide for the exit of a female prisoner who had proved to be no lady.

DESOLATE GRAVEYARD lies just below prison at junction of Colorado and Gila Rivers. Buried here are victims of riot, disease, murder and execution by hanging. Gallows was erected conveniently near ready, open grave. One man, when rope was adjusted around throat was seen to smile faintly. Asked the reason, he replied "Well, I was just thinking. You guys have got to walk back up there in this heat. I don't."

Old photo shows cemetery as it was with full complement of 104 graves. Since then Gila River has washed away some when in flood, encroaching highway claimed several more. All old headboards have been sneaked away by vandals. Curator at Prison Museum sadly commented to author "A visitor here once told me he had met a man who bragged of having accumulated seven boards."   Photo courtesy Arizona Dep't of Library and Archives.

THE HALLS OF MONTEZUMA

During the 1860s and 70s it was the custom for Arizona's savage Yavapai tribes to regularly raid their more peaceful neighbors, the agrarian Pimas. It was an easy way to acquire a fresh lot of girls and young women, of taking prisoners children who would be used as slaves. Usually these attacks were conducted without complications, the outcome predictable, surprised Pimas readily yielding to the aggressors.

This established pattern deviated one night in 1870 when a band of screaming Yavapais found their intended victims forewarned and prepared. Ordinarily submissive, the Pimas this time repelled the invaders, inflicting heavy losses. Emboldened at their unusual victory, the Pimas returned the raid next night, decimating astonished Yavapais and taking for themselves many prisoners, these including a six year old lad named Wassaja. Home for the tribe was the sparsely populated area along the Gila River, so the Pimas took their captives to Florence where there would be a more favorable market.

Put on display, the ragged group soon caught the eye of Carlos Gentile, an itinerant photographer. Gentile, an Italian, had come out to Arizona to take pictures of Indians and here they were. Eagerly he went to work photographing the Yavapais as a group. His attention was soon attracted by little Wassaja whose bright eyes and obvious awareness made him stand out among his dour tribesmen. Struck by the lad's appearance, Gentile decided to take him along to serve as companion and

model. He paid the required price of $30, then took the boy to his quarters.

Years later the Indian would relate how frightened he was at being plopped into a tub and vigorously scrubbed by his new master. Once cleaned up and his stomach filled, the lad managed to convey to Gentile that he had never had it so good. Then he received a new name, Carlos for his benefactor and Montezuma for a prominent peak on the horizon.

After a few days in Florence the two set out in the covered wagon that served as transportation and portable darkroom. They went to Camp Verde where Gentile took many pictures, finding the process expedited with the help of little Carlos who explained to the Indians what was required of them in posing. From Camp Verde the pair set out for Fort Apache, then worked east to Albuquerque and Santa Fe in New Mexico Territory. At this point Gentile concluded he had a sufficient supply of photographs and set out for Chicago and his studio.

He found the city devastated by the fire of October 8, 1871, his home and studio destroyed. Ruined, Gentile was faced with recouping, and now found the Indian lad a liability. He took the boy to friends in New York, gave the family some

NEAR CENTER of Indian cemetery at Fort McDowell is monument to Yavapai waif who grew up to become famous physician. Marker is easily most impressive in picturesque burial ground. Grave is venerated by present generation of Indians. Metal fence surrounds plot, though vandalism is unknown here.

TOWERING FOUR PEAKS form group in southern part of Mazatzals, scene of several skirmishes during Crook's campaign. After having left Fort McDowell in December of 1872, Captain James Burn's command scoured these mountains, killing several Apaches, then joined with Major William H. Brown's forces for concerted attack on Apaches cowering in Salt River Canyon cave. Unable to get natives into direct line of fire, soldiers sent volleys of bullets against roof of cave these ricocheting as deadly downward hail. Seventy-six Apaches were killed, 18 taken prisoners. Bones of slain hostiles remained at scene for many years, were eventually hauled here at instigation of Dr. Montezuma. Mass grave adjoins monument to Indian physician.

money and departed, saying he would return. He never was heard from again.

When funds for the boy's care ran out, the New York family sent him to a home for orphans. There followed several years of shift and neglect, but young Carlos eventually found himself in the home of Reverend and Mrs. Steadman of Urban, Illinois. Now he could go to school. He was conspicuous in his ready response to teaching, soon surpassing his white classmates. By the time he was 14 he was ready for enrollment at Illinois University.

At 17, Carlos Montezuma was graduated. His mind was now filled with the ambition to become a doctor. With funds from a part time job and some help from the kindly minister Carlos entered Chicago Medical School, receiving his degree when still 22 years old. The fledgling doctor was widely regarded a scholastic marvel.

Dr. Carlos Montezuma's first post was as resident physician at Fort Stevenson Indian School in North Dakota. There his scientific ministrations went mostly for nothing. He was to write later "The curse of savage life is the medicine man." The doctor might be called to treat a patient with a bad case of pneumonia. He would prescribe a course of treatment and leave medicines. As soon as his back was turned the family called in the medicine man who was likely to throw icy water on the sufferer, mumble some incantations, then destroy the drugs prescribed. When the patient died the doctor got the blame.

Frustrated, Dr. Montezuma applied for transfer to Carlisle Indian School in Pennsylvania and worked there for a time. Then he went to Colville in Washington State. Nowhere could he successfully pit his education against savage superstition. He quit the Indian Service to go into private practice in the East.

At first the going was rough. Although fastidiously groomed and perfectly mannered the Indian's aquiline features and penetrating black eyes frightened off prospective patients. But the women, at least, while repelled were also fascinated. They came back, at first singly, then in droves. The doctor's practice increased, his clientele mostly ladies in high society. Undeniably a good doctor, he began to attract male patients too. The one-time waif soon was wealthy enough to buy a large house loaded with fancy furniture and with a lawnful of marble statues. Then he found a bride in lovely Marie Keller of New York.

After a short honeymoon the young couple moved into the mansion and began a life of parties and brilliant social events. At the same time the doctor was teaching two courses at the medical school and steadily contributing to several medical journals. How high could a once savage Yavapai go? Actually, Dr. Montezuma had reached his zenith.

Carlos Montezuma now moved in the best circles of the white man's society, but he was still an Indian. He had never ceased to burn at the white man's injustices to the Indians. He had the feeling he was a traitor in enjoying the amenities of the white world while not working to advance the cause of his less fortunate brethren.

The feeling grew until it became near mania. He closed his offices, withdrew some meager funds, said goodbye to his wife and hit a sort of sawdust trail. He preached the cause of the Indian on streetcorners and halls, anywhere he could gain an audience. To save money he took quarters in the slums of towns where he talked. He spent many months pleading for Indian education and the right to vote.

Gradually Dr. Montezuma came to see that his struggle was useless. The authorities considered him a crackpot. They said the Indians were incapable of assimilating the educational advantages supplied for them. As for the franchise, how could the Indian vote if he couldn't read?

About the same time his money ran out, Dr. Montezuma realized he had contracted tuberculosis while living in airless rooms on a near starvation diet. He returned to his people, moving into a little brush wickiup on McDowell Indian Reservation. There he soon died of the disease then so little understood. His Indian friends gave him a savage funeral, speaking his name loudly, once and once only, never again to repeat it lest his soul suffer eternal unrest. Then the little shelter was burned. White authorities saw to it that Montezuma was properly buried, and later erected an impressive monument on his grave.

A few years later the "Great White Father" in Washington granted his Indian wards most of the educational and medical facilities so earnestly and futilely requested by the one time Wassaja.

PLEASANT VALLEY WAR

Young Mrs. John Tewksbury was waiting in the cabin for her husband to return home from the horse pasture. Unknown to her, John's mortal enemies the Grahams and Blevins were hidden in a thick patch of brush close by. Hearing footsteps she looked out to see her husband and his friend William Jacobs approaching. At that moment a hail of bullets came from the ambushing group in the brush riddling Tewksbury and Jacobs. The two men fell to the ground and lay there without moving. Now general firing broke out between the Graham men outside and Tewksbury forces in the cabin.

Mrs. Tewksbury stood at the window hoping there would be a pause in the firing so she could get to her husband, but when she saw the half wild hogs on the place move in and begin rooting at John's body she opened the door, screaming "I'm coming out!" She grabbed the shovel standing just outside and walked to the body. Astonished attackers and besieged held fire while the woman dug shallow graves beside the fallen pair, rolled the bodies in and lightly covered them. There was silence still while she knelt over the grave of her husband, said a prayer and walked back into the cabin. Shutting the door she heard the firing break out again, then quietly fainted. The affair was typical of a continuing series of fights that made up the Pleasant Valley War, actually a bloody feud between the Tewksburys and Grahams that was to cost 12 lives among those directly concerned in as many related incidents.

The patriarch of one of the warring factions was John D. Tewksbury, Sr. He had left his native Massachusetts to answer the call of gold in California, going by way of Cape Horn in a sailing vessel. Failing to make any rich strike in the Sierra foothills, he settled in Humboldt County and

TWO OF TEWKSBURY brothers are buried here. James went through war unharmed, his relative lack of activity credited to fact he was tubercular. Item from **Phoenix Herald**, Dec. 6, 1888 "Jim Tewksbury died of consumption at 5:30 P.M. Dec. 4, 1888 at his sister's home in Globe." Edwin Tewksbury, who was active in feud, also retired to Globe but lived active life there, fathering family. He died in fall of 1904. Neither grave can now be definitely located, old headboard being either gone or with inscriptions completely eroded away. Graves of descendants are on summit of hill at left.

married an Indian woman, either a Digger or Pitt River squaw. She bore her husband three sons, John Jr., James and Ed, dying soon after Ed was born.

The father took the sons to Arizona about 1885, settling in Globe. There he married an English widow, who bore him two more sons and a daughter. These latter offspring took no part in the ensuing feud. After a short period of living in Globe the family moved to a ranch in the cow country of Pleasant Valley, part of the Tonto Basin north and slightly west of Globe.

On the Graham side there also were three brothers, John, Tom and William. They had been born and raised on their father's farm in Boonesborough, Iowa, coming to Pleasant Valley around 1885. Their cabin was about 10 miles from that of the Tewksburys.

Both families acquired a few cattle, but not enough to keep all six boys busy, so they went to work for a man who did. This was James Stinson who had sold his fine ranch in Utah to Mormons who paid him the $11,000 asking price in cattle. Stinson was glad to have the half dozen young men as cowboys.

At first there was nothing unusual about the way the boys handled the animals at branding time, but after a few months they agreed that it was a shame Stinson had all those cows while they had so few. They agreed on what amounted to an informal partnership. Object — the quiet transfer of an occasional animal to their own herds, first identifying it with their own mutual brand. After a few

months of this very satisfactory arrangement the Grahams decided to alter it a little. Without consulting the Tewksbury boys, one of them went to Prescott and there officially registered the heretofore mutual brand as the exclusive property of the Graham tribe.

All went well as long as the rustlers were content to get away with only a few cows at a time. But when large numbers turned up missing, Stinson's foreman John Gilland got suspicious. Confronting Ed Tewksbury, Gilland expressed his suspicions, receiving a bullet in his leg during the ensuing battle. This was the first shooting in the Pleasant Valley War and the only one without fatal results.

After the fracas Ed went home and discussed the matter with his brothers. All agreed it was high time to divide the ill-gotten herd and dissolve the partnership. The Grahams laughed at them, and now boasted of their legal ownership of the brand.

During these years there had been a rigid ban against sheep in the valley. Two sheepmen, partners A. A. and P. P. Daggs of Flagstaff had for some time cast covetous eyes on the fat rangelands denied them by the Grahams and others. Now the Tewksbury brothers and friend William Jacobs came to them with a proposition. They would herd the Daggs sheep over the Mogollon Rim and protect them from the cattlemen, the Grahams in particular. The Daggs brothers eagerly accepted the arrangement, though in ignorance of the real reasons behind it. They provided the boys with

THE TEWKSBURY CABIN in Pleasant Valley, Arizona. This was the scene of the fight of September 2, 1887, in which John Tewksbury and William Jacobs were killed and their bodies left by Graham forces for the hogs to eat. Photo taken shortly after the close of the war. Photographer unknown.—Courtesy Arizona Pioneers' Historical Society.

THIS ADOBE HOUSE in Globe, Arizona was home to Tewksbury family after ending of feud with Grahams. Edwin Tewksbury was suspected of being involved in several "incidents", but not directly accused of murder until after slaying of Tom Graham. After his eventual release he sold holdings in valley, moved to Globe where he served most of remaining life in various capacities as peace officer. During 1888-89 he was Deputy Sheriff of Gila County under Sheriff Dan Williamson. Old home stands near cemetery at edge of Globe.

sheepherders who soon had thousands of woolies pouring into the valley.

The *Globe Silver Belt* of February 12, 1887 carried this news "Pleasant Valley Sheepherder's Death — The body of a sheepherder —— a Ute Indian in charge of the Daggs buck herd was found dead about ten days ago near his camp in Pleasant Valley, his body riddled with bullets. Some days previous to the murder, some unknown person fired at the herder in his camp. He returned the shots. His gun missed fire . . . or he would most certainly have killed his assailant." The story went on to say that the sheepherder's head had been removed, "evidently to make identification more difficult". Later it was reported that James Stinson had offered $500 for the head of any man caught bringing sheep into the valley, a statement vigorously denied by Stinson.

A few weeks later several horsemen tore into a herd of sheep, letting loose a fusillade of bullets that killed many and stampeded the rest to destruc-

tion. Repetition of such episodes discouraged the Daggs brothers who withdrew their sheep from the battleground. Apparently the Grahams had won the dispute and peace seemed to settle over Pleasant Valley.

During these years the Grahams had become friendly with "Old Man Blevins", sometimes referred to as "Mark". Blevins had four sons, Hampden, Charles, Huston and John. The Graham faction was growing formidable. One day the elder Blevins went out to hunt some lost horses in the direction of the Tewksbury cabin. He never returned. Several years later a human skull was found in the hollow of a tree near an upper fork of Cherry Creek. Thorough search revealed no other bones, but a rifle was found leaning against another tree nearby, the weapon identified as one belonging to Blevins.

John Payne was a tough, gun-slinging cowboy hired by the Grahams to help keep sheep off the range. It was rumored he attacked lone sheep-

JOHN TEWKSBURY who was killed with Bill Jacobs and left for the hogs to eat while the Grahams watched. Was father of John Rhodes, well-known rodeo rider and roper. His mother married John Rhodes when he was quite young, and young John Rhodes took his stepfather's name.—Courtesy Arizona Pioneer's Historical Society.

herders at night and beat them up. When "Old Man" Blevins turned up missing, he rode over to the Graham ranch to help in the search. He joined young Hampden Blevins, Bob Gillespie and Tom Tucker, the party riding toward a cabin on Middleton Creek. Reaching the dilapidated building they saw smoke coming from the chimney. One of the riders called out something about being hungry. A door opened a little and someone later identified as probably James Tewksbury called out that he wasn't running a boarding house and get the hell out of there. Almost at the same time several rifles were aimed from a window and fired at the four men outside.

John Payne and James Blevins fell from their horses and lay dead on the ground. Tom Tucker caught a bullet in the chest but managed to hang on to his horse long enough to get away to safety. Gillespie got a slug in a buttock, a painful but not fatal wound. He got away, but Tucker finally could hang on no longer, falling to the ground where he lay in a coma lasting all day and into the night. A cold hail and rainstorm revived him enough so that he was able to crawl to a ranch house where he was cared for. After a long convalescence he located his friend Gillespie and with him left the country, Gillespie riding slouched to one side. Historical files at Phoenix list a Thomas Covington (alias Eugene Clark) as having been

with the ill-fated search party, but fails to detail what happened to him.

The next victim of the feud was 18-year-old William Graham. He was shot while riding along a lonesome trail between Payson and Pleasant Valley. Several years after the war was over, a Tewksbury partisan J. D. Houck bragged while in his cups that he had shot young Graham. "I met William face to face on the trail", he related "we both drew at sight of one another, but I shot first and got him".

In 1931 Charles Perkins of the Perkins Store in the valley related the following to historian Will G. Barnes "Bill Graham was not alone when he was killed. He was with a cowboy named Ellenwood. Graham was some distance ahead of Ellenwood when the shooting took place. Ellenwood hurried away as fast as his horse would carry him. After everything was quiet he crawled back to the point where the shooting occurred. He met poor Bill seriously wounded and only able to crawl along with great suffering. Ellenwood with great difficulty helped the poor devil till they came to a ranch where he stayed with Graham for two weeks doing his best to save his life. He was too badly wounded, however and died at last." Ellenwood who wasn't particularly a partisan with the Grahams but only a footloose cowboy following the chuckline, now had something to remember.

Tom Graham felt the loss of his younger brother keenly and was now determined to wipe out the Tewksburys. To start with he joined forces with his brother John, the remaining Blevins boys and several other Graham partisans and went to the Tewksbury cabin. Surrounding the building, the Graham men concealed themselves in the brush and waited. When John Tewksbury and William Jacobs rode into the clearing they became easy marks.

Somehow the news got to Payson not far away and a posse was organized to go after the besiegers. With John Meadows, Payson Justice of the Peace at their head, the men rode right up to the cabin but found their quarry gone, having been amply warned by the cloud of dust raised by the posse. Meadows soon got the story from Mrs. Tewksbury and exhumed the bodies so recently buried, then holding an inquest on the spot.

Not long after this episode, Andy Cooper, a stepson of the elder Blevins, appeared in Holbrook and went straight to the saloon. After several drinks he bragged he had been the man who shot and killed John Tewksbury and William Jacobs. A warrant was issued for his arrest and "Commodore" Perry Owens, serving as sheriff was delegated to bring him in. Owens heard that Cooper was visiting his mother, Mrs. Blevins, at her home at the edge of town. Arriving there Owens managed to kill Cooper, friend Mose Roberts who sought to aid Cooper and Huston Blevins, a youngster in his teens. Mother Blevins had never allowed Huston to have a gun, but in the excitement he grabbed the fallen Cooper's weapon and attempted to shoot Owens, instead receiving a slug and falling back into his mother's arms to die. Huston's older brother John Blevins managed to survive the battle with a bullet in the shoulder. Owens, who had been subject to much joshing and criticism because of his affected fancy cowboy clothes and shoulder-length hair was now a hero, having killed three desperadoes and put another out of commission.

On September 17, 1887 the Graham faction, much decimated by loss of several Blevins allies made a raid on the Tewksbury ranch, but were themselves surprised by the intended victims, the Tewksburys having been warned. As the would-be attackers approached the cabin they were met by a volley of bullets from within. Graham and Henry Middleton fell dead and Joe Ellenwood (the same who had attempted to save the life of William Graham) was lightly wounded, falling from his horse. He made it to a tree which proved too small for cover. An exposed leg got a slug and he fell, but managed to crawl away in the grass. He eventually got to the San Carlos Agency where he was nursed back to health.

Shortly before this episode there had been a conference in the governor's office between Governor Zulich, District Attorney John C. Herdon and their respective sheriffs, constables and deputies. Something must be done to stop the trouble in Pleasant Valley, they decided. Nothing was done until after Middleton was killed. Then a posse was gathered for an all out assault on the principals. Since two Tewksbury friends, George Newton and Henry Houck had joined the posse, it was decided to go after the Grahams first.

The party holed up in the Perkins store, actually a onetime fort used in the Apache wars. The structure was in sight of the Graham cabin. Seeing the activity there, Charles Blevins and John Graham rode slowly up to the building and carefully made a circle around it. As they reached the corner Sheriff Mulvenon, who was in charge, stepped out with a leveled double-barreled shotgun. The riders attempted to whirl away, at the same time drawing their guns.

A charge from Mulvenon's gun tore a huge hole in the neck of Graham's horse, the sheriff after-

THOMAS H. GRAHAM, leader of the Graham faction in the Pleasant Valley war. Killed August 2, 1892, at the Double Butte school house, Salt River Valley, Arizona. Photo by "Worthington & Co., Red Bluff, California" in May, 1882.—Courtesy Arizona Pioneers' Historical Society.

wards explaining "I couldn't bear to kill Graham, I hoped he would surrender". Those men concealed inside, with no such scruples, put two holes clear through Graham's body and riddled that of Blevins. Blevins died instantly, Graham lingering on an hour or two.

Mulvenon's men then moved on to the cabin of Al Rose, another suspect in the war, arresting him and Joe Ellenwood who was recuperating from the wounds in his leg. Tom Graham, who had been hiding in the cabin made good his escape by crawling away through the grass.

Moving on to the Tewksbury cabin. Mulvenon surprised and arrested Ed and James and five others holed up there. All were taken to Payson where Rose and Ellenwood were soon released for lack of evidence against them. The Tewksburys were sent on to Prescott. There they appeared before the next grand jury, when they too were released.

During the short period the Tewksburys were languishing in Prescott jail, Tom Graham married Anne Melton near Tempe. Being now anxious to straighten out his record, he went to Phoenix to give himself up but was informed there was no warrant out for him. Mulvenon, however did still want him, and promptly went to Phoenix to arrest him. As with the other principals, however, the only remaining Graham was freed by the grand jury of Yavapai County.

In the meantime Rose was running, not from the law, but from the Tewksburys. A few days after the killing of Blevins and Graham, Al Rose was found dead over on Spring Creek. He had 11 bullet holes in his body.

Now 5 years went by in peace. Tom Graham was happily married and had a child. Apparently the war had come to a close through sheer decimation, but as one old timer said "There is still one Graham and one Tewksbury, the war ain't ended". He was right. On August 2, 1892 there came a rifle shot on a quiet country road and Tom Graham lay on the grain sacks piled in his wagon. He was dying.

Witnesses later told the story. Three young women and a boy, walking down the road saw and recognized Tom Graham driving a four horse team, his wagon filled with sacks of barley. Each heard a single shot, each saw two men with rifles in their hands, each identified the men as Ed Tewksbury and John Rhodes.

Graham's young wife was soon at his side. Her husband was lucid for some time and told her and other witnesses that he had been shot by Ed Tewksbury and John Rhodes. He died the same afternoon.

Rhodes was soon brought in and put on trial. One of the Phoenix dailies reported an incident in the courtroom, on the second day of the proceedings. Mrs. Graham was sitting beside her father near the reporter's table. Suddenly she put her hand into her dress, pulling out a .44 calibre revolver. She sprang towards the prisoner with the avowed intention of putting out his light. She would have succeeded had not her father held her back. "Let me shoot him, for God's sake let me shoot him" she screamed, "they will turn him loose". And they did, too. While it was proved that he

was indeed with Tewksbury, it could not be shown that he had fired a shot.

As for his partner Ed Tewksbury, he remained elusive for some time. There was wild excitement when Tewksbury appeared in Phoenix, charged with the murder of Tom Graham. The *Gazette* of August 1, 1916, 24 years afterward recapitulated the event thus "Ed arrived in the city armed to the teeth, 2 six shooters, a long rifle, bowie knife and everything. When the sheriff approached, Tewksbury threw down on him with his rifle and threatened to shoot him if he came a foot closer. Tewksbury, gun in hand, kept the officer at bay as he slowly backed down the street, up a flight of stairs and clear into the law offices of his attorneys. Here, on their advice he finally surrendered." The report is characterized by serious historians as "highly colored."

On December 3, 1892, Tewksbury was indicted by a Maricopa Grand Jury for the murder of Tom Graham. Formal trial brought a conviction, but was declared a mistrial through technicalities brought about by his attorneys. Declaring their client couldn't get a fair trial near the scene of the murder, the attorneys succeeded in getting a change of venue to Tucson. This time the jury disagreed because of seemingly incontrovertible evidence that the accused had been miles away at the time of the shooting. Date was set for still another trial, but before this could be held county authorities declared they could not afford any more trials for Tewksbury. They already were out $20,000, and a new trial probably would only result in another disagreement, the defense having located still more witnesses who would swear they saw Tewksbury 200 miles away from the scene when Graham was murdered.

Freed, Tewksbury returned to Tonto Basin, sold out his holdings in the valley and moved to Globe, where he died peacefully in 1904.

AT RIGHT ARE GRAVES of two grandsons of Tewsbury tribe, both named Edwin. Smaller markers at left locate graves of other members of numerous clan.

SOLACE IN STONE

Many a man who ventured west in the violent years met death in anonymity, his name and resting place known only to God. Perhaps passersby kindly mounded soil over him, possibly even erecting a wooden headboard at the end of the grave. If friends knew his identity his name may have been crudely inscribed on the surface of the marker. At best, however, such a monument proved transitory, crumbling under the slow erosion of time and weather. Now, even in established cemeteries there are many spaces known to be occupied by some departed pioneer, the record of his name and homeland now obscure or vanished.

The first permanently established stonecutters set up shop in the West around 1880, though transient craftsmen plied their trade long before that. Itinerants carried a stock of "blanks" from the East, their only tools a chisel and round-headed steel hammer. All carved the marble slabs exactly as statues were carved in ancient Greece, and with the same loving care. Each man had his own style and preferences in designs. Most artists signed their handiwork with honest pride. All this was before modern cemetery associations extended "permanent care", this involving the maintenance of green lawns between and around stones. To facilitate progress of mowers it now became necessary in most cemeteries to abandon the old standing slabs marking the graves instead with flat, flush-with-the-ground stones, these simply and efficiently inscribed with the sand-blaster. So passed a distinct art form, preserved now only in still remaining tombstones, these relics fast falling victim to vandals.

INTERESTING MONUMENT in Globe Cemetery is located halfway up hill, just below sections reserved for members of fraternal organizations.

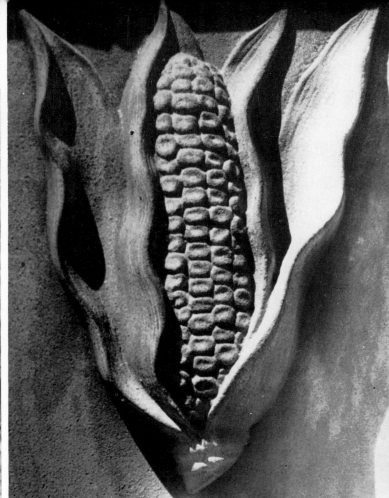

PRAYING ANGEL is motif often used to mark children's graves in old cemeteries. This one, with recently placed ribbon around neck, is in Milwaukie Pioneer Cemetery, Oregon. "English ivy" in background grows as if wild in moist Willamette Valley.

URN SYMBOL, beautifully carved, tops pedestal in old Mountain View Cemetery, Oregon City, Ore. Some form of urn has been used since ancient times to hold ashes of cremated dead, thus in itself figuratively, a grave.

UNIQUE SLAB of marble stands in old cemetery in one-time gold camp of Jacksonville, Ore. Sculptor seems to have been "carried away" with odd assortment of lettering styles, floral design.

BREECH-LOADING RIFLES with trowel bayonets are "stacked" as symbol of cessation of struggle for soldier James T. Barnes, veteran of Civil War. Locale is Jacksonville, Ore.

"GATES AJAR" symbol is shallow-etched in marble. God's welcoming hand extends from heavenly clouds, grasps olive branch to show peace prevails in world beyond gates. Handsome stone is in Pioneer Cemetery at Crawfordsville, Ore.

EAR OF CORN is variation from familiar sheaf of harvested wheat, unique in author's experience. Decoration is on marker in cemetery, behind old Providence Baptist Church, Scio, Ore.

FLORAL DESIGN, beautifully sculptured on stone in cemetery adjoining Providence Baptist Church, established 1853 near Scio, Ore. Here are combined roses, callas, morning glories, daisies and fern. Author does not recall ever seeing such bouquets without roses.

INDEX